D0207914

H. L. Mencken Revisited

Twayne's United States Authors Series

Joseph M. Flora, Editor

University of North Carolina, Chapel Hill

TUSAS 694

H. L. MENCKEN: "THE LION OF THE TWENTIES"
by Nikol Schattenstein

H. L. Mencken Revisited

William H. A. Williams

The Union Institute

Twayne Publishers
An Imprint of Simon & Schuster Macmillan
New York

Prentice Hall International
London • Mexico City • New Delhi • Singapore • Sydney • Toronto

Twayne's United States Authors Series No. 694

H. L. Mencken Revisited
William H. A. Williams

Twayne Publishers
An Imprint of Simon & Schuster Macmillan
1633 Broadway
New York, NY 10019

Library of Congress Cataloging-in-Publication Data

Williams, W. H. A.
    H. L. Mencken revisited / William H. A. Williams.
       p. cm. — (Twayne's United States authors series ; TUSAS 694)
    Includes bibliographical references and index.
    ISBN 0-8057-7837-3 (alk. paper)
    1. Mencken, H. L. (Henry Louis), 1880–1956—Criticism and
interpretation. 2. Mencken, H. L. (Henry Louis), 1880–1956—
Knowledge—Literature. 3. American literature—History and
criticism—Theory, etc. 4. Criticism—United States—History—20th
century.   I. Title. II. Series.
PS3525.E43Z914 1998
818'.5209—dc21   97-40633
                                                                                        CIP

This paper meets the requirements of ANSI/NISO Z3948–1992 (Permanence of Paper).

10 9 8 7 6 5 4 3 2

Printed in the United States of America

In Memory of my grandfather
Daniel Werner Hamm
And my parents,
William H. A. Williams and
Evelyn Hamm Williams

Contents

Preface

It has been almost 35 years since, as a graduate student in the history department of the Johns Hopkins University, I began my work on H. L. Mencken. I have not, I hasten to add, devoted my life to him. Yet he keeps turning up on my horizon, like some strange island, frequently visited, though never completely charted. Happily, each return to Mencken has been accompanied by masses of new material. When I wrote the original volume on Mencken for Twayne's United States Authors Series in the mid-1970s, I was able to make use of the vast collection of Mencken correspondence at the New York Public Library, opened at the beginning of that decade. Twenty years later, I have been able to delve into the recently published Mencken diary and memoirs (extracted from well over a million words hidden from the public for 25 years after Mencken's death). Each time I return, more is known about the man, and each time the mystery that lies at the center of his nature only deepens.

Mencken's first book came out in 1905, and new Mencken books have appeared in every decade of this century, although his career ended in 1948. While much of the subsequent material has been in the form of anthologies gleaned from his books and articles, new and previously unpublished material has appeared in the form of letter collections, as well as the aforementioned diary and memoirs. This continual flow of publications is what Mencken intended. No writer left a larger and better-organized collection of letters and manuscripts, all with an eye to posterity. "Larval Ph.D.s," as Mencken called them, burrow their way through the masses of published and unpublished works, leaving fresh dissertations in their wake. Books and articles regularly appear to keep Mencken in the public eye, where he has been for most of the twentieth century.

As a result, Mencken's influence has extended beyond the high-tide mark it reached in the 1920s, rippling through each subsequent generation of writers. In *Black Boy,* first published in 1937, a period when Mencken's reputation was at its nadir, Richard Wright left a memorable testimony of the visceral impact Mencken's writing made upon a young black man in the rural South. Almost half a century later, James J. Kilpatrick and Joseph Epstein spoke for many of their generation of writers when they acknowledged the effect Mencken's prose had on them when they first read him, about the time of his death in the mid-1950s.[1] A search of the World Wide Web in the late 1990s turned up personal home pages of individuals (apparently mostly young white males) who were enamored with Mencken's style and his libertarian views.

Not everyone reacts to Mencken with pleasure. Living or dead, he has always been a controversial figure. Even from the grave, Mencken has managed to reach out and "stir up the animals." When his diaries and memoirs were published in the early 1990s, it was discovered that Mencken, who was born in 1880, had been seriously deficient in those political and cultural sensibilities so necessary for survival in late-twentieth-century, multicultural America. In short, Mencken turned out to be a racist, a sexist, and a homophobe, or so many people thought. He was denounced and then defended in newspapers and journals around the country, all of which was not too bad for a man who was 40 years dead and who had spent his last years speculating gloomily that he and his works would be forgotten. Someday, no doubt, he will be forgotten, but not yet. We take Mencken with us into the new century, where he may continue for some time to startle the occasional unwary reader.

What is there about H. L. Mencken that keeps America coming back to him? Some commentators point to his humor. He was indeed a very skillful satirist, and his material can still make people laugh. He was a humorist, however, in the sense that Mark Twain was a humorist—it came with the job of scrutinizing America with what Mencken liked to call "a bilious eye." And like Twain, there was some dark energy pulsing away behind the facade of the "phunny phellow." Both Mencken and Twain laughed, perhaps, because the alternative would have been to face the grim void of a meaningless universe in silence.

What Henry Adams said of Theodore Roosevelt might also be said of H. L. Mencken: he was "pure act." Mencken's accomplishments were not translated, however, into the acts of statecraft: he led no armies, built no canals, and never invited millions of voters to stand with him at Armageddon to do battle for the Lord. Like "TR," however, "HLM" was a phenomenon. He was a force that went beyond any attempt to pen him within such easily defined categories as journalist, literary critic, popular philosopher, social and cultural critic, philologist, editor, auto-biographer, or satirist. Mencken was all of these things—and more.

But trying to define that phenomenon, searching for the sum of all of those seemingly disparate yet connected parts, can be difficult and con-fusing. For although Mencken transcended the limitations of compartmentalization, he did so without becoming the master of anything more than a highly idiosyncratic prose style. He was a good and very important literary critic but not a great one. As a commentator on American society, he was always observant and sometimes incisive, but he had no real theoretical or ideological approach to the subject. A pioneer in helping to introduce to Americans such European thinkers and writers as Friedrich Nietzsche and George Bernard Shaw, Mencken nevertheless saw ideas as gaudy banners to be waved instead of complex problems to be analyzed.

There may be a temptation, then, for the reader to lose patience with Mencken before coming to know him. The reader may begin to want a different Mencken from the one encountered—a better critic, a trained philologist, a genuine philosopher, a more consistent thinker. Mencken, the antispecialist, tends to displease most specialists in the various fields in which he sported.

Perhaps Mencken's disinclination to respect the academic proprieties is one of the reasons for his continuing appeal. After a century of specialization, one who leaps the fences of disciplines is a kind of outlaw—a modern Till Eulenspiegel, an intellectual Robin Hood. There have been others who have carried out this role more elegantly and with perhaps more impressive results than Mencken—I think immediately of Lewis Mumford or Edmund Wilson. But no one in twentieth-century America has done it with more verve and dash than Mencken. His energy, his humor, his irreverence, his satiric bite, and even some of his prejudices can still be refreshing and exciting.

Fortunately, there is more to Mencken than the noise and fireworks. Beneath the flash and thunder of his satiric prose, he evinces courage, conviction, and serious commitment to ideals. Deeper still, we catch glimpses of a sad, lonely man, unable to integrate the contradictory forces he tried to contain.

The previous five paragraphs have been lifted almost verbatim from the preface of the 1977 edition of this work. If the subject was other than H. L. Mencken, I might have at least a tinge of embarrassment in reporting that, although I have learned much from his published diary and autobiographies and from the recent work of many fine scholars, my approach to the man has not changed significantly over the past 20 years. Mencken had the utmost disdain for anyone who altered their opinions. It was a sign, he said, of "stupidity." I do not agree with him; yet in making my confession, I can take comfort that I have not offended his "gaseous vertebrate"—his ghost.

The present volume does, of course, contain new material—such as sections on Dreiser, the South, African Americans, and the question of racism—which has necessitated considerable rearrangement of the original text. Much of that text has been rewritten to accommodate new information and get rid of "the smell of the lamp," that academic odor Mencken found so offensive. I doubt that I have been entirely successful in the latter endeavor. Those who write about Mencken must submit to the unenviable contrast between their own solemn, doggedly determined prose and the lively style of the satirist whom they must quote.

In presenting Mencken the second time around, I have continued with my original goal: to write an intellectual biography of the man. I have shown how his ideas developed and, yes, in a few cases, changed, as he grappled with American society throughout the first half of the twentieth century. There remains the basic problem of dealing with Mencken's overlapping careers as journalist, magazine editor, and writer, with a minimum of repetition. Although this has become more difficult as new material has been added, I have done my best to keep the story moving, backtracking only when necessary. Nevertheless, a map might be in order.

Chapter 1 searches for the origins of Mencken's iconoclasm in his family, class, and city. The second chapter traces the development of his vision of the artist-iconoclast through his pioneering work on George Bernard Shaw and Friedrich Nietzsche. In chapter 3 I have looked at Mencken's prewar comments on American society and politics as gleaned from the articles he wrote for the Baltimore *Sun* from 1910 to 1915. The fourth chapter investigates Mencken's role as literary critic and then coeditor for the *Smart Set* magazine from 1908 to around 1917. Chapter 5 discusses his role in the "Battle of the Books," the name given to the cultural controversies that enlivened America during and immediately after World War I. The sixth chapter looks at Mencken's gradual shift from literary to social and cultural criticism, marked by his leaving the *Smart Set* and his founding of the *American Mercury* in 1924. Chapter 7 investigates various themes around which he developed his social criticism during the 1920s, such as free speech, Prohibition, the rural-urban conflict, the Fundamentalist movement, labor-capital relations, and the American Dream. In the eighth chapter, I discuss Mencken's views on democracy and character, as well as his libertarian politics. The ninth chapter follows Mencken as he tried first to ignore and then deal with problems arising from the Depression, the New Deal, and Nazi Germany. Chapter 10 looks at Mencken as revealed (yet still hidden) in his diary and the memoirs written in the 1930s and 1940s. This chapter also investigates the issue of racism. The final chapter attempts to explain Mencken's satire in terms of his own divided personality and seeks to find a place for him within the tradition of American critics of democracy.

Although many years have passed since I was the grateful recipient of their help, I would like to record my gratitude to the late Miss Betty Adler, bibliographer of Mencken and founding editor of *Menckeniana* from 1962 to 1973; and the late Mr. Richard Hart, former cochairman-in-charge of the humanities department of the Enoch Pratt Free Library in Baltimore.

For this new edition of my book, I am indebted to Dr. Joseph M. Flora, editor of the Twayne United States Authors Series, for his advice concerning this book. I am very grateful for the assistance of Ms. Mary Ray Worley, editorial coordinator for this book, and her staff. My thanks also to Mr. Mark Zadrozny, executive editor, as well as Anne Davidson, editor, both of Twayne Publishers.

I remember with great fondness, and still a certain awe, a very pleasant and enlightening evening in the spring of 1962, which I spent with the late Mr. August Mencken, the critic's brother, at the old house at 1524 Hollins Street in Baltimore. Near the end of the evening, Mr. Mencken, who had been as generous to me with his Jack Daniels as he had been with impressions and information, began to worry about Communists and radicals. He wondered if the John Birch Society did not have, after all, some point to their campaigns. Then looking at me with that wide-eyed glance so characteristic of his brother, he said, with the tone of one enunciating an obvious but basic truth: "But, of course, they are *all* frauds anyway." For an instant a ghost walked through the room.

Acknowledgments

All Mencken material is reproduced or reprinted by permission of the Enoch Pratt Free Library of Baltimore in accordance with the terms of the will of H. L. Mencken.

H. L. Mencken Papers, Rare Books and Manuscripts Division, The New York Public Library, Astor, Lenox, and Tilden Foundations.

From *Bode, New Mencken Letters* by Carl Bode. H. L. Mencken, Copyright © 1976, 1977 by Carl Bode and The Merchantile-Safe Deposit and Trust Company for the Estate of H. L. Mencken. Used by permission of Doubleday, a division of Bantam Doubleday Dell Publishing Group, Inc.

Quotations from the following works by H. L. Mencken are reprinted by permission of the publisher, Alfred A. Knopf Inc.:

> From *A Book of Prefaces,* copyright 1917 by Alfred A. Knopf Inc. and renewed 1945 by H. L. Mencken.
>
> From *The American Language,* copyright 1936 by Alfred A. Knopf Inc.
>
> From *Prejudices: First Series,* copyright 1919 by Alfred A. Knopf Inc. and renewed 1947 by H. L. Mencken.
>
> From *Prejudices: Second Series,* copyright 1920 by Alfred A. Knopf Inc. and renewed 1948 by H. L. Mencken.
>
> From *Prejudices: Third Series,* copyright 1922 and renewed 1950 by H. L. Mencken.
>
> From *Prejudices: Fourth Series,* copyright 1924 by Alfred A. Knopf Inc. and renewed 1952 by H. L. Mencken.
>
> From *Prejudices: Fifth Series,* copyright 1926 by Alfred A. Knopf Inc. and renewed 1954 by H. L. Mencken.
>
> From *Prejudices: Sixth Series,* copyright 1927 by Alfred A. Knopf Inc. and renewed 1955 by H. L. Mencken.
>
> From *Notes on Democracy,* copyright 1926 by Alfred A. Knopf Inc. and renewed 1954 by H. L. Mencken.
>
> From *Happy Days,* copyright 1939, 1940 by Alfred A. Knopf Inc.

Chronology

1880 September 12: Henry Louis Mencken born, Baltimore, Maryland.

1896 Graduates valedictorian from Baltimore Polytechnic Institute; end of formal education.

1899 Begins career in journalism as cub reporter on the Baltimore *Morning Herald*.

1903 City editor of the *Herald*.

1905 Managing editor of the *Herald;* publishes first book, *George Bernard Shaw: His Plays*.

1906 Begins association with the Baltimore *Sunpapers*.

1908 Publishes *Philosophy of Friedrich Nietzsche;* begins reviewing books for the *Smart Set;* meets Theodore Dreiser and George Jean Nathan.

1910 Publishes *Men versus the Man,* written with R. R. La Monte.

1911 Begins the daily "Free Lance" column in the *Evening Sun*.

1912 First trip to Europe.

1913 Writes "The American" series for the *Smart Set;* with George Jean Nathan assists Willard Huntington Wright in editing the magazine.

1914 Coeditor of the *Smart Set* with Nathan.

1915 End of the "Free Lance" due to anti-German feeling.

1916 Trip to the eastern front for the *Sunpapers*.

1917 Suspends work for the *Sunpapers;* publishes first book of criticism, *A Book of Prefaces*.

1918 Publishes *In Defense of Women*.

1919 Publishes first edition of *The American Language; Prejudices: First Series*.

1920 Returns to *Sunpapers* with weekly series of articles.

1923   Leaves the *Smart Set*.

1924   With Nathan, founds the *American Mercury*.

1925   Sole editor of the *Mercury;* covers Scopes trial for *Sunpapers*.

1926   Publishes *Notes on Democracy*.

1927   Brings out sixth and last book of the *Prejudices* series.

1930   Marries Sara Haardt; publishes *Treatise on the Gods*.

1934   Resigns editorship of the *Mercury*.

1936   Brings out fourth revised edition of *The American Language*.

1938   End of the weekly articles in the *Evening Sun;* February 8 to May 7: acting editor of the *Evening Sun*.

1940   Publishes *Happy Days,* the first of three volumes of memoirs about his youth and early career.

1941   Ceases writing for *Sunpapers;* remains on payroll.

1945   Brings out *Supplement I* to *The American Language*.

1948   Resumes writing for *Sunpapers; Supplement II* of *The American Language;* suffers stroke; end of career.

1956   January 29: dies in Baltimore.

Chapter One
The Making of an Iconoclast

Home Base

"A home is not a mere transient shelter: its essence lies in its permanence, in its capacity for accretion and solidification, in its quality of representing, in all its details, the personalities of the people who live in it. . . . I have lived in the one house in Baltimore for nearly forty-five years. . . . If I had to leave it I'd be as certainly crippled as if I lost a leg."[1] Written during the 1920s, when Henry Louis Mencken's reputation as a satirist, a skeptic, and, indeed, a cynic was at its height, this apotheosis of so traditional an institution as the home must have struck some of his readers as quite out of character. Yet no rebel was ever more conventionally and securely rooted. Three years after his birth on September 12, 1880, Mencken's family moved into the redbrick house at 1524 Hollins Street, Baltimore, Maryland, where, with the exception of the five years of his marriage, he lived until his death in 1956.

From this comfortable, middle-class home, Mencken's roots extended into the city of Baltimore, which even 20 years of commuting to his editorial offices in New York City never tempted him to leave. Writing in 1913 about the typical Baltimorean, Mencken essentially described himself: "There is a simplicity about him . . . which speaks of long habituation to his own opinions, his own dignities, his own class. In a country so largely dynamic and so little static that few of its people ever seem (or are) quite at home in their own homes, [the Baltimorean] represents a more settled and a more stately order."[2]

Mencken was an urbanite, born and bred. As such, he was one of the first American writers to champion the values of the city over those of rural America. If some of his urban values have a slightly bucolic ring about them today, this is because the Baltimore of his boyhood still retained something of the atmosphere of its preindustrial days. Mencken even professed to see some of the virtues of the old colonial planter in the Baltimore character, and some of the city's southern qualities appealed to him. Yet, even in Mencken's day, southern charm and pace

were inexorably mixed with the industrialism and the ethnically varie-
gated population typical of northern cities. The citizen of a border city
in a border state, Mencken was no more a southerner than he was a
Yankee. Although he later took a special interest in the culture of the
South, he had little experience with the region. In fact, except for summer excursions into the Maryland countryside, Mencken's youth was
bounded by the city limits of Baltimore.³

Mencken was a third-generation German American. Both of his
grandfathers came to America from Germany in 1848, not as fleeing
revolutionaries but simply as men in search of economic opportunity.
Grandfather Burkhardt Ludwig Mencken, a certified tobacconist,
founded the family cigar business in Baltimore. Henry remembered him
as a bearded patriarch who ruled the Mencken family with the firm
hand typical of the German *Bürger.* German *Kultur,* however, does not
seem to have played an especially strong role within the family.
Although his father probably understood German and his mother was
fluent in it, the language was not spoken much in the home. Moreover,
neither his grandfather Mencken nor his father showed any interest in
German-American organizations or activities.

It was class, more than ethnicity, that influenced the Menckens. As
biographer Fred Hobson explains, although the other sections of the
family—the Abhaus, the Gagners, and the McLellands—had little to
boast of, the Menckens belonged to an impressive line of seventeenth-
and eighteenth-century professors and philosophers. Thus old Burkhardt's shunning of his fellow *Landsmänner:* they were simply not of the
same class as the Menckens.⁴ During World War I, Mencken would discover his "Germanness," but until then any sense he had of separateness
from the mainstream of American life was derived more from a pride of
family and a sense of class than from an ethnic identity. As Mencken
wrote later in life: "I certainly did not think of myself as a German,
though I was already conscious of my differentiation from the common
run of Americans. If I ever pondered that differentiation at all, I probably thought of it, in the egotistic way of youth, as no more than the evidence of my superiority as an individual" (Hobson 1994, 48).

Mencken's father, August, solidly devoted to his family, his firm, the
Freemasons, and his baseball team (of which he was part owner),
appears to have been a typical American businessman of the late nineteenth century. A high-tariff Democrat with a particular dislike for
William Jennings Bryan, August held no-nonsense views on free-silver
radicalism and passed on to his eldest son, Henry, the economic and

social conservatism of the petit bourgeois entrepreneur. Looking back on this youth, Mencken traced his set of unchanging beliefs to the influence of his father, who was, in Mencken's words, "always the chief figure in his small world and hence inclined toward complacency, [therefore] I emerged into sentience with an almost instinctive distrust of all schemes of revolution and reform."[5]

In only one respect does Mencken's family seem to have deviated even slightly from the American middle-class norm of the period. As Mencken put it in 1939, "Religion was simply not a living subject in the house. It was discussed now and then but only as astro-physics might have been discussed. I grew up believing that it was unimportant and I am still of that opinion."[6] Although a basic element in Mencken's philosophy, his famous agnosticism was not the product of a rebellion against home and church. Rather, it was a part of that complex bundle of attitudes and prejudices that Mencken fashioned out of his family background.

In spite of his father's influence, the dominant personality in the household was Henry's mother, Anna Abhau Mencken, who lived at Hollins Street with her son until her death in 1925. The adult H. L. Mencken may have shaken the world of literary criticism and hurled his satirical dead cats at presidents, but at home his mother ruled with unquestioned authority. Mencken was very close to her, and she was the center of that domestic life that was so important to him. It is significant that he remained a bachelor until he was 50, five years after her death.[7] Some years later he described the passing of his mother as "pure disaster, for she had always stood by me loyally . . . and I owed to her, and to her alone, the fact that I had a comfortable home throughout my youth and early manhood. Her death filled me with a sense of futility and desolation."[8]

In the 1940s, when Mencken published his memoirs of childhood, he entitled the volume *Happy Days,* depicting his early years as "placid, secure, uneventful and happy." The Mencken children, he wrote in the introduction, were "encapsulated in affection" and kept "fat, saucy and contented." "Fat" is something of an exaggeration. By the age of seven, Mencken was slight, often ill, and was so round-shouldered that he had to wear a shoulder brace.[9]

Although *Happy Days* depicts an ideal life for a boy, Mencken differed from the majority of his contemporaries in at least one respect: his prodigious reading. "Altogether, I doubt that any human being in this world has ever read more than I did between my twelfth and eighteenth years."[10] Young Mencken was especially enamored with English literature. During his teens, he read the great eighteenth-century writers—Joseph Addison, Sir Richard Steele, Alexander Pope, and Samuel Johnson—who left the imprint of the Enlightenment on much of Mencken's thought and literary style. He also read William Makepeace Thackeray, Thomas Babington Macaulay, Lord Byron, and Rudyard Kipling. Among the British writers, however, it was T. H. Huxley who influenced him the most.[11] Of American authors, he read William Dean Howells, Henry James, Stephen Crane, and his first literary discovery, Mark Twain. *The Adventures of Huckleberry Finn* made such an impression on young Mencken that he reread it annually until he was 40. Appropriately, Mencken was one of the first critics to hail Twain as a great artist.[12]

In spite of Mencken's literary interests, he was also fascinated by science. He attended the Baltimore Polytechnic Institute, a high school emphasizing science and mechanics, from which he graduated valedictorian in 1896. By this time, however, letters had won the tug-of-war against chemistry for his mind, and Mencken announced to his startled family that he wanted a career in journalism. The result was an immediate, sharp conflict with his father, for August Mencken had plans of his own for his son. Henry could study law at the University of Maryland, enroll in the Johns Hopkins University, or, and here parental pressure was strongest, enter the family tobacco business. Since Polytechnic's valedictorian had had enough of pedagogues and classrooms, and since he was barred from journalism, Mencken unenthusiastically began to learn the dreary rudiments of the cigar trade.

The next months were unhappy ones for Mencken. "The very idea of selling revolted me," he later recalled. "I never got over my loathing."[13] Perhaps the whole episode offended his sense of dignity, for he suffered from no lack of business acumen in later life. As Hobson points out in his biography, Mencken was an almost compulsive record keeper and was very successful at managing the business side of his career (Hobson 1994, 55).

Whatever the reason for his difficulties at his father's firm, Mencken secretly took a correspondence course in writing and dreamed of the exciting career of a newspaperman. Although the young man's mother was sympathetic, August Mencken remained adamantly against journalism, and Henry could not bring himself to rebel against his father. Increasingly unhappy, Henry thought about suicide. Then, suddenly, the crisis was resolved with awful finality: his father died on January 13, 1899. This event, he wrote later, was "really a stroke of luck for me, for it liberated me from the tobacco business and enabled me to attempt journalism without his [August Mencken's] probable doubts and disapproval to hamper me" (*Thirty-five Years,* 154). Mencken wasted little time in taking advantage of his "luck." "On the Monday evening immediately following [the funeral]," Mencken noted crisply in *Newspaper Days,* "I presented myself in the city-room of the old Baltimore *Morning Herald,* and applied to Max Ways, the city editor, for a job on his staff."[14]

Mencken's pursuit of a career in journalism was an act of rebellion directed not so much against his father but, rather, against certain aspects of the bourgeois world that had nurtured him so well. Few careers deviated more dramatically from the respectable norm of the middle-class than what Mencken himself dubbed in *Newspaper Days* as the "maddest, gladdest, damndest existence ever enjoyed by mortal youth"—the world of the turn-of-the-century reporter (ix). At its gaudiest pinnacle, this career promised the romantic adventures of a Richard Harding Davis or a George Stevens. On its everyday level, journalism offered the colorful earthiness and excitement of night courts, waterfront brawls, political rallies, and city-hall skullduggery. In *Newspaper Days,* Mencken claimed, "[A]t a time when the respectable bourgeois youngsters of my generation were college freshmen, . . . affronted with balderdash . . . by chalky pedagogues, I was at large in a wicked seaport of half a million people, . . . getting earfuls and eyefuls of instruction in a hundred giddy arcana, none of them taught in schools" (ix).

Mencken's venture into journalism, then, was a rebellion against the middle-class insistence on gentility in culture and on respectability in professions. The door to Max Ways's office was an entrance into a new world and an escape from an old one. Yet Mencken never completely closed the door behind him. His was a halfway rebellion. If he rejected the surface of middle-class life, he was to cling tenaciously to its essentials. Although he would satirize bourgeois mores, Mencken took with him into journalism the discipline, the ambition, and the basic values of his class.

The influence of Mencken's background upon his later iconoclasm is paradoxical. The stable, prosperous, confident bourgeois atmosphere in which he grew up was itself the dominating influence on his development as an iconoclast. The strength of Mencken's roots in his home and his environment gave him the overwhelming self-confidence necessary for his later onslaughts against society. In his biography of Mencken, Fred Hobson states that the writer "was blessed with a superfluity of place, an overabundance of support and understanding" (Hobson 1994,

21). In a period when so many American writers were to pursue the you-can't-go-home-again theme, Mencken literally never left home. He used the psychological security of home as a basis from which to launch the barbs of his satire.

Journalism

Mencken's early experience as a journalist influenced him in several important ways, not the least of which was the reinforcement it gave to his already strong sense of self-assurance. Six years after he began working on the *Morning Herald* as a cub reporter, he had become the paper's managing editor. By then he had experienced practically every type of work the paper had to offer, from reporting, reviewing, and feature writing to editing. Mencken thus enjoyed the kind of rapid success that the myth of American individualism promises as the just reward for hard work and talent. It is little wonder that he never really questioned the basic tenets of this myth and would staunchly defend them in his later years.

Certainly, if Mencken's own statements are to be believed, no one was more self-consciously individualistic than the old-time journalist. In *Newspaper Days* he claimed that the journalist saw himself as "a free spirit and darling of the gods, licensed by his high merits to ride and deride the visible universe" (xi). Very often the visible universe under the newspaperman's nose was the rather sordid one of poverty, crime, prostitution, and political corruption. It was a rough training ground for a youthful mind, and to some extent Mencken's philosophical naturalism, like that of Theodore Dreiser and Stephen Crane, can be traced to the rather grim view of life encountered on the reporter's beat.

There were other aspects of turn-of-the-century journalism that played a more creative role in Mencken's development. "The daily newspaper," wrote novelist David Graham Phillips, "sustains the same relation to the young writer as the hospital to the medical student."[15] Certainly, the challenge of grasping and holding the attention of readers as they bolted their morning coffee often forced journalists to develop a colorful, racy style and an abrasive sense of humor. Unlike the middle-class magazines, with their genteel, largely feminine audience, the daily urban paper had a predominantly male readership that delighted in the dramatic, the satirical, and the vituperative.

Less encumbered by the taboos and restraints that influenced the genteel magazines, the reporter's language often echoed the tart slang of the streets where he found his stories. At a time when the universities and the "respectable" publishing houses were trying to maintain the English standard in American writing, newspaper writers, such as Finley Peter Dunne, George Ade, and Ring Lardner, employed the urban patois of immigrants, blacks, and sports figures. Creating a new brand of satire, these writers sought to unmask the foibles of their times through the use of dialect and slang.

Mencken was particularly impressed by George Ade and for a time tried to write his own imitations of Ade's "Fables in Slang."[16] Although the results were unimpressive, Mencken—like Ade, Dunne, and also Ambrose Bierce—learned to exploit the gap between genteel language and the vernacular of everyday speech. Much of the success of Mencken's satire depended upon dropping a pompous academic phrase into an ordinary sentence or exploding a slang term amid a line of ponderous Latinate words. The humor sprang from the contrast between "respectable" and "unrespectable" colloquial forms of speech. As one commentator has observed, such writing was a playing in the linguistic waters "where two strong currents, Standard and American English, met."[17] Mencken's allegiance lay with the American vernacular. The origins of his pioneering work, *The American Language,* are to be found in some of his early Baltimore *Sun* columns in which he delighted in publishing examples of pungent Baltimorese, which he had begun collecting while still a reporter.

Another journalistic influence that Mencken absorbed contributed directly to his development as a literary critic. During the 1890s, the ranks of the journalists produced a small group of critics who rejected the dominant genteel demand that literature and art had to reflect and support American moralism and idealism. At war with the genteel tradition, these journalist-critics turned their backs on the universities and the conservative publishing houses and looked to the avant-garde, particularly in Europe, to satisfy their yearnings for innovative art. Prophets of naturalism and apostles of aestheticism (although seldom of decadence), journalists like Percival Pollard, Vance Thompson, William Marion Reedy, James Gibbons Huneker, and Ambrose Bierce played an important role in helping to introduce Americans to the latest developments in art. Mencken, who knew Pollard, Huneker, and, briefly, Bierce, was part of this tradition. According to Henry F. May, "An unbroken line of newspaper iconoclasts stretches all the way from the pale aesthetes of the nineties to a surprising, improbable conclusion in H. L. Mencken."[18]

Mencken picked up and developed the impressionistic style of these journalist-critics. Unencumbered by either objectivity or academic formalism, these critics were completely subjective; they recorded their own impressions of the work of art. Their purpose was to make art come alive for the viewer or reader. As Mencken himself once explained, the critic was the "catalyst" between art and the public (see chapter 6). If the critic managed to entertain in the process, so much the better; for style was as important as ideas. Finally, Mencken also followed his mentors in their assumption that the artist of genius was usually at war with conventional society. Although Mencken did not accept the art-for-art's-sake doctrine held by some of the critics of the 1890s, he did posit a connection between art and iconoclasm, a point discussed in the next chapter.

Journalism provided Mencken with a training and a tradition quite at variance with what he would have received had he taken his father's halfhearted offer of a university education. In 1900, the universities were custodians of a nineteenth-century Victorian culture that was becoming increasingly irrelevant to an urbanizing, industrial America with its vast immigrant population. In the face of this raw, dynamic but troubled America, the universities, along with other bastions of the genteel tradition, preached a concept of art that either looked back to a simpler, rural past or to the heritage of European high culture, representing a noble idealism that was often sadly out of touch with reality. Genteel critics often tended to condemn or ignore contemporary art that called into question this idealism.

All of the influences that journalism brought to bear on Mencken were antagonistic toward this genteel tradition and its culture of idealism. If the first stage of Mencken's rebellion was the choice of a career in journalism, then the second—his development as an iconoclast—was a consequence of that choice.

Chapter Two
The Artist-Iconoclast, 1905–1909

Extremely well read with a wide range of interests, Mencken lacked the temperament to penetrate far below the surface of ideas. Although he liked to call himself a "critic of ideas," he was really more of a collector than an analyst. His writing always reflects the traits of the autodidact, the self-made intellectual: oversimplification, overconfidence, and rigidity. Throughout his life, he considered it a sign of strength that he seldom changed his ideas and opinions.

Nevertheless, Mencken was an intellectual pioneer. He helped to introduce and popularize writers, native and foreign, who were either unknown or deserved a wider hearing. In pursuit of this goal, his energy and enthusiasm were astounding. Between 1905 and 1908, he established a reputation as a promising critic, publishing the first book about George Bernard Shaw, the first popular work about Friedrich Nietzsche, and several interesting essays on Henrik Ibsen, all the while following the daily routine of a newspaper editor. Although the spread and the variety of his work warn against expecting very much depth, Mencken's writings on Shaw, Ibsen, and Nietzsche helped to break new ground. They also help us to trace in Mencken's criticism the evolution of his concept of the artist-iconoclast.

Theater and Iconoclasm

Although Mencken eventually built his national reputation as a literary critic by focusing on the American novel, he first entered the arena of criticism through the stage door, when he became drama editor for the *Morning Herald* in 1901. Eight years later, he gave up reviewing plays, allegedly as an act of mercy toward the local theater managers, who complained of his scathing notices (*Thirty-five Years,* 22).

At the turn of the century, Baltimore was a favorite place for pre-Broadway trial runs. Mencken, therefore, had an opportunity to sample a wide selection of American dramatic fare. Most of what he saw earned his contempt because few native playwrights in the early years of this century rose above the level of conventional competence. Dramatists like Bronson Howard, Augustus Thomas, Clyde Fitch, and William Vaughn Moody made some notable efforts to draw the American theater away from its endless diet of stereotyped historical plays, sentimental melodramas, and superficial comedies. Their attempts to come to grips with the reality of American life were, unfortunately, all too modest. As Alan S. Downer has asserted, "[E]ven the best of serious plays written by Americans before the First World War are not more than superficially true to life." It is little wonder that Mencken found more vitality in the irreverent low-comedy sketches of Joe Weber and Lew Fields, vaudeville being one possible source for his own style of humor.[1]

Even in his early reviews, Mencken demanded realism from both playwrights and actors. He wanted the theater to be "a field of action for personages resembling, in thought and act, the men and women we see about us every day."[2] Bored with romantic fantasy and the Victorian conventions of the well-made play, Mencken sought inspiration from the theater of ideas that had emerged in Europe during the late nineteenth century. In his own words, he wanted to see "human beings at their tricks; to witness combats between will and will, idea and idea, faith and faith, ideal and ideal; to attend a psychological peep show."[3] Wishing to go beyond the mere techniques of realism and naturalism, Mencken sought plays that would strip away the veil of sanctity and sentimentality from human institutions and customs, exposing them to the cold light of inquiry and doubt. The theater, he believed, should be a medium for iconoclasm, and in Henrik Ibsen and George Bernard Shaw he thought he had found his iconoclasts. This conception of the artist as an iconoclast is the essential idea behind Mencken's presentation of both playwrights.

Mencken's *George Bernard Shaw: His Plays* (1905) was intended primarily as a guide to the playwright's works, but it also provides an interpretation of Shaw's position as both an artist and a thinker. Mencken placed Shaw within the context of what he took to be the most important development of the nineteenth century: the gradual triumph of intellectual freedom over religious and secular orthodoxies. The key figure in this process of liberation was, according to Mencken, Charles Darwin. Mencken began his book on Shaw, then, not with the dramatist but with the evolutionist.

Before Darwin, Mencken claimed in *Shaw,* "[o]ne had to believe or be damned. There was no compromise and no middle ground." With the publication of *The Origin of Species,* however, "[r]amparts of authority that had resisted doubts fell like hedge-rows before the facts. . . . For six thousand years it had been necessary, in defending a doctrine, to show only that it was respectable or sacred. Since 1859, it has been needful to prove its truth." The spirit of the Darwinian liberation continued through the writings of Thomas Huxley and Herbert Spencer. "From [Darwin] through Huxley, we have . . . our affable indifference to hell. Through Spencer . . . we have Nietzsche, Sudermann, Hauptmann, Ibsen . . . and the aforesaid George Bernard Shaw."[4]

For Mencken, Shaw's importance lay in his satirical challenge to conventional thought. Mencken divided the characters in Shaw's plays into two categories: "the ordinary folks who represent the great majority, and the iconoclasts." Shaw himself was the perfect iconoclast: "Either he is exhibiting a virtue as a vice in disguise, or exhibiting a vice as a virtue in vice's clothing. In this fact lies the excuse for considering him a world-figure" (*Shaw*, xvi, xii).

Before writing about Shaw, Mencken had become interested in the plays of Henrik Ibsen. Mencken collaborated with a friend, the Danish consul in Baltimore, to translate some of Ibsen's plays into the American idiom. Two, *A Doll's House* and *Little Eyolf*, were published in 1909 with Mencken's introductions. Although he did not mention Darwin in his introduction to *A Doll's House*, Mencken continued to see modern drama as a force for liberating society from the chains of orthodoxy. He considered *A Doll's House* one of those works that helped men throw off the "crushing heritage of formalism and tradition, in art as well as in living." Ibsen's play was important because, by criticizing so sacrosanct an institution as marriage, it "served to prepare the way for an advance in human thought."[5]

From his commentary on Shaw, Ibsen, and later, Nietzsche, there emerges the outline of Mencken's ideal cultural hero: the artist-iconoclast. This coupling of art and iconoclasm dominated much of Mencken's early criticism. "As a matter of fact," he explained in 1909, "the world gets ahead by losing its illusions, and not by fostering them. Nothing, perhaps, is more painful than disillusion, but all the same, nothing is more necessary. . . . Because a horde of impious critics hang upon the flanks of our dearest beliefs today, our children, five hundred years hence, will be free from our present firm faith in political panaceas, unlucky days, dreams, hunches and the influence of mind over matter. Disillusion is like quinine. Its taste is abominable—but it cures."[6] For Mencken, the artist functioned iconoclastically by bringing into damning juxtaposition faith and reason, ideals and reality. By causing people to question their beliefs, the artist cleared the way for a more rational

society. Thus Shaw, a model iconoclast, "does a lot of good in the world."
He was an enemy to all "vile impediments to human progress."[7]

Mencken cast his artist-iconoclast in a romanticized and idealized
mold. He depicted him as an intellectual pioneer blazing trails into the
future, felling the shibboleths of outworn creeds and ideas, clearing
away the obstacles to the development of a rational, enlightened society.
Yet, although Mencken gave his iconoclast the negative power to attack
error, he withheld from him the positive function of building on the
ruins of error. "A preacher necessarily endeavors to make all his hearers
think exactly as he does," Mencken insisted in *Shaw*. "A dramatist
merely tries to make them think. The nature of their conclusions is of
minor consequence." The business of the artist is simply to "record the
facts of life as he sees them" so that the public could "deduce therefrom
new rules of human conduct" (xxiv, xiv).

In suggesting that the artist was to force society to rethink its values
and institutions but not to help it shape new ones, Mencken was trying
to avoid what he saw as the well-worn ruts of American literature and
criticism. He wanted to liberate American art from the genteel tradition's dictum that didacticism, not the critical evaluation of life, was the
essential function of good art. Mencken knew that when the artist
turned propagandist or tractarian, his art often suffered. Mencken's
artist, therefore, had both a creative and a social role. The casual connection between the two, however, rested on Mencken's uncritical faith that
art and intellect, creativity and truth seeking, iconoclasm and progress
were invariably bound together as natural allies in the long struggle of
the human mind against obscurantism. When this faith crumbled, so
did Mencken's confidence in the union of art and iconoclasm.

Darwinizing Nietzsche

Mencken's writings on Shaw and Ibsen developed naturally from his
own interests and experiences. His work on the German philosopher
Friedrich Nietzsche, however, began as a simple business proposition. In
1906, when the publishers of *Shaw* asked Mencken to try his hand at a
volume about Nietzsche, Mencken agreed. The result, *The Philosophy of
Friedrich Nietzsche,* was published in 1908. The book was a moderate
success, and Mencken brought out a new, revised edition in 1913. For
the next decade this book remained such an important source for the
young intellectuals that, during the early 1920s, *Vanity Fair* twice cited

Mencken in its "Hall of Fame" for having "contributed more to the popular understanding of Nietzsche than any other American."[8]

"Understanding" is not, perhaps, the most apt word. The Nietzsche that Mencken gave to American readers was essentially Mencken himself disguised as the German philosopher. This should not be too surprising. Those few Americans who turned to Nietzsche in the prewar years treated his works like a philosophical ragbag from which they carefully selected the appropriate aphorisms to support their own presuppositions. As a result, Nietzsche appeared in such unlikely guises as a liberal Christian or even a Marxist. At least Mencken's insistence on presenting Nietzsche as an enemy of Christianity, democracy, and middle-class idealism conveyed something of the philosopher's authentic voice.[9]

At the time of Nietzsche's death in 1900, the *New York Times* had dismissed the idea that he was a serious philosopher as "preposterous" and had compared him to the "devil-worshippers" of Paris. Because Nietzsche's philosophy challenged so many basic American values, Mencken faced a formidable task in trying to make him palatable to an American audience. He needed some familiar frame of reference within which Nietzsche might be fitted. Therefore, Mencken forced the German into the one mode of American popular thought that Mencken himself enthusiastically accepted: social Darwinism. By Darwinizing Nietzsche, Mencken also Americanized him.[10]

As a teenager, Mencken had absorbed many of the social Darwinist attitudes popular in late-nineteenth-century America. He had cut his intellectual eyeteeth on such Darwinian apostles as Thomas Huxley and Herbert Spencer. He had been especially impressed by William Graham Sumner and had retained a lifelong admiration for his works.[11] As a result, Mencken accepted unconditionally the concept of progress through competition. He firmly believed that "we are still being driven forward and upward, unceasingly and willy-nilly, by the irresistible operation of the law of natural selection."[12] The idea of the struggle for existence so captured Mencken's imagination that he proclaimed in his book on Nietzsche: "If victory comes not, let it be defeat, death and annihilation—but, in any event, let there be a fair fight. Without this constant strife—this constant testing—this constant elimination of the unfit—there can be no progress."[13]

Mencken romanticized the Darwinian struggle for existence because he conceived of it in intellectual, and not just social and economic, terms. The joy of the "highest caste man," he wrote, was to be found "in effort, in work, in progress. A difficulty overcome, a riddle solved, . . . a fact proved, an error destroyed." Mencken's social Darwinism was, therefore, something more than an apologia for capitalism. "My own private view . . . is that the idea of truth-seeking will one day take the place of the idea of money-making" (*Men,* 119–20, 205). In this way Mencken managed to turn the Darwinian concept of the struggle for existence into the iconoclast's attack on orthodoxy. He viewed Nietzsche, therefore, through the twin lenses of Darwinism and iconoclasm.

The best illustration of this approach is Mencken's interpretation of Nietzsche's famous cultural dualism, symbolized by the apposition of the mythical figures of Apollo and Dionysus. Nietzsche believed that there were two forces in life: the Apollonian, which was philosophical and contemplative, and the Dionysian, or the dynamic element. Mencken blurred the many subtle distinctions between the two. The Apollonian spirit appeared to him to be nothing more than the timid conservative's defense of the intellectual status quo, whereas the Dionysian spirit represented iconoclastic rebellion. Or, as Mencken stated in *Nietzsche,* "the apollonians . . . stood for permanence and the dionysians . . . stood for change." The former insisted on a "strict obedience to certain invariable rules, which found expression as religion, law, and morality." The aim of the latter was to "adapt themselves to changing circumstances, and to avoid the snares of artificial, permanent rules" (*Nietzsche* 1913, 72).

Nietzsche had not given unqualified assent to either Apollo or Dionysus. Instead, he sought a synthesis of the two forces. Mencken may have been vaguely aware of this, but he clearly admired what he took to be the superior and more vital virtues of Dionysus: "Dionysus may fall short of triumph to the end of the chapter, but so long as he wages his war upon Apollo fiercely and intelligently there need be no fear of the perils of sloth, of vegetation, of bigotry, of authority, of standing still. . . . Today, the preacher who thunders from the pulpit and the statesman who howls from the rostrum must take thought of and give heed to the doubter who arises in his place and demands to know wherefore and why" (*Nietzsche* 1908, 293–94).

Summarizing the philosophy of his Darwinized (and thus Americanized) Nietzsche, Mencken called it the "gospel of prudent and intelligent selfishness, of absolute and utter individualism" (*Nietzsche* 1908, 102). Mencken often seemed less interested in plumbing the depth of Nietzsche's philosophy than in extolling a ruggedly individualistic gospel of Rooseveltian strenuosity. Indeed, he even insisted that Nietzsche's philosophy was identical to that expressed by Theodore

The King's Library

Roosevelt in *The Strenuous Life*. "There is no denial of the law of natural selection in this thunderous sermon of the American dionysian" (*Nietzsche* 1908, 271).

An extreme individualism colors Mencken's attempt to explain Nietzsche's concept of the *Übermensch*. Mencken totally missed the poetic ecstasy of the philosopher's vision—what Nietzsche called the "urge toward unity, a reaching out beyond person . . . reality, beyond the abyss of perishing."[14] Anxious to present the German as a realistic, practical philosopher, Mencken played down Nietzsche's Zarathustran prophesies about the *Übermensch*. As far as Mencken was concerned, Nietzsche's superman was "merely man raised to perfect efficiency . . . , man absolutely healthy, absolutely unfettered, absolutely undeluded, absolutely immoral."[15]

Mencken seemed convinced that Nietzsche's philosophy could encourage the establishment of a "new aristocracy of efficiency," which would function in a state of "ideal anarchy." Under such conditions the world would witness the ascendancy of powerful figures—"[s]ham-smashers and truth-tellers and mob-fighters"—such as Abraham Lincoln, Otto von Bismarck, Darwin, and Huxley. Such men would "re-establish the law of natural selection firmly upon its disputed throne, and so the strong would grow ever stronger and more efficient, and the weak would grow ever more obedient and tractile" (*Nietzsche* 1913, 198, 197).

The emotional and psychological storm center flashing behind Nietzsche's work was totally lost upon Mencken. He was poorly equipped, both philosophically and temperamentally, to understand the existentialist side of the German's thought. Comfortably and uncritically immersed in social Darwinism and a firm believer in progress, Mencken was completely insensitive to the spiritual crisis of the nineteenth-century intellectuals who had agonized over the challenge that science and materialism had presented to the metaphysical and spiritual side of their culture. Oblivious to the sense of crisis, Mencken missed the heart of Nietzsche's work and found it relatively easy to gloss over the philosopher's condemnation of Darwin as a nihilist.

Mencken *used* Nietzsche, as he used Shaw and Ibsen and almost every other writer he ever championed. The philosopher became another model of the perfect iconoclast whose mission was, as Mencken explained it, "to attack error wherever he saw it and to proclaim truth wherever he found it. It is only by such iconoclasm and proselyting that humanity can be helped." Nietzsche, Mencken insisted, had been a fighter against the "only real crime in the world . . . unreasoning belief"

(*Nietzsche* 1913, 201, 4). Instinctively, Mencken also used Nietzsche to shore up social Darwinism against the stresses of its own inner contradictions. No philosophy, not even the loose and informal doctrines of American social Darwinism, could long maintain in combination such contradictory elements as naturalistic determinism, laissez-faire economics, Protestant idealism, and native individualism. By the turn of the century, social Darwinism was beginning to break apart as an intellectual force. The harsh competitiveness and extreme individualism of Sumner and the benign determinism of Spencer were being challenged by a more liberal emphasis on cooperation and social intervention— what Richard Hofstadter called the "transition towards solidarism" and Eric Goldman denoted as "Reform Darwinism."[16]

Reform Darwinism held little attraction for Mencken, who believed that progress could result only from the triumph of "those strong, free, self-reliant, resourceful men whose capacities are so much greater than the mob's that they are often able to force their ideas upon it" (*Nietzsche* 1913, 197). He wanted to turn social Darwinism into an apologia for pure elitism. In trying to graft what he took from Nietzsche onto social Darwinism, Mencken sought to use the former to purify the latter by reestablishing individualism at the center of social philosophy. Nietzsche helped Mencken rid social Darwinism of the "corrupting" influences of Christian altruism and Progressive idealism. At the same time, Mencken sought to arm Nietzscheism with the Darwinian weapons of the struggle for existence and the law of natural selection, which he hoped would provide the liberating force for his aristocracy of iconoclasts.

On the surface, Nietzsche served Mencken well. By presenting his iconoclastic hero as the harbinger of progress, Mencken was pushing his way into the intellectual vanguard. His work on Shaw, Ibsen, and especially Nietzsche placed him for a time at the forefront of the cultural debates in America. Mencken's encounter with Nietzsche also helped him to put his own ideas into a roughly consistent, if limited and highly simplistic, framework. It is true, as D. C. Stenerson has shown, that most of Mencken's prejudices had already been formed by the time he had completed his apprenticeship as a journalist and well before he started work on the philosopher (Stenerson 1971, 117–18). Admitting that he had been working out his own ideas by writing the book, Mencken also acknowledged, "Even so, those ideas were plainly *based* on Nietzsche; without him, I'd never have come to them."[17] Nietzsche provided Mencken with "*certification* of those ideas, a philosophical framework into which to place them" (Hobson 1994, 91).

Mencken's Darwinized Nietzsche gave him the nearest thing he would ever have to an ideology. He viewed society in terms of the eternal struggle between the talented individual and the ignorant, venal mob. This conflict contained certain dramatic possibilities, which Mencken certainly exploited in his satire. Would this stark and crudely simple approach be enough to enable Mencken to understand a complex and rapidly changing American society? This question was not yet a crucial one for him in 1908, as he strove to ensure the survival of nineteenth-century romantic individualism in the twentieth century. Mencken's heaven-storming hero, the artist-iconoclast, would drag the human race forward into the searing light of rationality. What this light might reveal did not yet trouble him.

The initial importance of Mencken's book on Nietzsche was that it clearly stamped Mencken as a cultural rebel. Nietzsche, no matter how garbled, was a challenge to American thought, especially to genteel idealism. The final rebellion that was to overthrow the genteel tradition was only beginning in 1908. With Mencken's book on Nietzsche, as Henry F. May has noted, "a lonely glove was thrown down and a whole period of revolution foreshadowed" (May, 209).

Chapter Three

Social Criticism in Prewar America, 1910–1915

The "Free Lance"

All the while Mencken was inventing his artist-iconoclast and laying the foundations for his reputation as a critic, he was fully engaged as a newspaperman in Baltimore. Starting as a cub reporter for the city's *Morning Herald* in 1899, he was city editor by 1904 and already tiring of office routine. On February 6 of that same year, a fire started that, within a week, burned out a square mile of the city. Like the Chicago Fire of 1871 and the San Francisco Earthquake of 1906, the Great Baltimore Fire was one of the major urban disasters of the period. It was also the kind of opportunity of which young newspapermen dreamed. With little sleep, no change of clothes, and traveling between three cities, Mencken worked for a solid week to bring out the paper. The fire marked his rite of passage from youth to maturity. "It was brain-fagging and back-breaking, but it was grand beyond compare," he wrote in *Newspaper Days,* "an adventure of the first chop, a razzle-dazzle superb and elegant, a circus in forty rings. When I came out of it at last I was a settled and indeed almost a middle-aged man, spavined by responsibility and aching in every sinew, but I went into it a boy, and it was the hot gas of youth that kept me going" (277–78). Nothing could ever be as exciting again, least of all newspaper editing.

While the fire tempered Mencken, it ruined the *Morning Herald.* Burned out of its building, the paper was financially weakened beyond repair. As managing editor and secretary of the paper's board of directors, the 25-year-old Mencken found himself presiding over a sinking ship.

When the *Herald* went out of business in June 1906, Mencken's problem was not finding a job but finding a job in Baltimore; several New York papers had made good offers, but Mencken's sense of responsibility toward his widowed mother and his attachment to Baltimore ruled out any such move. After barely a month on the Baltimore *Evening*

News, Mencken joined the staff of the city's *Sunpapers* in July 1906, inaugurating a connection he would maintain for most of the remainder of his career.

By 1910, as an editor of the *Evening Sun,* Mencken had begun to attract attention. In 1911, his editorials for the *Evening Sun* (signed "H. L. M.") caught the eye of one of the paper's owners, who suggested that Mencken be given his own daily, signed column and a free hand to write about whatever he wished. The result was the "Free Lance," which Mencken himself described as a "private editorial column devoted wholly to my personal opinions and prejudices."[1]

The "Free Lance," which first appeared on May 8, 1911, provided Mencken with a limited but untrammeled platform from which to exercise the iconoclasm and philosophical skepticism he had developed in his work on Shaw and Nietzsche. Looking back over the column in later years, he believed that it had been very beneficial for him: "[I]t not only rid me of the last vestiges of [editorial] work, but also served to clarify and organize my ideas. Before it had gone on a year I knew precisely what I was about and where I was heading. In it I worked out much of the material that was later to enter into my books, and to color the editorial policy of the *American Mercury*" (*Thirty-five Years,* 33).

Mencken's iconoclasm soon generated a steady stream of protest letters. Consistent in his love of controversy, Mencken asked for and received control of a column next to his in which he printed the most vigorous of the attacks against him. "This was partly mere bombast and braggadocio," he later recalled, "but also partly genuine belief in free speech" (Adler, 49).

Mencken's opinions about politics and society were derived from an amalgam of his social Darwinism, his Nietzscheism, and his dedication to the idea of an iconoclastic elite. In 1910, he and Socialist editor R. R. La Monte published a dialogue entitled *Men versus the Man,* which contains the rudiments of Mencken's social philosophy. Although the book attracted little attention, Mencken later claimed that its preparation "clarified and crystallized my ideas and by the time our correspondence was at an end . . . I was ready to take on something on the order of leadership in the long war against utopianism" (*My Life,* 35).[2]

In *Men versus the Man,* Mencken defined society as the battleground between the superior individual and the inferior mob. In one of his contributions to the collaboration, Mencken argued that the prime quality of the superior man was "a sort of restless impatience with things as they are—a sort of insatiable desire to help along the evolutionary process"

(113). Because the inferior man lacked these virtues, he deserved the place to which nature had assigned him—the bottom of the heap. Invoking a parody of the American Dream, Mencken described the average man: "He is forever down-trodden and oppressed. He is forever opposed to a surrender of his immemorial superstitions, prejudices, swinishness, and inertia. He is forever certain that, if only some god would lend him a hand and give him his just rights, he would be rich, happy and care-free. And he is forever and utterly wrong" (112). Any political system based on the participation of the masses was, therefore, doomed by its false doctrine that a man, "merely by virtue of being a man, is fitted to take a hand in the adjudication of all the world's most solemn and difficult causes" (151).

Already highly critical of democracy in 1910, Mencken had not yet begun to associate the worst aspects of democracy with the American system. The United States fell short of its democratic ideals, Mencken noted in *Men versus the Man,* and rightly so. "Once a year we reaffirm the doctrine that all men are free and equal. All the rest of the twelvemonth we devote our energies to proving that they are not" (152). Should a real democracy actually be instituted, Mencken insisted, "[t]here would be an end to all progress. Emotion would take the place of reason. It would be impossible to achieve coherent governmental policies" (153).

At this point in his career, Mencken was torn between his libertarian, antigovernment instincts and his hope for a modern form of government based on rationality and efficiency. During the early days of the "Free Lance," his main target was that of corrupt and inefficient government led by self-serving politicians who played upon the stupidity of the masses. Mencken advocated instead a government that would be efficient, honest, enlightened, and *active;* it would cut away the old, fraudulent pieties of special privileges and emotional party ties and thereby run society along intelligent, modern lines. Although Mencken clearly rejected Bryanesque liberalism, which equated better government with increased democracy, he sought, like many others during the Progressive Era, the path to effective government.

For example, he championed the idea of a strong executive over what he considered venal and stodgy legislatures. Along with many urban reformers, he wanted to curtail the powers of rural-dominated state legislatures over the cities. In urban "home rule" he saw the first essential step toward improving city government. In fact, Mencken even argued that state legislatures and city councils should be stripped of their powers. They were the "headquarters of all governmental incompetence, stupidity and corruptions," he insisted in his *Evening Sun* column of May 22, 1911. "What state will be the first to abolish its legislature?" In place of representative bodies, Mencken advocated the strong use of executive power by mayors, city managers, governors, and even presidents. In 1911, he welcomed the election of reform governor Woodrow Wilson in New Jersey; for with the people behind a strong leader, "not even a dubious legislature can affront or defy him."[3]

It is significant that Mencken's political hero at this time was Theodore Roosevelt. Commenting on TR's European trip in 1910, Mencken suggested that Europeans saw the ex-president as "a visible symbol of all the great qualities which enter into the spirit of Americanism. They regard him . . . as the archtype of the energetic, resourceful, idol-smashing American." Roosevelt was the spokesman of American efficiency, and this spirit was "the one thing that sets the United States apart from all other nations. We are sworn foes to formalism in all departments of thought and life. Our one god is progress—and Colonel Roosevelt is the high priest in the temple."[4]

Like Roosevelt, Mencken believed that America needed efficient and dynamic leadership to introduce modernizing reforms. Public health was a prime example. A well-informed layman on medical matters and acquainted with some of Baltimore's best medical professionals, Mencken used his "Free Lance" column to campaign for improvement in the city's dismal record on fighting malaria and typhoid. Typically, he blamed the problem on the backwardness of the public and on the disinclination of timorous politicians to support unpopular and vigorous reforms.

When local politicians and civic boosters complained that Mencken's publicizing of Baltimore's health problems was hurting the city's image, the "Free Lance" lashed out on January 3, 1913, at those who seemed to believe "that every raid upon established custom, and particularly upon established hoggishness, hurts business, and that no city can survive such damage. Their ideal is commercial prosperity, and they are determined to get it if half of humanity must rot for it." Although an unrepentant supporter of capitalism, Mencken was far from enamored with the progress of industrialism in his city; nor did he admire the values upon which it seemed to thrive. "The time will come, no doubt, when a man who proposes to put 500 women to work in a factory at four dollars a week will be sent to jail as an enemy to society, instead of being fawned upon as a public benefactor, as at present. . . . We still estimate all such enterprises by the money they produce and not, as we should, by the human beings they produce" (June 23, 1911).[5]

Mencken's iconoclasm enabled him to cut across ideological bound-aries. Although not a liberal on racial issues, Mencken did ask Balti-moreans to consider both the justice and the wisdom of the growing policy of housing segregation that forced blacks, no matter what their status, to remain in slums, the breeding grounds for typhoid and tuber-culosis. Other areas of reform also interested the "Free Lance": Mencken vehemently attacked capital punishment. He gave cautious approval to the "Oregon Plan," which provided for the initiative, referendum, and recall at the state level. He supported the direct primary and even the new state of Arizona in its proposal for the recall of judges. "The one way to prove the good or evil of new schemes of government is to test them in practice. And the best place to test them is in the new states, where the insecurity and fluency of institutions are taken for granted and comparatively little harm can be done by sudden change."[6]

This tolerance for experimentation was a part of the general reform atmosphere of the Progressive Era. Some of Mencken's ideas, however, clearly ran counter to the mainstream of reformist thought. He contin-ued to warn against the dangers of democracy, claiming in one "Free Lance" article that "[u]niversal manhood suffrage is the cancer that eats at the vitals of the republic. No improvement will ever be real until that cancer is cut out" (July 23, 1912). The great masses of people, he con-tended, "are against all those varieties of change which involve risk and sacrifice. . . . [The masses'] proper function is to execute the ideas of their betters. It is highly dangerous to let them manufacture ideas themselves." Those who were too ignorant to mark their ballot slips properly, he maintained, should not be disqualified in an election but permanently disfranchised (June 5, 1913).

Even here, however, Mencken also managed to be more progressive than many dedicated democratic-minded reformers. He condemned the various attempts to disfranchise Maryland blacks as totally dishonor-able. He also supported women's suffrage, although not on the usually idealistic grounds that women voters would somehow purify politics. He saw it as simply a matter of justice that women, particularly working women who suffered under the "double slavery" of brute marriage and industrialism, should have a right to help frame the laws that affected their welfare. He was, in fact, opposed to arbitrary restriction of the franchise by race or sex. He insisted that "[a] black Lincoln would be just as much a Lincoln as Abe himself, and a Pasteur in skirts would still be worth hearing and heeding. . . . Before we may begin to edit and denaturize democracy, we must first give democracy a fair trial, and it has not yet had that fair trial." In the end, however, Mencken remained convinced that society would eventually be forced to consider the franchise not as a right but as "a thing the citizen must earn by his ability and his industry" (June 5, 1913).

Mencken's attitudes during the Progressive period seem so idiosyncratic, so lacking in either liberal or conservative consistency, that it is tempting to consider him a complete maverick. Yet Mencken did support many of the reforms dear to the hearts of urban Progressives— clean government, executive leadership, administrative efficiency, political experimentation, urban home rule, civic improvements, and public health initiatives. Mencken's support for such reforms based on modernization and efficiency marks him as a Progressive, but his suspicion of democracy places him at the conservative end of the Progressive spectrum.

The idea of a conservative Progressive might seem a contradiction in terms if one assumes that all reform is the product of liberal movements only. Bismarck's Germany and the Britain of Benjamin Disraeli and Arthur Balfour suggest that, in other countries at least, reform sometimes has been a conservative phenomenon. Although it may be argued that the liberal elements predominated in America during the Progressive period, Progressivism was by no means a monolithic force. William Jennings Bryan's demands for more direct democracy were very different in spirit from the Rooseveltian approach to reform, which placed its faith in decisions made by experts and technicians and implemented by a strong executive. Progressivism was so diverse in terms of people and ideas that it is better described as a mood than as a movement.[7]

In this light, Mencken's support for Roosevelt, an avowed Progressive, has added significance. As mentioned earlier, Mencken saw Roosevelt as an American Nietzsche who, despite his playing fast and loose with public emotions, still had "great foresight and sagacity. . . . He is not an orthodox man, true enough, but he is at least a man who supports his reasoning intelligently, and shows intellectual hospitality and alertness." The Rough Rider would be dangerous, Mencken concluded, if he believed his own democratic "balderdash," but "what reflective man accuses him of believing it?" (June 11, 1912). Even as late as 1920, Mencken remained convinced that Roosevelt had never been moved by Bryanism or Wilsonian democratic liberalism, observing that

> Roosevelt, for all his fluent mastery of democratic counter-words, democratic gestures and all the rest of the armamentarium of the mob-master,

had no such faith in his heart of hearts. He didn't believe in democracy; he believed simply in government. His remedy for all the great pangs and longings of existence was not a dispersion of authority, but a hard concentration of authority. He was not in favor of unlimited experiment; he was in favor of a rigid control from above, a despotism of inspired prophets and policemen. He was not for democracy as his followers understood democracy, and as it actually is and must be; he was for a paternalism of the true Bismarckian pattern . . . a paternalism concerning itself with all things. . . . His instincts were always those of the property-owning Tory, not those of the romantic Liberal. (*Prejudices* 2, 123–24)

Mencken voted for Roosevelt in 1912. Woodrow Wilson defeated the Rough Rider, however, and as the liberalism of the New Freedom waxed, Mencken's interest in reform quickly waned.[8] Mencken, of course, had never embraced the term "Progressive," which to him represented the democratic side of the reform mood. As early as July 23, 1912, he quipped in the "Free Lance" that "[a] progressive is one who believes that the common people are both intelligent and honest; a reactionary is one who knows better." By June 20, 1914, he was so disgruntled with the turn that reform had taken that he issued a manifesto of reaction. "Up with the black flag! The time has come for honest men to throw off all disguises. The uplift has failed in politics as it has in morals. The country has been made ridiculous abroad and darn near ruined at home. . . . Down with direct elections! Down with muckraking! Down with the new freedom! . . . Down with mob rule! . . . Down with bogus progressivism! . . . Up with Civilization! . . . The people are ripe for rescue."

Mencken's reference to the "uplift," a popular term for moral reform during the Progressive Era, suggests that he felt that reform had saddled the country with something more than an excess of democracy. It had created, in his view, a militant, intolerant, moralistic spirit that not only invaded the privacy of the individual but threatened the sanctity of the individual as well.

Crusade against Crusades

The pressure for moral reform that accompanied the movement for political and social reform after 1900 is, perhaps, one of the most important cultural phenomena of the Progressive period. As historian Clyde Griffen has observed, "The progressives grew up with a moral consensus so clear and unquestioned that they tended to assume this consensus was characteristic of human nature whenever it was permitted to develop freely. This assumption easily fostered righteous indignation against violators of the consensus; personalities with an authoritarian warp carried this to the blind intolerance of 'sinners' which not infrequently appears in progressive crusades against intemperance, gambling, and prostitution."[9] With industrialization, urbanization, and immigration, the old rural Protestant values, which were the core of this moral consensus, began to come under attack. As a result, the moral reformers within the Progressive ranks were driven not only by faith in their values but also by an aggressive attempt to meet the challenge of urban secularization and cultural pluralism.

Mencken's Baltimore experienced its share of this conflict. Protestant evangelists, Anti-Saloon Leaguers, and vice crusaders preached proscriptive laws as a cure for social ills. Using the "Free Lance" as his platform, Mencken sought to organize local resistance against the drive for moral legislation. Under the banner of libertarianism, Mencken waged a crusade against the moral crusaders. Attempts to censor books or the theater drew from him the accusation that such laws were "revolutionary and dangerous" and could turn the policeman into "the most lawless man among us." Angered at efforts to curtail secular entertainments on Sundays, Mencken complained, "Virtue, once it grows militant and tyrannical, tends to become a vice" (June 1, 1911). It also tended to be self-defeating. Mencken pointed out that when vice crusaders attempted to destroy the old "red light" district, they simply spread prostitution throughout the city. "Nothing has ever been accomplished in Christendom," he warned, "by proceeding upon the theory that sin is a purely volitional phenomenon, to be stamped out by invective. All the moral progress we have made has been based upon frank acceptance of human frailty, and common-sense endeavor to diminish the evil in its inevitable effects" (November 7, 1912).

While some people viewed moral legislation as merely an inconvenience and a nuisance, Mencken believed that such laws endangered liberty. On January 11, 1913, he accused the militant moralists of trying to "steal liberty and self-respect, and the man who has lost both is a man who has lost everything that separates a civilized freeman from a convict in a chain gang." Mencken went so far as to urge Baltimoreans to defy all proscriptive legislation whenever and wherever it was possible to do so. This statement bothered Charles Bonaparte, a former member of Theodore Roosevelt's administration and the leader of the Baltimore Reform League. In a public letter printed in the *Evening Sun,* he informed the "Free Lance" that a citizen was duty bound to obey all laws as long as they remained on the books. Responding on January 8, 1913, Mencken insisted that laws that invaded the citizen's rights and privacy were beyond obedience. The citizen "is bound to resist such laws to the full extent of his courage and ingenuity, so long as the chances of success remain in his favor. . . . In brief, the decent citizen has to protect himself against legislative snouting and tyranny, for it is only by protecting himself that he can protect civilization. The law, when it falls into the hands of moral maniacs, becomes itself a desperate criminal."

Mencken regarded the drive for social control through the legislation of morals as a real threat to individualism and to traditional American ideas of liberty. Moreover, he was convinced that moral crusades were an extension of Progressive reform, control of which, in his opinion, had drifted from the rational leadership of the few to the democratic emotionalism of the masses. Mencken, therefore, turned so vehemently against Progressivism that he conveniently ignored his previous support for many Progressive reforms.

"The American": 1913

Occurring between 1912 and 1913, this change in Mencken's attitude toward reform paralleled a much more significant shift in his rhetorical position toward America. Although increasingly critical of many aspects of American culture and society, Mencken had always criticized his country from the inside: that is, he adopted the persona of the bemused but concerned citizen who accused his society of violating its own value system. By 1913, however, his persona had undergone a simple but dramatic change. Mencken suddenly appeared to be criticizing America from the outside, using a value system that, he implied, was exterior and superior to America's. In terms of style, he accomplished this shift by a simple alteration in his employment of possessive pronouns: where he had previously written about "we" Americans and "our" problems, he now used the terms "the" American and "his" problems.

Several factors contributed to the hardening of Mencken's critical attitude toward American society: his struggle to improve American literature in the face of mediocrity and cultural conservatism, his disillusionment with reform, and his concern about militant moralism. Another factor was his trip to Europe in the spring of 1912. For the first time, he came into direct contact with old societies that had a tradition of high culture extending back for centuries, providing a dramatic contrast to America. At first he was just one more Yankee tourist making the obligatory rounds of Gibraltar, Rome, Paris, and London, but when he arrived in Germany, the land of his forebears, Mencken's ideal of the superior society suddenly materialized before him. In Germany he thought he had discovered a land of beauty, tradition, and order, which had, at the same time, a powerful sense of modern efficiency.[10]

Within a year after his return from Europe, Mencken began to publish in the *Smart Set* magazine a series of articles about American society and the national character. The articles were intended to be the basis for a book. That book was never published, but the articles mark Mencken's most ambitious attempt thus far at satiric social and cultural criticism. Running intermittently from June 1913 to February 1914, the series began with an introductory essay entitled "The American." Subsequent pieces were subtitled "His Morals," "His Language," "His Idea of Beauty," "His Freedom," and "His New Puritanism."[11]

The effectiveness of Mencken's satire in this series was based on two innovations. One, already noted, was the adoption of the persona of the outsider. The other was the constant inversion of the myths that Americans cherished about themselves. For example, Mencken took the myth of American individualism and converted it into an image of American conformity. In perhaps no other country in the world, he claimed in October 1913, was any deviation from the accepted norm met with such "utter social and political extinction" as in the United States. In his view the American was "so little the soul-free individualist that it is almost impossible for him to imagine himself save as a member of a crowd. All of his thinking is done, and most of his acts are done, not as a free individual, but as one of a muddled mass of individuals. . . . He does not stand for something; he belongs to something" (85). Mencken similarly inverted the myth of American liberty, declaring, "[T]here is probably no civilized man who knows less of genuine liberty, either personal or political, than the American." Surrounded by so many prohibitions concerning morals, "it has become almost impossible for a citizen . . . to get through a day without violating at least one of them. . . . In every relation of life the private conduct of the American is minutely regulated" (82).

Mencken also denied his fellow citizens' proud belief that their government was the most advanced in the world. Americans, he wrote in June 1913, enjoyed the opportunity to change old platitudes for new ones, "[b]ut certainly not opportunity to tackle head on and with a surgeon's courage the greater and graver problems of being and becoming, to draw a sword upon the time worn and doddering delusions of the race, to clear away the corruptions that make government a game for thieves and morals a petty vice for old-maids and patriotism a last refuge of scoundrels" (94). Instead of freeing the individual, Mencken insisted in October 1913, American democracy placed the citizen under the tyranny of the majority. "A democracy made up of assertive individualists, each reacting upon all the others, would be a democracy extremely jealous of human rights and extremely sensitive to new ideas." In the United States, however, democracy consisted of the maneuverings of political parties that were little more than "two disorderly mobs, each wholly careless of the rights of the other" and "highly resistant to purely intelligent suggestion" (86).

The American who emerged from Mencken's articles was a far cry from the national myth of the courageous, self-reliant individualist. In the new Menckenized version, he became a figure haunted by fears: fears of the minority groups below him, of the powerful and wealthy above him, of the beauty he could not appreciate, and of the new and different ideas that disturbed him. Primarily, however, Mencken's American of October 1913 was afraid of *himself*. "His dominant passion is not for self-expression, but for self-effacement. He performs the function of a citizen, not as a free ego, but as a mere cipher, a nameless soldier in a large army" (87).

Mencken blamed this failure of spirit on Puritanism, or rather the "New Puritanism," as the title of his final article in February 1914 suggested. According to Mencken, the Puritanism of seventeenth-century New England was based on an introspective concern for the individual's spiritual well-being and upon renunciation and asceticism. Modern Puritanism, however, was aggressive; it sought to dominate society, not with spiritual ideals but with moral coercion. Puritanism had become a debased form of Nietzsche's "Will to Power." It was nothing more than "a wild scramble into Heaven on the backs of harlots" (89).

The "New Puritanism" was the result, Mencken argued, of the accumulation of industrial wealth following the Civil War. "In brief, puritanism has become militant by becoming rich" (89). As a result of this "trustification" of religion, the Puritan could "combat immorality with the weapons designed for crime" (91). Imposed upon an undisciplined democracy, Puritanism, by means of "uplift" or moral reform, had made its assault on culture, order, and individual liberty.

Although Mencken's attempt to combine Nietzschean psychology with an economic interpretation of Puritanism is not without interest, he clearly had only a superficial grasp of American religious history.

Those characteristics that Mencken associated with "Puritanism"—sentimental evangelical piety, bourgeois moralism, the business ethic, excessive reforming zeal—had little or nothing to do with Puritanism as a historical force. Mencken was not alone in this error, however. Many Americans of the period believed that something called "Puritanism" constituted the core of the national culture. Mencken himself agreed that it was the central factor in the American tradition, but, in his final myth inversion, he condemned it as dangerous and stultifying. Puritanism, in Mencken's hands, had become a tradition that had to be destroyed.[12]

Although almost all of Mencken's "American" articles constituted a sustained denunciation of the American character and society, there was one exception. "The American: His Language" was the only article about an aspect of American culture that Mencken wholeheartedly admired. He believed that American speech had developed so many new words and phrases, had become so altered in syntax and pronunciation, that it was becoming a separate language. This article, appearing in August 1913, was the basis of what was to become the enduring work of his lifetime, *The American Language.* Suddenly, Mencken dropped the satirical tone that dominated the rest of the series in the *Smart Set.* "The distinguished trait of the American is simply his tendency to use slang without any false sense of impropriety, his eager hospitality to its most audacious novelties, his ingenuous yearning to augment the conciseness, the sprightliness, and, in particular, what may be called the dramatic punch of his language. It is ever his effort to translate ideas into terms of overt acts, to give the intellectual a visual and striking quality" (95). For a brief moment Mencken's American became an iconoclast, if not in his acts, then at least in his speech, which was "a language preeminent among the tongues of the earth for its eager hospitality to new words and no less for its compactness, its naked directness, and its disdain of all academic obfuscations and restraints" (95).

The Two Nations

"The American" series dates the emergence of that satirical line of attack that was to make Mencken both famous and infamous in the 1920s. Although his satire became more bitter after World War I, Mencken's rhetorical stance toward his country had been formed before the guns sounded. By assiduously inverting America's most cherished myths, Mencken created countermyths, reverse images of the American:

homo boobiens—the citizen as mob-man. This powerful but distorted image was to dominate his writings in the 1920s.

Mencken's insistence that the essential weakness of America was to be found in the very essence of Americanism gave a tremendous force to his satire. It also created a serious artistic and intellectual problem for him. All satirists dredge up the evils and follies of their societies. Some, unfortunately, choose scapegoats from among minority groups to bear the burden of those evils. Others, like Sinclair Lewis, concoct national stereotypes—such as Babbitt, the businessman, or Elmer Gantry, the evangelist—to personify folly. Some, like Mencken, distill all their society's shortcomings and offenses into a series of negative images. Few satirists, however, have gone as far as Mencken in identifying by name this anticountry as their own. The lands in which Gulliver traveled resembled with painful clarity Jonathan Swift's own islands, but Swift never actually labeled those lands "England" and "Ireland." He maintained the necessary artistic distance between reality and his satiric vision.

Mencken, then, took the ultimate step as a social satirist. He herded the fools and follies of his country into a cage and labeled the cage "America." But if America was in the cage, where was the satirist standing as he viewed the show? If everything that Mencken disliked in his society was American, then by what means could he identify and defend those national virtues that he did admire and to which he was deeply committed? Mencken was in danger of being isolated by his own rhetorical gesture.

The "American" articles were not the result of a deep sense of alienation from America; they were the product of Mencken's impatience, his elitist arrogance, and his satiric instinct for the jugular. He had inverted American myths, but he did not really devalue American ideals. Mencken denied that Americans were freedom-loving, intelligent, honorable, or courageous, but he did not condemn the values of freedom, intelligence, honor, or courage. Moreover, when he dealt with the American language, he momentarily changed from critic to celebrant of *another* America, covertly expressing his admiration for some of those American traits—audaciousness, conciseness, liveliness, impatience with formalism and restraint—that his newly adopted satiric persona did not allow him to identify as part of the national character.

In a sense, Mencken had unconsciously impoverished his vocabulary. He had made the word "American" stand for everything he was against, and, as a result, he later found it difficult to revalue the word when he wished to defend those national values to which he was deeply attached. He had, in effect, created two nations: the America of his satiric image, which he overtly attacked, and an America that he covertly loved and wanted to preserve. Unfortunately, World War I was to magnify the weaknesses of the first and to make him even more unconscious of his attachment to the second.

Chapter Four

The *Smart Set* Years: Mencken as Literary Critic and Editor

The period between 1908 and the outbreak of World War I in 1914 was one of the most decisive in Mencken's career. In those half dozen years, he solidified his satirical style and made himself a leader in the opposition to the conventional literary culture of the period, laying the basis for a national reputation as a literary critic. The two key developments in this period were the establishment of the "Free Lance," and his association with the *Smart Set* magazine.

In the spring of 1908, Mencken was invited to write the book review section for the *Smart Set,* a monthly magazine with a dubious but sophisticated reputation. A somewhat tarnished remnant of New York's fin de siècle days, the *Smart Set* had been founded in 1900 by the self-styled Colonel William D'Alton Mann, an ambitious publishing buccaneer and scandalmonger. The magazine was the outgrowth of an earlier periodical, *Town Topics,* which had successfully combined literary bohemianism and international bon vivant criticism with spicy gossip concerning New York's "four hundred." Eventually freed from the colonel's activities, if not from the taint of his reputation, the *Smart Set* published such authors as O. Henry, Clyde Fitch, David Belasco, James Branch Cabell, Frank Norris, Jack London, Edgar Saltus, and Anatole France.[1]

With its tradition of combining works of solid literary merit with a light sophisticated touch, the *Smart Set* initially seemed well suited to Mencken's satirical style and his adventurous approach to literature. Moreover, his work on the magazine brought him into contact with George Jean Nathan, a young drama critic who shared many of Mencken's tastes and who was to become his alter ego in one of the most famous editorial partnerships in American magazine history.

The year 1908 also marked the coming of age of the rebellion against the dominance of the genteel tradition in American letters. In addition to Mencken's and Nathan's appearance in the *Smart Set* (and Mencken's book on Nietzsche), the year also saw the publication of Van Wyck Brooks's first book, *The Wine of the Puritans*. Dissent also came from more conservative quarters with the appearance of Irving Babbitt's *Literature and the American College*. In the same year, Babbitt's fellow Humanist Paul Elmer More was preparing to exchange his position as literary editor of the New York *Evening Post* for the editorship of a more influential magazine, the *Nation*.

The literary scene these emerging critics faced was anything but encouraging. Unlike the decades that bracket it, the period from 1900 to 1910 was neither exciting nor momentous for American literature. True, realism continued to gain acceptance, and some writers made genuine attempts to come to grips with the economic and social realities of life in industrial America. Nonetheless, the artistic results were seldom impressive. Except for the work of Henry James, who lived in England and who was not highly regarded at home, the "Strenuous Age" produced few books of permanent importance. Theodore Dreiser's magnificent *Sister Carrie* (1900), although not quite suppressed as legend has had it, did not make a great impact at the time. Apart from a few other notable exceptions such as Frank Norris's *The Octopus* (1901), Jack London's *The Call of the Wild* (1903), Edith Wharton's *The House of Mirth* (1905), and Upton Sinclair's *The Jungle* (1906), little of permanent value was published during the decade.

Indeed, many critics of the period felt that the American novel was facing a crisis. James E. Collins, commenting in the *Bookman* in 1906, saw American writing falling into four basic categories: the "fashion plate," the "cosmic monotone," the "strenuous," and the "optimo-platitudinous." "Poverty" and "dullness" were the judgments handed down by Charles Moore in the *Dial* in 1910. Contemplating the state of the American novel in 1905, a critic in the *Forum* insisted that "[t]here is no other kind of literary work . . . in which the level of performance is so low."[2] Van Wyck Brooks mulled over the tasteless wine of the Puritans and the lack of a "constructive force" in American culture. Mencken himself characterized the situation in his own inimitable fashion in the *Smart Set* when he declared in August 1910 that "our American manufacturers of best sellers, having the souls of fudge-besotted high-school girls, behold the human comedy as a mixture of fashionable wedding and three-alarm fire, with music by Francois Frédéric [*sic*] Chopin" (153).[3]

The defenders of the literary status quo did not, of course, desire to espouse the cause of mediocrity. Some of them were painfully aware that something was wrong with the American novel, but they were trapped by their assumptions that art had to reflect not reality but the ideal, not doubt and questioning but moral and civic affirmation. They were ill-equipped to search out and appreciate the newer kinds of writing that could revitalize American literature. For their part, dissenting critics like Mencken felt they worked in a void. There were few contemporary American writers whom they could hold up as models, and there was only a vague sense of where each critic stood in relation to his fellows. In his last *Smart Set* review in December 1923, Mencken recalled that there had been no concerted effort among writers and critics who were seeking to overthrow the old literary order. Critics had to work out, more or less on their own, what was wrong with American literature and what kind of writing and imaginative insight was needed to bring in a new era.

This problem was not, as Percy Boynton later pointed out in 1927, a purely aesthetic one. "Criticism in America is implicitly an attempt by each critic to make of America the kind of country he would like, which in every case is a better country than it is today. . . . As he achieves a sense of values he adopts them, and declares them, and tries to make them prevail."[4] Obviously, American critics in 1908 were not engaged in purely academic debates. Assuming that literature was the product of culture, they ranged beyond art to consider the society out of which it arose. Mencken's literary criticism, then, should be seen both as a bid to encourage the emergence of a vital, vibrant national literature and as an attempt to provide a sharp critique of American society and culture. In Mencken's case, as with most of his fellow critics of the time, the two tasks were deemed inseparable.

Mencken's criticism, especially before 1917, reveals a threefold strategy for the improvement of American letters. First, he tried to identify and attack those characteristics of American culture that seemed to obstruct writers in their efforts to come to grips with their society. He also cautioned American writers not to look to the past for their inspiration. Rather, he urged them to look to contemporary Europe for their models of excellence and to contemporary America for their material. Finally, he turned his reviews in the *Smart Set* into an ongoing seminar on the novel, extolling the kind of philosophical approach that would enable writers to look at life through clear rather than rose-colored glasses.

Clearing the Ground

Toward the end of his 15-year domination of the *Smart Set* book department, Mencken commented, "My business, considering the state of the society in which I find myself, has been principally to clear the ground of mouldering rubbish, to chase away old ghosts, to help set the artist free."[5] Sentimentality ranked high on Mencken's list of literary taboos. Reviewing William Allen White's *A Certain Rich Man,* in the *Smart Set* in October 1909, Mencken complained that the Kansas editor-turned-novelist saw human existence as nothing more than "a good excuse for a sentimental orgy." "Sentimentality," Mencken moaned, "is our national weakness, as bigotry is our national vice" (153, 155). As a result, writers all too frequently failed to depict the reality of American life, and shallow optimism was often preferred to penetrating insight. "The purpose of novel writing, as that crime is practiced in the United States, is not to interpret life, but to varnish, veil and perfume life" (January 1911, 163).

Mencken frequently complained that even when a novelist did attempt to depict reality, his story was often spoiled by the American tendency to turn fiction into an exercise in moralistic didacticism. In his first review in the *Smart Set,* in November 1908, Mencken castigated Upton Sinclair, the muckraking novelist, for having allowed his novel *The Moneychangers* to degenerate into an economic and political tract. Sinclair, he complained, had "hopelessly confused the functions of the novelist with those of the crusader. His story, despite its interest and its craftsmanship, is not a moving picture of human passions, . . . but a somewhat florid thesis in sociology, with conclusions that were stale in the days of St. Augustine" (156).

It was one thing to attack an important figure like Sinclair, but Mencken mustered equal enthusiasm for assaults against the confectioners of mawkish best-selling romances. While he obviously enjoyed exercising his satiric bludgeon, there was a certain seriousness behind his decision to devote five long paragraphs of a review to Marjorie Benton Cooke's *Bambi* and half a review to *Innocent,* by Marie Corelli. In his last *Smart Set* piece, in December 1923, Mencken fumed, "If a critic has any duty at all, save the primary duty to be true to himself, it is the public duty of protecting the fine arts against the invasion of such frauds. They are insidious in their approach; they know how to cajole and deceive; unchallenged, they are apt to bag many victims. Once they are permitted to get a foothold, however insecure, it becomes doubly hard to combat them. My method, therefore, has been to tackle them at first sight and with an ax" (143).

Europe and America

Although much of Mencken's criticism was devoted to trying to eradicate the bad and the banal from American fiction, it would be a mistake to regard him as a negative force. While identifying and decrying those factors in American literature and culture that hampered literary innovation, Mencken also sought to keep his readers abreast of the best material coming from Britain, Ireland, and the Continent. If, as he thought, models for excellence were lacking at home, then they had to be sought abroad. In suggesting this turn toward Europe, Mencken was urging upon his *Smart Set* readers the pattern of his own self-directed education. With almost the single exception of Mark Twain, Mencken had found his inspiration in such European figures as Huxley, Hardy, Conrad, Shaw, Ibsen, and Nietzsche. Mencken continued this transatlantic focus after he joined the *Smart Set,* and, for a time, few important figures in Europe escaped his notice.

Mencken's European orientation did pose some potential problems. In calling attention to the innovative and superior quality of European writing, Mencken ran the double danger of seeming to encourage American writers to imitate Europeans or to pessimistically conclude that America was inimical to art. He frequently defined as European those qualities he most admired in his favorite American authors and critics. In praising Theodore Dreiser's *Jennie Gerhardt,* Mencken found the novel "so European in its method, its point of view, its almost reverential seriousness, that one can scarcely imagine an American writing it."[6]

Yet, although he frequently despaired of the state of American literature, Mencken never urged native writers to imitate European material or even styles. Nothing infuriated him more than what he called the "absurd fear of nationalism" in American arts. Americans, he believed, could learn from Europe, but they had to write about their own country, in their own voices. Therefore, as a critic, Mencken was a nationalist. When commenting on contemporary music in 1909, he noted that "[a]n American trying to write like a German is essentially an absurdity. But an American trying to write as an American might conceivably thrill the world."[7]

Therefore, when the English drama critic William Archer complained that American playwrights had made little progress in their craft, Mencken admitted that his country had not yet produced a Shaw or a Pinero. But he believed that progress would be made. "Around the corner the first really great American play may be waiting. Let us assume that it is and so prepare ourselves to receive and recognize it."[8] For this reason, Mencken frequently withheld his satiric invective when he came across a young American writer whose flawed work nevertheless showed promise. "I read novel after novel without encountering a single idea," he wrote in the *Smart Set* in January 1911. "Therefore, when I happen upon one that is full of ideas, I rejoice and am exceedingly glad, and shout the news at the top of my voice" (164).

On the other hand, Mencken considered established "respectable" literary figures fair game. One of his favorite targets was William Dean Howells, a prolific novelist and "the dean" of American criticism. Although Howells had played an important role in furthering the cause of American realism, Mencken criticized him for his alleged "paralyzing surrender to Boston notions of what is nice" and for having surrounded Mark Twain with a "pink fog" of gentility. Henry James also came under fire. James, Mencken thought, had made the grave mistake of leaving America for London. The expatriate would have done better had he gone west to Chicago, where he would have been "vastly improved by a few wiffs from the . . . stupendous abattoirs."[9]

All of this was a part of Mencken's strategy as a critic. Not only did he think that contemporary European literature could be used as a model and inspiration for American writers, but he was equally adamant that the established figures of the previous generation of American writers had become obstacles in the paths of young and non-conforming authors. He once suggested that American novelists would learn much more from Sherwood Anderson's *Winesburg, Ohio* than they would from the works of Howells or James (Nolte *Smart Set,* 274).

Mencken's reviews rapidly took on the aspect of a symbolic battlefield where European excellence was arrayed against American mediocrity, the young literary rebels against the old respectability, unpopular and dissenting voices against conventional sentimentality and moralism. He gave the younger generation of writers literary heroes and villains to stir their imaginations. A simplistic and often misleading approach, it was instrumental in polarizing the literary attitudes during the years from 1910 to 1925. Nevertheless, it did help to create a critical environment in which the cultural tensions of the nation were thrown into stark, if not always accurate, relief.

This tendency to play off Europe against America, or the new against the old, temporarily obscured for Mencken the need to discover or create a viable national cultural tradition upon which young American writers could build. He was largely unmoved by Van Wyck Brooks's call for a "usable past." Because Mencken's own usable past lay in his special and idiosyncratic reading in the European tradition of cultural iconoclasm from Voltaire through Huxley to Shaw, he felt no need during the prewar years to seek out native precursors. In fact, whenever he referred to American nineteenth-century writers of stature, such as Walt Whitman or Edgar Allan Poe, Mencken usually depicted them as standing quite outside the mainstream of American literature. They were, in his opinion, isolated figures in a cultural desert in which they had no meaningful place. They had been misunderstood and rejected by their society.

The Romantic Realist

One of the factors that entitled Mencken to the status of a literary critic, as opposed to a mere reviewer of books, was his conscious attempt to instruct both his readers and the younger generation of writers in those philosophic qualities he regarded essential for good literature. While his ideas were not especially original, they were usually aesthetically sound, and, given the uncertain state of American criticism and writing in the prewar years and in the early 1920s, they were useful. Reviewing a Gertrude Atherton novel in September 1912, Mencken voiced one of his major complaints. The author had, he asserted, "neglected the first business of a serious novelist, which is to interpret and account for her characters, to criticize life as well as to describe it" (153). The novelist's task involved more than inventiveness and style: he or she needed an intellectual and philosophical point of view. A novel had to "make comprehensible the philosophy of life of a whole community or race of men by showing us how the philosophy accords with the impulses and satisfies the yearnings of typical individuals."[10]

In Mencken's view, a single basic insight lay at the heart of all good fiction: the essential meaninglessness of life. In *A Book of Prefaces* he stated that "human life is a seeking without a finding, . . . its purpose is impenetrable, . . . joy and sorrow are alike meaningless."[11] In his *Smart Set* review of Dreiser's *Jennie Gerhardt,* Mencken noted with approval "the same profound pessimism which gives a dark color to the best that we have from Hardy, Moore, Zola and the great Russians—the pessimism of disillusion . . . that pessimism which comes with the discovery that the riddle of life . . . is essentially insoluble" (November 1911, 155).

Although Mencken never clearly defined this "European" point of view, he did call attention to "that 'obscure inner necessity' of which Conrad tells us, that irresistible creative passion of a genuine artist, standing spell-bound before the impenetrable enigma that is life . . . [and] challenged to a wondering and half-terrified sort of representation of what passes understanding" (*Prefaces,* 147). By adopting this philosophical attitude, Mencken believed that American writers could rise above sentimentality, moralism, and optimism, thus enabling them to present a more complex, challenging, and disturbing view of life. "The aim of a genuine novel," Mencken claimed, "is not merely to describe a particular man, but to describe a typical man, and to show him in active conflict with a more or less permanent and recognizable environment— fighting it, taking color from it, succumbing to it" (June 1914, 153).

It was this element of romantic individualism that kept Mencken from embracing the school of European naturalism, the "flea-hunting naturalism" of Zola and his followers. What was left out of their "scientific pornographies," Mencken complained, was the "realism" that stressed the "failure of society to fit into an orderly scheme of causes and effects, virtues and rewards, crimes and punishments. What [naturalism] leaves out is the glow of romance that hangs about that failure— the poignant drama of bland chance, the fascination of the unknowable." The naturalists were bad artists, Mencken concluded, because they did not appreciate beauty.[12] What Mencken wanted the artist to depict was not the naturalist's vision of man as a mere pawn, the helpless victim of a deterministic universe, but rather man's doomed rebellion against that universe—what he called the "eternal struggle between man's will and his destiny" (February 1910, 158).

There is a distinctly romantic quality, absent in European naturalism, in Mencken's insistence that all great fiction concerned "one man's struggle against fate." Praising Frank Norris's *Vandover and the Brute* in August 1914, Mencken agreed with the author's estimation of himself that he was "something of a romanticist . . . as every great realist always is" (158). As Mencken attempted to explain to Marion Bloom in 1920, at a time when the two lovers were engaged in one of their many quarrels. "It doesn't surprise me that you dislike old Mark [Twain]. He was the eternal skeptic and you are the eternal believer. You are in error, however, when you assume that he was an utter materialist. He was a mechanist, but that is something different. He, too, had his dreams, as you will see plainly in Joan of Arc, and as you must also see in the lyrical passages of Life on the Mississippi and Huckleberry Finn."[13]

Theodore Dreiser

Among American novelists, it was Theodore Dreiser who came closest to Mencken's ideal. In *A Book of Prefaces* (1917), Mencken denied that the novelist was either a naturalist or a realist. "He is really something quite different, and, in his moments, something far more stately. His aim is not merely to record, but to translate and understand; the thing he exposes is not the empty event and act, but the endless mystery out of which it springs; his pictures have a passionate compassion in them that it is hard to separate from poetry" (136).

It was Dreiser who seemed to elicit Mencken's most heartfelt comments on his philosophy of life and literature. The two men first met in 1908, when Dreiser was a magazine editor. Although Mencken contributed little to Dreiser's magazines, he and the older man became fast friends, the friendship being enhanced by Mencken's admiration for Dreiser's first novel, *Sister Carrie,* which had been published in 1900, eight years before Mencken began reviewing books. Half suppressed by its publisher, who suddenly feared the controversy the novel was stirring up, *Sister Carrie* still managed to attract some attention. Mencken tried to keep the book in the public's mind, using it in his reviews as a kind of literary benchmark: "one of the most thoughtful and impressive novels in our latter-day literature" (*My Life,* 124).

The failure of his first novel had shaken Dreiser, and it was 11 years before he finished his second. When Mencken read the manuscript for *Jennie Gerhardt* in 1911, he wrote to Dreiser: "The story comes upon me with great force; it touches my own experience of life in a hundred places; it preaches (or perhaps I had better say exhibits) a philosophy of life that seems to me to be sound; altogether I get a powerful effect of reality, stark and unashamed. It is drab and gloomy, but so is the struggle for existence. It is without humor, but so are the jests of that Great Comedian who shoots at our heels and makes us do our grotesque dancing" (Forgue 1961, 12).

In Dreiser, Mencken had found an American novelist who could express his own profound sense of "the meaninglessness" of the universe. He had also found something else. In his memoirs, Mencken recalled that as early as 1909, "I had been on the lookout for an author who would serve me as a sort of tank in my war upon the frauds and dolts who still reigned in American letters." He wanted a good writer to champion and set against the "fakers" supported by the literary establishment. The writers Mencken had championed up to that point had been mostly foreigners or established Americans, like Twain and James Huneker. "What I needed was some American, preferably young, to mass my artillery behind, and I gave a good deal of diligence in the search for him" (*My Life,* 127–28).

Mencken had a few false starts. Some young writers such as Henry Milner Rideout and Owen Johnson quickly failed to follow up on early promise, and James Branch Cabell, whom Mencken much admired, was "too precious in both his style and ideas to make much progress with the generality of readers. What [Mencken] needed was an author who was completely American in his themes and his point of view, who dealt with people and situations of wide and durable interest, who had something to say about his characters that was not too obvious, who was nevertheless simple enough to be understood by the vulgar, and who knew how to concoct and tell an engrossing story" (*My Life,* 129).

Mencken thought he had found his "tank" with the publication of David Graham Phillips's *The Hungry Heart* in 1909. Unfortunately Phillips was murdered shortly afterward. "But luck was still with me, for exactly a month after this tragedy Dreiser finished *Jennie Gerhardt.*" The novel was, Mencken recalled, "my new Trojan horse." For five or six years, "Dreiser was the stick with which I principally flogged the dullards of my country, at least in the field of beautiful letters" (*My Life,* 128, 129, 131).

It is not clear to what extent Mencken's memoirs accurately reflect the ambitious calculations of his younger self or the extent to which an aging writer was carefully preparing for posterity an image of himself as a successfully self-made man always in charge of his own destiny. According to his memoirs, Mencken's genuine delight and admiration for *Jennie Gerhardt* fitted in with his plans to launch himself as a major critical force. He was aware of Dreiser's defects as a writer and thinker (which he made plain in his reviews), but his loud support for the older writer was soon being echoed in the national press. "I had by this time acquired a considerable following among newspaper reviewers, and had learned by experience that they had very few ideas of their own, and were always willing to follow a resolute lead." Dreiser himself appears to have been aware of how much his younger colleague had riding on his championing of *Jennie Gerhardt.* "It looks to me," Dreiser wrote Mencken, "as though your stand on *Jennie* would either make or break you." Indeed, by coupling his name to Dreiser's and booming his novels, Mencken himself became noticed, which "appreciably enhanced [his] position as a reviewer" (*My Life,* 131).

This symbiotic relationship, which both men enjoyed, had a profound effect not only on their careers but also on the atmosphere in which the cultural debates in America would take place during and after World War I. The Mencken-Dreiser relationship was based on Mencken's myth of the embattled artist-iconoclast fighting against an entrenched old-guard literary establishment. As Thomas P. Riggio has pointed out, "In

[Mencken's] hands, Dreiser became the model for the artist for whom creative expression was inseparable from the politics of cultural confrontation." In his reviews and letters Mencken often used words associated with warfare when writing about artists' struggles. Sometimes these passages took on biblical proportions, as when Mencken wrote to Dreiser, "Don't despair. The philistines will never run us out as long as life do last. Given health & strength we can shake the American Jericho to its fourth sub-story." According to Riggio, the two men "helped establish a model for literary discourse . . . more militant and more tied to social realities" than older forms of cultural dialogue, one that was to dominate American cultural debates for much of the twentieth century.[14]

The militant metaphors and similes that Mencken employed in his criticism were soon to become even more relevant than he could have expected. It was one thing for Dreiser to write, and Mencken to aggressively defend, novels that in peacetime seemed to negate so thoroughly the idealism of American genteel culture. It was quite another to do so after 1914, when many of the defenders of the Anglo-American cultural establishment depicted the war as a struggle between barbaric materialism on the one side and idealism and civilization on the other. Cultural tensions within America increased. In 1916, the publishers of Dreiser's new novel, *The Genius,* were threatened with prosecution if they brought out the book. Mencken immediately launched an "author's protest," enlisting help on both sides of the Atlantic for Dreiser. Mencken clearly saw this as an opportunity both to support his friend and to advance the liberation of American letters by forcing American writers to declare which side they were on. Mencken, for one, never forgot the lineup.

Editing the *Smart Set*

The war years would have been a much bleaker period for Mencken had it not been for the *Smart Set.* The magazine not only offered him an outlet for his writing but also enabled him to play a direct role in the cultural conflict that the war exacerbated. Under the coeditorship of Mencken and his partner, George Jean Nathan, the *Smart Set* became one of the best-known organs of the literary rebellion. The Mencken-Nathan editorship was, however, actually the second act of the *Smart Set*'s involvement in the cultural struggle of the period. The first act began in 1913, when Mencken talked the magazine's new owner, George Adams Thayer, into engaging Willard Huntington Wright as editor. Wright, a young West Coast critic, was already a staff member of both the *Smart Set* and *Town Topics.* He and Mencken had been attracted to each other through a shared interest in Nietzsche and by a common hatred of Puritanism. Wright, Mencken, and Nathan, the magazine's theater critic, agreed to work in close cooperation. Although the arrangement was a triumvirate, Wright undoubtedly gave the magazine his own stamp and was ultimately responsible for both its brilliant success and for the crisis that ended his brief tenure as editor.[15]

The new regime began with high hopes and a good budget, and for a while everything went well. Under Wright, the *Smart Set* began to blossom with contributions from such figures as Theodore Dreiser, Louis Untermeyer, Ludwig Lewisohn, Harriet Monroe, Robinson Jeffers, and Floyd Dell. From Europe, material arrived from Ezra Pound, W. B. Yeats, Frank Wedekind, Arthur Schnitzler, August Strindberg, D. H. Lawrence, George Moore, and Joseph Conrad. At the same time, Mencken and Nathan sharpened their reviews and began a series of satirical articles under the joint pseudonym of Owen Hatteras. Mencken's series on "The American" also appeared during this period. The whole magazine gained a reputation for excellence, innovation, and satiric bravura.

Unfortunately, Wright's initial success and enthusiasm led him to ignore the sensibilities of both his readers and his publisher, Thayer, who was soon appalled by the rising costs and the falling circulation. Although the "sex" stories Wright printed seem tame by present-day standards, they were daring enough in 1913. In fact, Mencken was soon counseling more discretion and less sensation. The war against the Puritan could not be turned into a war against the reader. By the end of the year, Thayer had become impossible to placate, and Wright refused to compromise. Mencken suggested that editor and owner part company.

Wright left the magazine in January 1914, and, for a brief period, the *Smart Set,* under the editorship of Mark Lee Luther, became, in Mencken's words, "as righteous and decrepit as a converted madame." Thayer soon sold the magazine, and the new management offered the editor's chair to Nathan. Nathan insisted that Mencken be made coeditor, and the *Smart Set* entered its most famous decade, in the summer of 1914, just as war was breaking out in Europe. Because Mencken still refused to leave Baltimore, Nathan, who refused to live anywhere but New York, became the senior editor, supervising what passed for the magazine's office routine. Mencken, who was primarily responsible for soliciting material, acted as first reader, selecting the manuscripts that were sent to Nathan to accept or reject. Each editor, therefore, had a veto over what went into the magazine without any need for debate or negotiation. Mencken made regular trips to New York to help work out the final details for each issue.

Even without the difficulties that World War I soon imposed in terms of rising paper costs and the threat of censorship, the vehicle that Mencken and Nathan inherited was far from promising. Unlike the *Little Review*, the *Dial, Poetry*, and the *Masses* ("little magazines" whose reliance upon philanthropic backers made them independent of popular tastes), the *Smart Set* was and remained a commercial venture. As such, it was unique among the periodicals of the literary rebellion. Not only was the magazine supposed to make a profit, Mencken's and Nathan's own livelihood was at stake because they had accepted stock in lieu of part of their salary.

This factor placed the editors in a difficult position. The funds at their disposal were very limited. At the same time, Wright's debacle made it clear that the *Smart Set* was tied to a readership with only a limited toleration for the wilder shores of literary innovation. To turn the *Smart Set* into the kind of magazine the editors wanted meant attracting a new audience while holding the old readers long enough to survive the transition. The problem was never really solved. Subscriptions continued to decline, and the *Smart Set* remained, for Mencken in particular, a halfway house, a curious mixture of iconoclasm and sophisticated conventionality. Nonetheless, the editors did what they could, relying on a combination of snobbery and satire, mixed with enough good-quality literary material to see them through. In an attempt to hold on to the magazine's traditional readership, the editors sought to cultivate an elitist image for the *Smart Set*. "A Polite Magazine for Polite People"; "A Magazine of Cleverness"; "We don't buy names, we make them"—these were some of the mottos that appeared on the *Smart Set*'s covers and in advertisements attempting to capture the snobbish sophisticate.

Like elitism, satire was an extension of the personality and style of the editors themselves. Not only did satire constitute one-fifth of the *Smart Set*'s contents, it characterized most of the contributions, and the public's image, of the two editors. Mencken and Nathan ran the magazine with a showman-like combination of cabaret and burlesque, which did not fail to attract attention. They set up a "free lunch" table for starving poets in the magazine's garishly decorated editorial offices. Would-be contributors who pressed their cases too hard and too often were solemnly informed that Mr. Mencken (or Mr. Nathan) had entered a Trappist monastery and was not available for consultation. In 1923, the editors announced their joint candidacy for the presidency (they would flip a coin to see which of them would actually occupy the White House). Even in their darkest days at the helm, when financial restrictions forced them to marshal a stage army of noms de plume and write half the magazine themselves, satire kept the *Smart Set* afloat. As Mencken told Theodore Dreiser in 1915, "We guessed that satire would save it [the *Smart Set*], and we guessed right" (Forgue 1961, 70).

Meanwhile, both editors were anxious to fill the magazine with as much good writing as their meager budget could support. Because of their much-publicized war against gentility and conventionality, the editors could get material from established writers, American and foreign, that would not fit into more popular and respectable periodicals. In addition, the *Smart Set* did have one advantage over the avant-garde little magazines: although its rates were among the lowest in New York, it did pay something, whereas the little magazines were largely mutual charity efforts on behalf of editors and contributors. Moreover, the editors paid upon acceptance, and checks were cut every week. Offering prompt decisions as well as swift payment, the *Smart Set* editors managed some occasional "firsts": excerpts from James Joyce's *Dubliners* (marking the first appearance of his work in America); Somerset Maugham's "Rain" (the original of the Sadie Thompson story); and an excerpt from James Branch Cabell's *Jurgen* (one of the most widely talked about books of the early 1920s).

Obviously, such coups were hard to achieve. A more typical source of good material was the young writer for whom breaking into print (and getting a small check) was a driving ambition. Because the editors wisely catered to such unknowns, they made some first-rate "discoveries."[16] They published three plays by Eugene O'Neill and some of F. Scott Fitzgerald's first stories, as well as articles and short fiction from such figures as Maxwell Anderson, Thomas Beer, S. N. Behrman, Ruth Suckow, and Ben Hecht—all of whom became regular contributors. By cultivating these new writers, Mencken and Nathan made a particularly valuable contribution to the rebellion.

The *Smart Set*'s involvement with the rebellion, nevertheless, had its limits. Neither editor had any interest in experimental writing of any sort, especially in poetry, and they largely ignored the avant-garde prose that followed in the wake of James Joyce's *Ulysses* (serialized by the *Little Review*). Nor did they have much sympathy for the "bread and roses" radicalism of the Greenwich Village bohemians. Finally, despite the editors' anti-Puritanism, both Mencken and Nathan looked askance at attempts to take the gates of prudery by a full frontal assault on sexual taboos. "No man in the world is hotter for artistic freedom than I am . . . ," Mencken once told Dreiser, "but I know that there are certain rules that can't be broken, and I am disinclined to waste time trying to break them when there is so much work to do in places where actual progress can be made." Partly due to his fear of censorship (which could have barred his magazine from the mails), Mencken's disinclination to publish suggestive, much less sexually explicit material was also a matter of conservative tastes. "My dissents," Mencken once said, "are from ideas, not from decorums."[17]

There was one area in which the *Smart Set* matched or even surpassed the efforts of the little magazines. Continuing a policy begun by Wright, but also reflecting Mencken's own interests, the magazine sought to introduce the new writing of Europe to Americans. Frank Harris in London, Ezra Pound in London and Paris, and, for a time, Ernest Boyd in Dublin acted as scouts for overseas material. Half of this new writing came from English and Irish authors such as Joyce, Yeats, Lord Dunsany, Padraic Colum, Maugham, Aldous Huxley, and Hugh Walpole. Although few of these foreign writers were regular contributors, their work was usually of a high caliber. Carl Dolmetsch, the *Smart Set*'s historian, believes that in terms of both the volume and the quality of the foreign works produced, the magazine was "unsurpassed and even unequalled" by the little magazines (Dolmetsch 1957, 121).

Chapter Five
The Battle of the Books, 1914–1924

Mencken and the War

"War is a good thing because it is honest, because it admits the central fact of human nature. Its great merit is that it affords a natural, normal and undisguised outlet for that complex of passions and energies which civilization seeks so fatuously to hold in check." With these words the "Free Lance" greeted the outbreak of World War I on August 4, 1914. Although the remark seems preposterous today, many people on both sides of the Atlantic held this tragically fallacious belief in the power of war to purge Western civilization of the complexities that seemed to plague it. Idealists of the genteel tradition, confident that America would not become involved in the fighting, greeted the war with a kind of wistful longing. President John Grier Hibbon of Princeton University, for example, feared that neutral America might be denied the spiritual and cultural chastening that Europe was about to experience. Novelist Robert Herrick was sure that the young men who were dying in Flanders had "drunk deeper than we can dream of the mystery of life" (May, 365). Mencken, of course, saw the situation in Darwinian terms. In his "Free Lance" article of August 4, 1914, Mencken claimed, "The American people, too secure in their isolation and grown too fat in their security, show all the signs of deteriorating national health." While Europeans were "preparing to fight out the great fight that must inevitably select and determine, in man no less than among protozoa, the fittest to survive," Americans were surrendering their ruthless vigor and their joy of life for a false idealism and repressive moralism.

This tendency of American intellectuals, to use the war to focus attention on the social and cultural tensions within their own society, suggests why the war years, even before America's direct involvement in the fighting, became a time of cultural crisis for the country. America's ethnic diversity by itself was enough to ensure that its citizens would be divided in their sympathies for the belligerents. Among the intellectuals, powerful cultural loyalties, as well as ethnic ties, governed their attachment to one side or the other. Many Americans, like many Europeans, were convinced that the war was a struggle in which the very survival of civilization was at stake. Thus, depending on whether they believed in the ideals of Anglo-American "culture" or of Germanic *Kultur*, they identified with either the Allies or the Central Powers. The dominant voice in this cultural debate in America belonged to the genteel tradition, which was naturally sympathetic to Britain, the cultural motherland. Under increasing pressure from the young rebels in art and literature, the defenders of the old cultural order found it all too easy to depict Germany as the source of all the literary and philosophical heresies they were so earnestly combating in America.

By 1914, Mencken, on the other hand, had come to identify German culture with those artistic and iconoclastic values that he had been championing for almost a decade. What stirred him was not the kaiser and the Second Reich but rather that Nietzschean, romantic view of *Kultur*, which had been reenforced upon his imagination by his visit to Germany in 1912. "There can be no doubt," he wrote to Ellery Sedgwick of the *Atlantic Monthly*, "that Neitzscheism has been superimposed upon the old, unintelligent Prussian absolutism" (Forgue 1961, 49). In an article entitled "The Mailed Fist and Its Prophet," published in Sedgwick's magazine in November 1914, Mencken insisted that Nietzsche's *Herrenmoral* was "hailed by all the exponents of the new order as the voice of the true German Spirit. . . . a perfect statement of the theory and practice of sound progress!" This new order was no longer the old Prussian aristocracy of the court and the barracks but a new aristocracy, an "Athenian democracy" of "the laboratory, the study and the shop." A "democracy at the top" with experts instead of vote-hungry politicians in command, Germany was "the great test of the gospel of strength, of great daring, of efficiency."[1] Mencken's enthusiasm for this "New Germany" had been growing since he had met Percival Pollard in 1911. "But it remained for the shock of World War I to carry me all the way," he wrote in the 1940s. "It suddenly dawned on me, . . . that the whole body of doctrine that I had been preaching was fundamentally anti-Anglo-Saxon, and that if I had any spiritual home at all it must be in the land of my ancestors" (*My Life*, 173–74).

Conversely, Mencken saw England, whose literature had once been so important to his development, as the champion of ill-directed democracy, sentimentality, and moralism. Writing in the "Free Lance" of September 29, 1914, he stated: "For the manly, stand-up, ruthless, truth-telling, clean-minded England of another day I have the highest respect and reverence. It was an England of sound ideals and men. But for the smug, moralizing, disingenuous England of Churchill and Lloyd-George, . . . England, by Gladstone out of Pecksniff, I have no respect whatever. Its victory over Germany in this war would be a victory for all the ideas and ideals that I most ardently detest, and upon which, in my remote mud-puddle, I wage a battle with all the strength I can muster."

The battle became much more fierce than Mencken could have anticipated. Outraged by the successful Allied propaganda that depicted the Germans as barbarous Huns, Mencken undertook to portray the German side of the war. Although he continued to print attacks against himself in the column next to the "Free Lance," he soon discovered that a free and open discussion of the war was going to be difficult, if not impossible. Pro-Allied sympathy, played upon by Britain's increasingly effective propaganda machine, helped to create strong anti-German sentiment, even in Baltimore. The unabashed *"hoch, hoch, dreimal hoch!"* with which the "Free Lance" greeted news of each German victory was more than most of the readers of the *Sunpapers* could stand. Nor did many of them appreciate Mencken's contention that President Wilson's declaration of American neutrality was essentially dishonest because it allowed Britain's control of the seas to channel American material exclusively into the Allied camp. The *Sunpaper*'s management, Wilsonian and pro-Allied itself, was under great pressure to control Mencken. Finally, in late October of 1915, at Mencken's suggestion, the "Free Lance" was killed. In retrospect, Mencken claimed that the column was in danger of outliving its usefulness and that he was ready for a change. The truth was, however, that unable to respond to the debate about the war in a freewheeling manner, Mencken was no longer interested in the column.[2]

Mencken continued to contribute occasional pieces to the *Sunpapers*. In December 1916, he was sent to Germany to cover the war on the eastern front. His tour was cut short, however, by the break in diplomatic relations between Germany and the United States. He left Germany in January 1917, stopping off in Cuba to cover a sudden and brief revolution there. Back in Baltimore, he discovered that most of his dispatches from Germany had been suppressed. With a declaration of war against the Central Powers imminent, he and the *Sunpapers* parted company for the duration.

Efforts to write for other journals became increasingly difficult. Even as early as 1915, Mencken had complained to Sedgwick, "It is, in fact, out of the question for a man of my training and sympathies to avoid the war. . . . How can I preach upon the dangerous hysterias of democracy without citing the super-obvious spy scare, with its typical putting of public credulity to political and personal uses" (Forgue 1961, 76). After America entered the war, Mencken tried to contribute some satirical pieces to Sedgwick's *Atlantic Monthly* but found it impossible. For a while, he did manage to write a series of literary pieces for the New York *Evening Mail;* but when that paper folded as the result of a charge of espionage against its management, Mencken's only outlet remained the nonpolitical *Smart Set.*

Mencken's support of Germany over the Anglo-French alliance was a direct outgrowth of the cultural values he had been propagating well before the war. He had never intended to champion Germany's interests above those of his own country, and he denied that he held any political loyalty to Germany. "The fact is that my 'loyalty' to Germany, as a state or nation, is absolutely nil," he wrote in reply to a correspondent in 1918. "It would do me no good whatsoever if the Germans conquered all of Europe; it would do me a lot of damage if they beat the United States. But I believe I was right when I argued that unfairness to them was discreditable and dangerous to this country, and I am glad I did it" (Forgue 1961, 128).

The experience of being silenced and spied upon during the war so embittered Mencken that the tone of alienation from American society, largely rhetorical in 1913, took on a new depth. He resented the suppression of free speech and the attacks on German Americans. On February 16, 1915, before the "Free Lance" was closed down, he warned that German Americans were being pushed into "a separateness which, before the war, had never marked them." It was useless, he claimed, "to denounce them for imaginary offenses against their Americanism; they have already received plain notice that they stand in a separate class, and haven't the rights of other Americans." Such statements made him the unwanted object of gratitude from Baltimore's German Americans, a group whom he had always regarded as "ignoramuses of the petty trading class" to be sedulously avoided. "But now, surrounded by hostile neighbors, they turned to me as one of them, . . . I was, of course, no more a German patriot than I was an American patriot, but it was impossible to make them understand and believe it, so I had to suffer their attentions" (*Thirty-five Years,* 54). He also had to suffer the attentions of spy hunters, amateur and professional, and according to his Justice Department file reviewed by his biographer Fred Hobson, Mencken was watched more closely than even he in his most paranoid moments suspected (Hobson 1994, 161).

The war years were unfortunate in another way for Mencken. Disinclined to submit his opinions to critical reevaluation, his wartime experiences simply reinforced the negative image of America already articulated in 1913. Fred Hobson suggests that the war provided an "intellectually defensible reason" to continue the process of detachment from Anglo-American values (Hobson 1994, 134). Certainly, the war strengthened his belief that he was, indeed, an outsider. In his unpublished "Autobiographical Notes" written in 1925, he claimed that the experience gained from the war had benefited him: "I was being purged of the last remaining vestiges of patriotic feeling. Since then I have viewed the United States objectively, and without the slightest sentiment. . . . It was a great joy to be thus set free" (188). Mencken was wrong, however. Far from being set free, he was, after 1914, more involved with America than he would ever allow himself to realize.

The Cultural Rebellion

In the emotionally charged atmosphere of the war years, cultural tensions, which had been building within the society for a generation, were suddenly unleashed with such ferocity that it was not until the mid-1920s that they began to subside. Questions of artistic traditions, aesthetic values, and literary style were transformed into questions involving patriotism, ethnicity, morality, even civilization itself. The literary debates, in fact, became so overheated during the decade from 1914 to 1924 that critics dubbed the controversy the "Battle of the Books."[3]

The genteel tradition stood at the center of the fray as the dominant cultural construct. This American version of Victorian culture had survived, seemingly intact, into the new century. As noted earlier, however, challenges to the hegemony of the genteel tradition increased year by year from 1908 until 1914. Intensely Anglophilic, many of the custodians of the genteel tradition—the established novelists, artists, poets, editors, publishers, and college professors—could not resist the temptation to see in imperial Germany the source of all of the philosophic materialism and the literary naturalism threatening their cultual values. Nor could they resist branding as unpatriotic and under alien influence those writers, artists, and critics at home who seemed hostile to the Anglo-American tradition. By 1917, when America entered the war against Germany, the genteel tradition was prepared to see that the war to make the world safe for democracy abroad became a struggle to make culture safe for genteel idealism at home.

Those arrayed against the genteel tradition represented a wide spectrum of opinion and ideas and may be roughly divided into two groups: those on the cultural right who wanted a homogeneous national culture based on moral discipline and conservative ideals, and those on the left who wanted a pluralistic culture that would encourage diversity and would liberate, rather than discipline, the human spirit. The most articulate group on the right was known as the Humanists, whose principal spokesmen were Paul Elmer More, Irving Babbitt, and, during the war years, Stuart Pratt Sherman. The Humanists rejected the genteel tradition because they thought it had compromised the cause of cultural conservatism through its overly optimistic confidence in democracy, in progress, in shallow sentimentality, and in romantic idealism. At the same time this small but highly articulate group of Humanists attacked the cultural rebels on the left with even greater vehemence.

Whereas the Humanists were a fairly cohesive group with clearly expressed ideas, the rebels on the left were much less unified. In politics, their ideas ran from the vaguely liberal to the vaguely radical. Intellectually, their work included the sharp, probing criticisms of Randolph Bourne and the nebulous, Whitmanesque effusions of Vachel Lindsay. Within their ranks were such diverse talents as those of Floyd Dell, Margaret Anderson, Van Wyck Brooks, Marianne Moore, Sherwood Anderson, Max Eastman, Carl Sandburg, and Walter Lippmann. Nevertheless, according to Henry F. May in *The End of American Innocence,* these men and women, mostly of the younger generation, shared enough opinions and goals to constitute what May denotes as "the Rebellion." Their rebellion was, as May suggests, an "innocent," or a "cheerful," one. It was innocent in that the rebels retained a highly optimistic and idealistic view of life. In fact, May goes so far as to suggest that the rebellion unconsciously accepted the cultural framework of the genteel tradition, but it redefined concepts such as progress, morality, idealism, and the social efficacy of the arts in new and radical ways (219–329, 333–34). As Walter Lippmann put it in 1914, "*The rebel program is stated.* Scientific invention and blind social currents have made the old authority impossible in fact, the artillery fire of the iconoclasts has shattered its prestige. We inherit a rebel tradition."[4]

Paul Elmer More once asked Stuart Pratt Sherman, "Why do [the young liberals] and a man like Mencken consort together so readily, when as 'democrats' and 'aristocrat' they ought to be at one another's throats?" (Ruland, 116). More was right, up to a point. Mencken was not a member of the rebellion. His elitism obviously set him off from the majority of the rebels, who believed in the democratic spontaneity of art and whose politics were liberal or even radical. Nor did Mencken have much time for the rebels' tendency to follow such strange gods as Henri Bergson and Sigmund Freud. Mencken's pessimistic view of the meaninglessness of life and his sense of irony were not a part of the basic tone and style of the rebellion. The rebels' roots lay primarily in the optimistic Progressive Era in which they came of age; Mencken's lay in the aesthetic and naturalistic movements of the 1890s. As May noted, Mencken's was "a somewhat older and quite separate voice in the rising chorus of the liberated" (215). It was a voice, however, raised consistently against both the genteel tradition and the Humanists. It sounded such enthusiastic support for the younger rebels that, for a time, many of them did not realize that Mencken fought under his own flag.

The War against Puritanism

Mencken's enforced silence about the war was frustrating. But freed from daily newspaper work, he suddenly had an opportunity to concentrate on his long-term goals. First of all, he had time to bring out the first edition of *The American Language* in 1918. More important, he was able to focus on the *Smart Set* and on his literary criticism. As he noted in his memoirs, however, "these [literary] things, after all, were not my principal business in life, and I chafed against the restraints that gradually hedged me in. Thus, for the first and last time in my life, I suffered from a feeling of bafflement. I knew where I was headed, but I had not yet formulated a definite programme of writing" (*My Life,* 121). Nevertheless, by 1917, the year America entered the war in Europe, Mencken had launched the vehicle that would take him to the next stage in the cultural war at home.

A Book of Prefaces (1917), Mencken's first book of literary criticism, was the most significant factor in establishing his reputation as a dissident critic during the war years. In retrospect, he thought *Prefaces* was the most important book of his career: "It gave me a kind of authority that I could never have got from my *Smart Set* reviews alone, and brought me a large number of new readers." Anticipating its potential impact, Mencken had planned the book for a long time. "Back in the first months of the war I had begun to think of a book that would set forth my objections to the whole Puritan *Kultur* in a large and positive way" (*My Life,* 186, 174).[5]

The book contained four essays or "prefaces." The first three dealt with figures Mencken had closely associated himself with: Joseph Conrad, Theodore Dreiser, and James Gibbons Huneker. The last essay, "Puritanism as a Literary Force," was the longest and, at the time, the most important piece because it gave the book its overall unity. It was also one of the most aggressive documents filed on behalf of the cultural revolt. Taken as a whole, *A Book of Prefaces* was a gauntlet thrown down before all those who sought to impede the progress of American letters.

In his hands, Conrad and Dreiser became the exemplars of the romantic naturalism that to Mencken characterized his artist-iconoclast. Each of Conrad's heroes, Mencken claimed, "goes down a Greek route to defeat and disaster, leaving nothing behind save an unanswered question" (12). Yet, "[s]earch where you will, near or far, in ancient or modern times, and you will never find a first-rate race or an enlightened age, in its moments of highest reflection, that ever gave more than a passing bow to optimism" (14). The austere, ironic pessimism of the Polish-born Conrad gave Mencken a chance to attack what he called "the Anglo-Saxon mind," which "is essentially moral in cut; it is believing, certain, indignant; it is incapable of skepticism . . . as it is of wit" (20). American novelists burdened with such a mind floundered when they tried to depict life. "No other country can parallel this literature, either in its copiousness or in its banality. It is native and peculiar to a civilization which erects the unshakable certainties of the misinformed and quack-ridden into a national way of life" (28). By contrast, Conrad's aim "is not to edify, to console, to improve or to encourage, but simply to get upon paper some shadow of his own eager sense of the wonder and prodigality of life as men live it in the world, and of its unfathomable romance and mystery" (29).

Even more than Conrad, Theodore Dreiser represented for Mencken the lone artist pursuing his vision in the face of his society's disinterest, even hostility. "Out of the desert of American fictioneering," Mencken begins the second essay, "so populous and yet so dreary, Dreiser stands up—a phenomenon unescapably visible, but disconcertingly hard to explain. . . . how has he managed to hold out so long against the prevailing blasts—of disheartening misunderstanding and misrepresentation, of Puritan suspicion and opposition, of artistic isolation, of commercial seduction? There is something downright heroic in the way the man has held his narrow and perilous ground, disdaining all compromise, unmoved by the cheap success that lies so inviting around the corner" (67). By contrast, the work of most American novelists "takes colour from the national cocksureness and superficiality. . . . a somewhat infantile smugness and hopefulness, a habit of reducing the unknowable in terms of the not worth knowing" (69).

Mencken had, of course, initially deployed his "tank" in his *Smart Set* reviews. Now, launching his first book of literary criticism, he appears to have been anxious to demonstrate his independence from and his critical superiority over Dreiser. He made clear his dislike of some of the novelist's recent work, especially *The Genius*. Calling attention to Dreiser's shortcomings as a stylist, Mencken lamented his "endless piling up of minutiae, an almost ferocious tracking down of ions, electrons and molecules, an unshakable determination to tell it all. One is amazed by the mole-like diligence of the man, and no less by his exasperating disregard for the ease of his readers" (83).

Nor did Mencken spare the novelist's tendency to try to seek out some cosmic, mystical meaning behind the apparent meaninglessness of life. On the one hand, Mencken maintained, Dreiser's approach to life was similar to Conrad's: "Both novelists see human existence as a seeking without a finding; both reject the prevailing interpretations of its meaning and mechanism; both take refuge in 'I do not know' " (88). But beneath the surface, Conrad was more "resolute" than Dreiser. "He is, by birth and training, an aristocrat. He has the gift of emotional detachment. The lures of facile doctrine do not move him" (92). Dreiser, on the other hand, was eternally divided. "He is intelligent, he is thoughtful, he is a sound artist—but there come moments when a dead hand falls upon him, and he is once more the Indiana peasant, snuffling absurdly over imbecile sentimentalities, giving a grave ear to quackeries, snorting and eye-rolling with the best of them" (93). Dreiser was "still in the transition stage between Christian Endeavour and civilization, between Warsaw, Indiana and the Socratic grove, between being a good American and being a free man" (93).[6]

The relationship between the two men was already strained, and this kind of fun at the novelist's expense caused Dreiser to temporarily break off contact with Mencken. But Mencken, ever the strategist, knew what he was doing. By putting some distance between himself and the writer he had done so much to promote, the resulting appearance of objectivity added weight to his positive assessment of Dreiser's stature. Mencken still praised *Sister Carrie* as something beyond a novel: "It is at once a psalm of life and a criticism of life" (97). "One does not arise from such a book . . . with a smirk of satisfaction; one leaves it infinitely touched" (98). Dreiser might have been a flawed artist, but he was nonetheless an artist, one who rose far above the herd of American novelists.

Inferior novelists were not the only target against which Mencken deployed his Dreiserian tank. Several sections of this long essay are taken up with the problem of censorship, with Dreiser presented as a frequent victim of hostility from the defenders of American morality. In his counterattack, Mencken singled out the Humanist reviewer Stuart Pratt Sherman, "not because his pompous syllogisms have any plausibility in fact or logic, but simply because he may well stand as archetype of the booming, indignant corrupter of criteria, the moralist turned critic" (138). Just as America was about to enter the war in Europe, Mencken raised the stakes in the cultural war at home—perhaps a bit higher than he anticipated.

If *Prefaces* had been a symphony, then the third section on the critic James Gibbons Huneker would have been the scherzo. For the last time, Mencken indulged himself in the kind of exuberant style he had cultivated during the prewar years (a style that certainly owed something to Huneker himself). Describing one of Huneker's less serious books on music, Mencken's gleefully claimed: "On the one hand, he is a prodigy of learning, a veritable warehouse of musical information, true, half-true and apocryphal; on the other hand, he is a jester who delights in reducing all learning to absurdity. Reading him somehow suggests hearing a Bach mass rescored for two fifes, a tambourine in B, a wind machine, two tenor harps, a contrabass oboe, two banjos, eight tubas and the usual clergy and strings" (172).

The subject of these verbal pyrotechnics was a well-traveled critic who took in a remarkable range of art, literature, and music, and who commented on them with knowledge and spirit. Mencken had long admired Huneker and enjoyed many hours and steins of pilsner with the older writer. Huneker's place in *Prefaces,* however, had little to do with friendship or sentiment. First of all, by including a critic in his pantheon of excellence, Mencken was, by inference, announcing his own arrival as a critic. Second, Huneker's breadth, style, and knowledge placed him as far above the average American critic as Conrad and Dreiser stood above the average novelist.

Indeed, in Mencken's eyes, Huneker's work was hardly American at all. Although Huneker was born in Philadelphia, Mencken insisted that the critic was essentially European in his cultural outlook: "There is something about him as exotic as a samovar, as essentially un-American as a bashi-bazouk, a nose-ring or a fugue" (187). Comparing him to most American critics, Mencken insisted that Huneker "stands for a *Weltanschauung* that is not only un-national but anti-national; he is the chief of all curbers and correctors of the American Philistine; in praising the arts he has also criticized a civilization" (190–91).

Conrad, Dreiser, and Huneker; each in his own way was made to stand as an example of excellence and, thus, as an indictment of an American culture that seemed hostile to the independent, free imagination of the true artist and critic. All three, according to Mencken, shared a philosophical approach to life that stood in sharp contrast to Anglo-American facile optimism and eternal moralizing.

The final essay in *Prefaces*, "Puritanism as a Literary Force," was built around two themes. The first, the development of Puritanism as the dominant literary and cultural tradition in America, was drawn largely from one of Mencken's earlier articles in "The American" series. The second theme was censorship, which Mencken contended was nothing less than Puritanism writ large in the nation's law books. The defenders of Puritanism had called censorship and moral legislation into play to defeat the enemy at the gates. By citing specific cases and court decisions, Mencken depicted Puritanism as a formidable obstacle to the emergence of a modern American literature. Referring to his own experience as a magazine editor, he claimed that before he could consider the artistic merits of a story submitted to him, he had to ask himself "whether its publication will be permitted—not even whether it is intrinsically good or evil, moral or immoral, but whether some roving Methodist preacher, self-commissioned to keep watch on letters, will read indecency into it." Indeed, he went on to complain, "Not a week passes that I do not decline some sound and honest piece of work for no other reason" (277). Although the tone of the essay was pessimistic, it was, nevertheless, a call to arms. "We have yet no delivery, but we have at least the beginnings of a revolt, or, at all events, of a protest. . . . Maybe a new day is not quite so far off as it seems to be, and with it we may get our Hardy, our Conrad, our Swinburne . . . our Moore, our Meredith and our Synge" (282–83).

With the possible exception of Van Wyck Brooks, Mencken did more than any other critic to make Puritanism a central issue in the cultural debates of the 1910s and 1920s. Why did Mencken choose this label to identify the cultural forces that he sought to overthrow? Basically, the label was chosen for him by his opponents, for both the defenders of the genteel tradition and the Humanists looked to a vaguely defined Puritan heritage as the foundation of American culture. The Humanists were even more insistent on claiming the Puritan spirit as essential to the survival of proper civilized values. To Paul Elmer More, in particular, Puritanism was *the* American tradition: it was the source of moral restraint and discipline that enabled the individual to preserve his inner spirit amid the alluring but dangerous demands of nature.

Mencken agreed that Puritanism lay at the heart of the American tradition. Typically, he stood the argument on its head, however, by revealing Puritanism not as a vital but as an unhealthy force. If Puritanism was centered on morality, then morality itself was repressive and destructive. If Puritanism had produced the best in American culture, then this culture was a stunted and twisted growth. If Puritanism was *the* American tradition, then the national tradition smelled of sickness and decay. Puritanism, in Mencken's hands, became an *un*usable past.

Mencken was thus drawn, perhaps unwittingly, into an attack on the American cultural past. The proponents of the genteel tradition and of Humanism, having staked out the past in their own terms, made it seem a burden to Mencken and to literary rebels such as Van Wyck Brooks and Randolph Bourne. Instead of questioning the conservative reading of the past, Mencken and the other opponents of Puritanism slipped into a pattern frequently seen in American cultural history: the proponents of the new culture accepted the terms of the debate as presented to them by the old guard. As a result, the cultural rebellion fell all too easily into seeing itself as simply the anti-Puritan culture resulting from the reversal of the Puritan image.

This problem was exacerbated by another factor, also typical of American cultural rebels: a surprising ignorance of the past. Even Van Wyck Brooks, one of the few rebels who recognized immediately the need to build the new literature on the foundation of a tradition, worked against his own goal because, in the prewar years, he lacked a deep, sound understanding of American literary history.[7] His early books were so damning in their portrayal of the American cultural heritage that he was unconvincing when he called upon his fellow rebels to build a bridge to the literary past.

Mencken was in an even more difficult position because he knew less than Brooks did about the development of American literature. Moreover, he was so preoccupied with his Puritan ogre that it was not until the 1920s that he sensed the need to tie the cultural rebellion to a national tradition. Even then, he lacked both the knowledge and a sustaining interest in the problem to do more than sketch a possible connection between past and present.

Taking On the Humanists

A most striking example of the confusion surrounding the "Battle of the Books" is Mencken's protracted debate with the Humanists. A preliminary to what became known as the "Humanist Controversy" during the late 1920s and early 1930s, it was, unfortunately, one of Mencken's major concerns—unfortunate because Mencken misunderstood or chose to misrepresent much of the Humanist position, thereby adding to an atmosphere already marred by ignorance and suspicion on all sides.[8]

Mencken carelessly assumed that the intense conservatism of Babbitt, More, and, for a time, Sherman made them the most articulate spokesmen for the genteel tradition. He was quite wrong. That the Humanists attacked the genteel tradition as vehemently from the right as the younger writers did from the left never seems to have interested the Baltimore critic. Nor did he recognize how many attitudes he shared with the Humanists. Elitist, suspicious of democracy, and economically conservative, Mencken and the Humanists alike abhorred sentimentality, optimism, shallow idealism, and moralism.

Several issues, however, did create a deep and genuine gulf between them. The Humanists, rooted in their classical training, rejected the idea of cultural liberation for both the arts and the human spirit. To them, civilization was possible only through the imposition of a rigid control on the natural instincts, control provided by continual introspective restraint. When Babbitt preached his idea of the "inner check" and More his *frein vital,* both hoped to keep the dangerous human ego on a short tether. To them, self-discipline and restraint could take hold only in a culture committed to tradition. For Babbitt this was the tradition of classicism; for More and Sherman, it was the Puritan heritage.

Following the point of view he had expressed in his books about Shaw and about Nietzsche, Mencken believed in the free, untrammeled play of the ego in intellectual matters (although he too was a strong believer in self-discipline). Moreover, just as his political conservatism was tempered by a libertarianism, which the Humanists found dangerous, so his attitude toward culture was quite radical in comparison to theirs. To Mencken, culture was not to be bound to tradition but was to be allowed to evolve freely, reflecting contemporary needs and attitudes.

Mencken naturally rejected the Humanist attempt to impose preconceived and rigid standards upon the arts and on literature. "To More and
Babbitt," he wrote in *Prejudices: Second Series,* "only death can atone for
the primary offense of the artist" (22).

The Ethnic Issue

Despite Mencken's efforts to tempt the two scholars into a direct public
debate with him, More and Babbitt refused to be drawn. It remained to
Stuart Pratt Sherman, Babbitt's pupil and More's protégé, to cross
swords with the Baltimore iconoclast. The result not only continued the
generation of more heat than light but also helped carry the literary war
into the volatile area of ethnicity. Mencken must share some of the
blame for this development, even though he himself was a victim of the
ethnic issue during the war. His tendency to identify as "foreign" those
qualities of excellence he found in American writing helped to highlight
the non-Anglo-Saxon background of such writers as Dreiser and
Huneker. Mencken's own celebrations of central European culture made
it all too easy for overzealous patriots to focus on his German-American
origins and to question his allegiance.

Although Sherman was by no means the most virulent of those who
used the ethnic attack, his ability to command space in such prestigious
journals as the *Nation* and his power as a polemicist (which at times
rivaled Mencken's) made him a dangerous foe during the war. The ex-
professor of English who had turned critic did not enter the "Battle of
the Books" against Mencken directly. His initial target was Mencken's
friend Theodore Dreiser, who was also a German American. Sherman
condemned Dreiser's naturalism as alien to the moral vision of the
American Puritan heritage. In a review of Dreiser's *The Genius* in the
December 2, 1915, issue of the *Nation,* Sherman sarcastically pilloried
the novelist's work as representative of "a new note in American literature, coming from that 'ethnic' element of our mixed population which
. . . is to redeem us from Puritanism and insure our artistic salvation."[9]

Mencken, who was soon actively engaged in helping to organize a
writers' protest against the subsequent banning of *The Genius,* eventually replied on Dreiser's behalf in 1917, first in an article in *Seven Arts*
and then in *Prefaces.* Consistent with his strategy as a critic, he turned
from defending Dreiser to attacking Sherman. "What offends him," he
wrote in *Prefaces,* "is not actually Dreiser's shortcomings as an artist, but
Dreiser's shortcomings as a Christian and an American" (138).

When Sherman reviewed Mencken's *Prefaces,* he again stressed the ethnic theme by depicting Mencken and those associated with him as part of a Hunnish plot against American culture. To link together men with names like Mencken, Huneker, Ludwig Lewisohn, Louis Untermeyer, Peter Viereck, Dreiser, George Jean Nathan, and Alfred Knopf (Mencken's publisher) was hardly of innocent intent in the heady days of 1917. To Sherman, Mencken's "continuous laudation of a Teutonic-Oriental pessimism and nihilism in philosophy . . . of the *Herrenmoral,* and of anything but Anglo-Saxon civilization, is not precisely and strictly *aesthetic* criticism; an unsympathetic person might call it infatuated propagandism."[10] Mencken considered such attacks on himself and Dreiser as hitting "below the belt," for he found it almost impossible to reply to them in an atmosphere that was dominated by patriotic hysteria and censorship. He maintained a grim silence and waited for the war to end.[11]

The Mencken-Sherman debate was renewed vigorously in 1919 when the latter reviewed Mencken's *Prejudices: First Series.* Sherman satirically depicted Mencken as the barbarous spokesman of the cultureless descendants of the immigrant masses—the "Loyal Independent Order of United Hiberno-German-Anti-English Americans."[12] Although the war was over, the rising demand for an end to immigration put a nasty edge on Sherman's argument. Now, however, Mencken decided to meet the ethnic issue head on. In *Prejudices: Second Series,* published the following year, he avidly admitted that the American cultural tradition as defined by Sherman was indeed under attack from the non-Anglo-Saxon part of the population. Standing Sherman's Anglo-Saxonism on its head, Mencken predicted that the so-called ethnic writers would eventually triumph over an inferior Anglo-Saxon culture. Without "this rebellion of immigrant iconoclasts," Mencken concluded, "the whole body of national literature would tend to sink to the 100% American level" (50). Mencken was so eager to document the downfall of Anglo-Saxon culture that he urged novelist Percy Marks to make a study of the grandparents of contemporary American writers. "The inquiry would show, I believe, that there has been a steady displacement of the Anglo-Saxon strain" (Forgue 1961, 244).

Because critics of the time did not divorce art from society, their reviews and essays reflected the very real cultural debates taking place in their society. One question, which seems endemic in American history, revolved around the very nature of American culture: Should it be homogeneous in its character or reflect a pluralism of values and ideas?

Sherman, who was among those who believed in cultural homogeneity, sincerely believed that it was necessary and desirable that all Americans conform to that single set of values supposedly defined by the Puritan tradition. Mencken, who spoke for cultural pluralism, demanded the right to diversity: all groups and all individuals in America should be free from the pressure of conformity. "Laws are passed to hobble and cage the citizen of the newer stocks in a hundred fantastic ways," he wrote in *Prejudices: Fourth Series* (1924). "Every divergence from the norm of the low-caste Anglo-Saxon is treated as an *attentat* against the commonwealth, and is punished with eager ferocity" (30).

The Sage of Harlem

As both critic and editor, Mencken was anxious to uncover and to help give voice to writers of various ethnic minorities, not to "honor" diversity for its own sake but to reveal it as a part of American culture. For Mencken, the diversity of American life countered what he saw as the depressing sameness taking hold of much of American culture. He was particularly attracted to African-American writers, partly because of his interest in the South, but also because they represented an aspect of American life about which most whites were absolutely ignorant.

There may have been another reason for his focus on black writers. In *The Sage of Harlem* Charles Scruggs suggests that Mencken, because of his experience during World War I, suddenly "discovered himself to be a Negro." Certainly, Mencken's finding himself and other German Americans the target of WASP suspicion and anger may have made him more sensitive to and certainly more curious about the situation of African Americans. As Scruggs points out, Mencken, 13 years after the Armistice, referred to himself "as a member of a race lately in worse odor among 100% Americans than either Jews or Negroes."[13]

Mencken reviewed books by black authors and opened the pages of his magazines to their stories and essays. In reviews, in articles in black periodicals, and in his extensive correspondence with black writers, Mencken encouraged them, urging them to tell the truth about themselves and about the America in which they lived.[14] Among African-American writers with whom he talked and corresponded were James Weldon Johnson, Walter White (of the NAACP), the poet Countee Cullen, W. E. B. Du Bois, and George Schuyler. He entertained black writers in his offices in New York and in his home in Baltimore.

Mencken's interest in African Americans did not lead him to follow the trail of white New York liberals who made pilgrimages into Harlem in search of good jazz and black exoticism. Nor did he sentimentalize black Americans. As Scruggs has noted in *The Sage of Harlem,* Mencken treated them as he treated other writers—and, as with other writers, he did not hesitate to advise them on what to write (6–7). He urged them to bring the techniques of realism and satire to bear on what they knew best: themselves and their situation. Black writers had "the privileged view"; only they could write about black America. But they could only exploit this view if they gave up the trappings of gentility and ceased to portray blacks as virtuous victims of white America. Mencken wanted black authors to write novels composed of "characters seen with compassion, and characters who are true to life—real men and women with faults and virtues" (146–47). Blacks also had a unique view of the white man. Writing in the NAACP's *Crisis,* in 1926, he urged black writers to satirize the average white man. "He looks ridiculous even to me, a white man myself. To a Negro he must be a hilarious spectacle."[15]

Black writers were very much aware of Mencken's interest in them, and some tried to heed his call for black realism and satire. Walter White rated Mencken as an important influence in the emergence of the Harlem Renaissance.[16] Younger African-American writers in particular were taken by Mencken's call for black satire and some, journalist George Schuyler, for example, began to write like him.

Like their white counterparts, some of the Harlem writers welcomed Mencken's war against gentility and idealism. They accepted Mencken's claim that too many black writers were "so intent upon depicting the Negro as the hero of a moral melodrama that they fail to show him as a human being." Inevitably, Mencken's demand for internal scrutiny and satire aimed at black life became caught up in a growing split between the older guard of the Harlem Renaissance and what Scruggs calls the "black Menckenites" (Scruggs 1984, 126, 131–32). Yet even those African-American writers who admired Mencken's work were fully prepared to criticize his opinions when they reflected ignorance of the reality of black life in America.[17]

The Lonesome Artist

The "Battle of the Books" was not only about ethnicity and culture. It was also about the nature of the relationship between the artist and his society. Sherman spoke for a strong popular tradition in American literature when he called upon the artist to "express the profound moral idealism of America" and to "slip a spiritual gold piece into the palm of each of his fellow countrymen."[18] Mencken, however, believed that the artist's role was to question, not reinforce, the dominant values of American society. Artist-iconoclasts were supposed to be at war with society, which, if the artists were genuine, was at war with them.

Mencken's elitism constituted another area of disagreement between himself and Sherman. In spite of Sherman's Humanist background, his instincts were basically those of a liberal and a democrat. Once he had escaped the passions generated by the war, Sherman's liberalism began to assert itself over the doctrines of Babbitt and More. He took a much more tolerant view of the new literature and, by the time of his death in 1926, had even begun to praise some of the very authors Mencken himself had long supported.

Mencken, of course, had not changed his opinions. In a long essay entitled "The National Letters" in the second book of *Prejudices* (1920), he tried to diagnose the problems facing American literature. "A great literature is . . . chiefly the product of doubting and inquiring minds in revolt against the immovable certainties of the nation" (101). In America, however, artists could not rely on any class or on any institution to protect and support them. The mob was against them. The press and universities were in the hands of the plutocracy, which was fearful in its turn of any dissent from the status quo. To Mencken's elitist mind, this isolation of the genuine artist suggested the real problem facing the development of American culture: "the lack of a civilized aristocracy, secure in its position, animated by an intelligent curiosity, skeptical of all facile generalizations, superior to the sentimentality of the mob, and delighting in the battle of ideas for its own sake" (65). Without a real aristocracy, there could be no "mantle of protection around eccentricity." The artist had to carry out the rebellion alone. The "lonesome artist" was rejected by society and fought without any allies.

Cutting the Painter

Looking back over the "Battle of the Books" from the vantage point of 1923, Mencken believed it had been the war that had broken the back of the genteel tradition. "The bald fact that the majority of the adherents of that old tradition were violent Anglomaniacs, and extravagant in their support of the English cause . . . was sufficient in itself to make most of the younger writers incline the other way. The struggle thus became a battle royal between fidelity to the English cultural heritage of the country and advocacy of a new national culture that should mirror, not only the influence of England, but also that of every country that had contributed elements to the American strain."[19]

An oversimplification of a very complex problem, Mencken's statement does explain why critics in the 1910s and early 1920s were still debating the question of America's cultural independence. It also explains why Mencken, who had once been an enthusiastic champion of English writers such as Thomas Hardy and H. G. Wells, should have become almost Anglophobic after 1914. In "The National Letters" (*Prejudices: Second Series*), he claimed: "The essence of a self-reliant and autonomous culture is an unshakable egoism. It must not only regard itself as a peer of any other culture; it must regard itself as the superior of any other" (93). American culture, however, had always existed in the shadow of England. "Here the decadent Anglo-Saxon majority still looks obediently and a bit wistfully toward the motherland. No good American ever seriously questions English judgment on an aesthetic question." This situation added to the difficulties of the American artist: "Looking within himself, he finds that he is different, that he diverges from the English standard, that he is authentically American—and to be authentically American is to be officially inferior. He thus faces dismay at the very start" (94–95). America, Mencken maintained, was a cultural colony of England; the artist was as yet undelivered by a declaration of independence in art and literature.

As usual, Mencken was exaggerating; but his anti-English tactic was useful to his critical strategy. If the defenders of the old order were going to wrap themselves in the Anglo-American tradition, Mencken was willing to turn the tables on them by portraying them as mere colonials. At the same time Mencken's own sense of cultural nationalism was very real. When it became clear that American literature was finding its own distinct voice, he jubilantly proclaimed that British writers had fallen behind their American cousins. When British novelist Hugh Walpole took issue with this view in an open letter in the *Bookman* in 1925, Mencken merely intoned, "If I violate English pruderies I can only regret it politely. I am not an Englishman but an American." "The Republic," he announced, "has cut the painter, and has begun to go it alone."[20]

Fortunately, Mencken's most powerful and original contribution to the controversy over the Anglo-American literary tradition went beyond polemic. In 1919, he published the first edition of what was eventually to become his most enduring work, *The American Language*. Expanding an idea originally expressed in "The American" articles, Mencken intended the work to be another salvo in the "Battle of the Books"— and it was received as such. Stuart Pratt Sherman condemned *The American Language,* as "designed as a wedge to split asunder the two great English-speaking peoples" (Sherman 1922, 10). The book's very title challenged the old assumptions of strong cultural ties between Britain and America. American speech, Mencken insisted, was developing its own vocabulary and syntax to such an extent that it would eventually be a separate language, one totally incomprehensible to an Englishman. Here was cultural nationalism with a vengeance.

By describing how American speech had taken on a life of its own despite ridicule from abroad and pedagogical strictures at home, Mencken was also putting forward a concept of language hotly disputed by conservative scholars. In line with his literary criticism, Mencken saw language as a continually evolving phenomenon, constantly reflecting social change and the contemporary face of culture. The attempt to fix it to unchanging laws of grammar and other academic restraints was not only futile but denied the richness and inventiveness—the very Americanness—of the language.

Naturally, Mencken was an unrepentant and enthusiastic defender of slang. "Given the poet," he wrote hopefully in the first edition of *The American Language,* "there may suddenly come a day when our *theirins* and *would'a hads* will take on the barbaric stateliness of the peasant locutions of old Maurya in [Synge's] 'Riders to the Sea.' " It was wrong, Mencken maintained, to view slang as grotesque or the people who used it as absurd. "In all human beings, if only understanding be brought to the business, dignity will be found, and that dignity cannot fail to reveal itself, soon or late, in the words and phrases with which they make known their high hopes and aspirations and cry out against the intolerable meaninglessness of life."[21]

Neither Mencken nor his publisher, Knopf, expected *The American Language* to sell many copies. Nevertheless, coming as it did at the end of World War I and at a time when the "Battle of the Books" was beginning to attract wide attention, the first printing rapidly sold out. As hundreds of contributors from all over the country sent him new material on local usages, Mencken began to expand the work. A revised edition appeared in 1921 and a third edition in 1923. Mencken again rewrote and enlarged the book in 1936 and followed it with two supplements in the 1940s.[22]

In the preface to the 1936 edition, Mencken had to admit that his prediction of the parting of the ways of American and British English had not occurred. But he remained adamant in his cultural nationalism. The connection between the two modes of speech had continued unbroken because British English was becoming "a kind of dialect of American, just as the language spoken by the American was once a dialect of English" (vi).

The American Language is a work of solid, painstaking research and a compilation of voluminous primary materials contributed by hundreds of correspondents, among them many eminent academicians. As Owen Dudley Edwards has pointed out, Mencken's collaborations with linguists and dialectition led to the founding of *American Speech* (1925) and of the American Dialect Society and its journals.[23] Although some philologists and linguists have viewed Mencken's work as, at best, that of a gifted amateur, he had never intended to pose as an academic. The value of his work lies in its attempt at synthesis. Yet his success produced something more than a gloss on the work of professional language scholars. As a historian of language, Mencken was also a historian of an important aspect of American culture. That he produced such a brilliant and original work years before American cultural history had become a recognized and established field is merely one token of his achievement.

The Iconoclastic Tradition

D. C. Stenerson has suggested that "*The American Language* reinforced Mencken's efforts to create an American as opposed to an Anglo-Saxon tradition" (Stenerson 1971, 219). By allowing his opponents to set the terms of the debate, Mencken had come close to rejecting the very idea of a usable national tradition in letters. By the end of the war, however, Mencken seems to have been aware of the need to establish a reading of the American literary tradition in opposition to that claimed by the cultural conservatives.

Although Mencken took a while to put together his own version of the American cultural tradition, its shape is suggested in his essay "The National Letters" in the second *Prejudices* collection (1920). Looking about the literary scene, "One observes an undercurrent of revolt" against the "intrinsic childishness of the Puritan *Anschauung*. The remedy for that childishness is skepticism, and already skepticism shows itself: in the iconoclastic political realism of Harold Stearns, Waldo

Frank and company, in the groping questions of Dreiser, Cabell, and Anderson" (100). Mencken's task was to project this tendency toward cultural and literary revolt back into the past. He did this in a negative way in the essay when he depicted Poe, Whitman, Hawthorne, and other nineteenth-century writers as "lonesome artists" who had been ignored or misunderstood in their own country and who had thereby been forced to work and think in isolation. Even earlier, in *Prejudices: First Series* in an essay on Emerson, Mencken had claimed that, despite all the enthusiasm for the Concord sage among the conservatives, America had forgotten Emerson's "unheeded law": "defer never to the popular cry" (192).

Not until Mencken wrote his final essay for the *Smart Set* in December 1923, however, did he sketch the bare foundations of an American iconoclastic tradition. Returning again to Emerson, he could now confidently claim, "It was obviously Emerson's central aim in life to liberate the American mind—to set it free from the crippling ethical obsessions of Puritanism, to break down herd thinking, to make liberty more real on the intellectual plane than it could ever be on the political plane." Although Emerson had become a saint in the heaven of gentility, he nevertheless "paved the way for every intellectual revolt that has occurred since his time" (144).

In "The American Tradition" in *Prejudices: Fourth Series* (1924), Mencken maintained that subservience to the Anglo-Saxon norm went against the grain of the real American cultural heritage. "The ancient American tradition . . . was obviously a tradition of individualism and revolt, not of herd-morality and conformity. If one argues otherwise, one must inevitably argue that the great men of the Golden Age were not Emerson, Hawthorne, Poe and Whitman, but Cooper, Irving, Longfellow and Whittier" (18–19). One may appreciate Sherman's surprise as he noted that his opponent was now loudly calling up a literary tradition that included some of the most respected figures in American letters. Yet all Mencken had done was to extend his tradition of iconoclasm, which he had previously found only in European literature, westward across the Atlantic. Obsessed as he had been with Puritanism, it was not until it appeared to crumble that he could see the possibility, even the need, for an alternative reading of the past.

That Mencken responded to that need is a sign both of his cultural nationalism and of what Sherman, satirically but perceptively, denoted as his "passion" for "moral propaganda."[24] Mencken's ministry was to the young writers, but by the early 1920s he seemed afraid that they, in their newfound freedom and in their rejection of idealism, might swing the pendulum too far in the other direction. They might be so caught up in cynicism and skepticism as to forget the essential sense of humanity upon which good literature depended. Moreover, Mencken was anxious to keep their attention focused on their America and to suggest that even as rebels they were part of a great national tradition. Unfortunately, Mencken developed this idea too late. By the mid-1920s, the "Battle of the Books" was coming to an end and with it Mencken's own interest in literature. The essay "The American Tradition" was nothing more than the sketch of an idea. Had he pursued fully its implication, he might have realized just how much he himself belonged to the tradition of the American rebel.

Chapter Six

From the *Smart Set* to the *American Mercury:* A Farewell to Art

Mencken and the Literary Rebellion

As we have seen, a tacit accommodation existed, during the war, between Mencken and the young rebels, whose cheerful innocence did not impel them to pick fights easily with those who lent them support. At the same time, Mencken's generosity to these writers and his obvious commitment to the liberation of American letters overrode his suspicion of some of the flags, political and literary, under which the rebels marched. The battle against the common enemy took precedence over what he would have regarded as the political naïveté and philosophical frivolities of writers who were so clearly in need of encouragement.

Mencken was not, however, free from criticism within the rebel ranks. A few of them, for example, felt he was too cautious about actually challenging censorship. Unsympathetic with the compromises Mencken and Nathan believed they were obliged to make to keep the *Smart Set* afloat, Theodore Dreiser (an older voice in the rebellion) gruffly told Mencken that "for a man with your critical point of view[,] the stuff you are publishing is not literature and there are those who are getting it under your nose," a sentiment also echoed by Ezra Pound.[1] Randolph Bourne, one of the most radical of the younger rebels, expanded on this point in his review of *Prefaces* in 1917. Noting that Mencken, by his own admission, rejected worthy stories because of his fear of the censor, Bourne asked, "But what is this but to act as busy ally to that very comstockery he denounces? If the Menckens are not going to run the risk, in the name of freedom, they are scarcely justified in trying to infect us with their own caution" (Bourne, 165). Bourne had a point, but so did Mencken. The *Seven Arts,* an excellent periodical with which Bourne was closely associated, folded that same year because its sponsor was frightened by the staff's refusal to temper their antiwar opinions.

In the same review, Bourne raised a question that came closer to defining the differences between Mencken and at least some of the rebels. Bourne complained, rightly, that Mencken's concentration on Puritanism had created an ogre of exaggerated proportions. The trouble with Mencken was that he was too preoccupied with the Philistine majority, wrote Bourne. "Why cannot Demos be left alone for awhile to its commercial magazines and its mawkish novels? All good writing is produced in serene unconsciousness of what Demos desires or demands. It cannot be created at all if the artist worries about what Demos will think of him or do to him. The artist writes for that imagined audience of perfect comprehenders. The critic must judge for that audience too" (Bourne, 164).

Writing from Europe, Ezra Pound put the same criticism to Mencken personally in a letter in 1919. Commenting on the iconoclast's *In Defense of Women* (1918), Pound scolded, "What is wrong with it, and with your work in general is that you have drifted into writing for your inferiors. . . . We have all sinned through trying to make the uneducated understand things. Certainly you will lose a great part of your public when you stop trying to civilize the waste places; and you will gain about fifteen readers" (Pound, 146).

Although there was a good deal of truth in their criticisms, Bourne, Pound, and Dreiser ignored Mencken's most valuable role in the rebellion. Despite his pose as an elitist, Mencken had no desire to turn his back on "Demos" or to seek out a small devoted coterie. His whole purpose as a critic and a writer was to take the leadership in civilizing the waste places. If this intention made him, as Bourne complained, more concerned at times with the Philistine than the artist, or, as Pound saw it, more of a popularizer and less of an intellectual, it also made Mencken a powerful figure in the "Battle of the Books." As a popularizer *and* as a critic, as the schoolmaster to the culturally unwashed, as well as the champion of the artist, Mencken dominated for over a decade that vital middle ground of criticism where the new writing could be brought before a new and wider audience.

If, by the end of World War I, the rebels were beginning to voice doubts about Mencken, the critic was by then prepared to turn his attentions to what he considered *their* weaknesses. In "The National Letters" from *Prejudices: Second Series* (1920), he showed his disapproval of the avant-garde side of the rebellion as symbolized by the artist enclaves in Greenwich Village. He depicted the average *literatus* of the village "in corduroy trousers and a velvet jacket, hammering furiously upon a pine table in a Macdougal street cellar . . . his discourse full of insane hair-splittings about *vers libre,* futurism, spectrism, vorticism, *Expressionismus*" (27). The fruits of such labors were seldom worth Mencken's notice: "I have yet to hear of a first-rate book coming out of it [the village], or a short story of arresting quality, or even a poem of any solid distinction." The work of the young experimentalists was "jejune and imitative" (29).

Nor was Mencken pleased with the postwar tendency of the young writers to become expatriates. Although he himself was briefly tempted to leave America, his cultural nationalism soon reasserted itself.[2] In *Prejudices: Third Series* (1922), he satirically, but accurately, described his position: "Yet I remain on the dock, wrapped in the flag, when the Young Intellectuals set sail. Yet here I stand, unshaken and undespairing, a loyal and devoted Americano, even a chauvinist" (11). Most of Mencken's last essays on literature were really sermons urging young writers to recognize the *American* iconoclastic tradition, to focus on their own society, and to draw their material from American character types.

In his last article in the *Smart Set,* in December 1923, Mencken announced that the literary battle for the liberation of letters had finally been won. But what use had the American writer made of his new opportunities, he asked. "Certainly not the worst use possible, but also certainly not the best. He is free, but he is not yet, perhaps, worthy of freedom" (142). To drive home his criticism of the young writers, he commissioned the Irish critic Ernest Boyd to write a devastating, satirical composite portrait of the Greenwich Village "aesthetes" for the first issue of the *American Mercury.* When Boyd's "Aesthete: Model 1924" appeared in the January 1924 issue, its contents infuriated its victims, and they bombarded the unfortunate Boyd for days with epithets and stink bombs. They even published a single issue little magazine, *Aesthete: 1925,* the following year, which was full of anti-Mencken barbs.[3] The old literary alliances of the "Battle of the Books" had come to an end.

Irony and Pity

Well before Mencken broke with the rebellion, he had been struggling to realign his ideas on literature with his growing interest in social and cultural criticism. By the end of the war, Mencken had embarked on a voyage of exploration that would leave literary criticism behind.

Mencken had always rejected the naturalist's belief that art could be an objective, scientific representation of life. Like most realists, he believed that art involved the selection and ordering of reality. "Art can never be simple representation," he noted in *Prejudices: First Series* (1919). "It must, at least, present the real in the light of some recognizable ideal; it must give to the eternal farce, if not some moral, then at all events some direction" (44). Mencken the critic was a realist. However, Like Norris and, indeed, Dreiser, he was also something of a romantic. His search for those qualities of the "endless mystery" of life and the "passionate compassion" in the handling of characters inspired the best moments in his criticism.

Yet, apart from Mencken's commitment to the style of realism and his philosophical approach to fiction, his prewar criticism does not reveal any comprehensive theory of the novel. In fact, he had difficulty deciding whether the main emphasis in a work should lie with the characters or with their background and environment. After World War I, however, Mencken tried to pull his ideas together and ended up with a very narrow concept of the form and function of the novel. In one of his last pieces of criticism, published in *Prejudices: Fifth Series* (1926), Mencken insisted that the good novel is always "a character sketch of an individual not far removed from the norm of the race" (219). In the best contemporary American novels, he claimed, it was not the story line or the ideas that stood out, but the characters. He believed that American society had produced more lively and diverting character types than all other nations taken together. He therefore urged American novelists to depict the "particular richness of the American scene in sharply-outlined and racy characters" (220).

This emphasis on character types moved Mencken toward a sociological view of the novel. It is significant that among his favorite authors of the 1920s were Ring Lardner and Sinclair Lewis. Mencken urged Lardner, Lewis, and even F. Scott Fitzgerald to immortalize the moralists and evangelists, the politicians, and the confidence men who peopled the American scene. Yet he never lost sight, as some of his admirers occasionally did, of the need to keep the romantic element in focus. For him, the great gap between aspiration and attainment was the most dramatic and poignant element in American life.

Mencken's main criticism of Ring Lardner, for example, was that the author's characters only amused him; he did not pity them in their stupidity. In *Prejudices: Fifth Series,* Mencken suggested, "The moron, perhaps, has a place in fiction, as in life, but he is not to be treated too easily and casually. It must be shown that he suffers tragically because he cannot abandon the plow to write poetry, or the sample-case to study opera" (53). Urging American writers to take up the moral reformer as a subject, Mencken warned that such a type had to be seen as one "eternally in the position of a man trying to empty the ocean with a tin-dipper. He will be mauled, and the chance he offers thrown away, if the novelist who attempts him in the end forgets the tragedy under his comedy. . . . A novelist blind to that capital fact will never comprehend the type. It needs irony—but above all it needs pity" (232).

This concept of irony and pity became not only the major theme of Mencken's criticism in the 1920s but also an aesthetic counterbalance to the kind of sociological and satirical fiction that he himself, as a critic and as an editor, was helping to promote. That he made the point so obviously and often suggests he may have feared that, with the passing of the genteel tradition with its idealism and its sentimentality, some of the younger writers were swinging to the other extreme and were depicting life as nothing but a shallow farce. Indeed, Mencken is still often accused of having fathered an easy cynicism among the younger writers of the postwar years. Yet, no other critic worked harder to maintain a balance between satire and sympathetic understanding. In his *Prejudices: First Series,* he took the English author Arnold Bennett to task for depicting his characters as only "mean figures in an infinitely dispersed and unintelligible farce, as hopeless nobodies in an epic struggle that transcends both their volition and their comprehension." Nothing in Bennett's stories suggested "the responsive recognition, the sympathy of poor mortal for poor mortal, the tidal uprush of feeling that makes us all one" (38).

A Critic Is a Critic Is a Critic

Although Mencken did manage to come to some conclusions about the novel, his various attempts to define criticism and his own place as a critic tended to change with the ever shifting focus of his interests. For the most part Mencken distrusted labels and categories, and he did his best to squirm out from under them when he could. Thus, he claimed in his "Autobiographical Notes" of 1925, "I am simply an eclectic" (173). Certainly Mencken's tastes were broad. At one time or another he championed such dissimilar writers as Conrad, H. G. Wells, Bennett, Dreiser, Sinclair Lewis, Fitzgerald, and James Branch Cabell. Usually he tried to spread the blanket of realism over as many of his favorites as he could. He even claimed Cabell (whose imaginary medieval kingdom of Poictesme might seem be be pure fantasy) as a realist in spirit, if not quite in style. "Realism is simply intellectual honesty in the artist. . . . He makes no compromise with popular sentimentality and illusion. He avoids the false inference as well as the bogus fact. He respects his material as he respects himself."[4]

Mencken shied away from pinning down his own critical position, partly because he placed the freedom of the artist above everything else, including his own critical dictums. "The test, to me, is not the man's programme, but his honesty. If he is making a sincere effort to do something worthwhile I am disposed to allow him a wide latitude in the choice of the means. This attitude, I find, is incomprehensible to many persons. They cannot grasp the concept of liberty" ("Notes" 1925, 173). Admittedly, even Mencken's toleration often weakened when he read works that lay beyond the limits of his own tastes and comprehension. Thus he frequently took the expatriate writers of the 1920s to task for having abandoned the fecund material of their native heath in order to carry out surrealistic experiments in the garrets and cafes of Europe. His attitude toward poetry, though not as uninformed as his critics have contended, made him totally unresponsive to such complex writers as Robert Frost and T. S. Elliot.[5]

On the whole, however, Mencken's concern for the freedom of the artist was genuine; thus his interest in Joel Spingarn's influential book *Creative Criticism* (1917). Spingarn, in an essay entitled "The New Criticism," held that the critic's first and foremost duty was to discover what the artist's intentions were in a given work. Mencken agreed with Spingarn's basic premise that the author's work should be judged, not in terms of preexisting theories or ideologies, but in terms of itself. In his essay "Criticism of Criticism of Criticism," in *Prejudices: First Series,* however, Mencken issued an early warning against carrying Spingarn's "New Criticism" too far. "[B]eauty as we know it in this world is by no means the apparition *in vacuo* that Dr. Spingarn seems to see. It has its social, its political, even its moral implications." Brahms, Mencken noted, "wrote his Deutsches Requiem, not only because he was a great artist, but also because he was a good German" (18).

Few American critics before the mid-1920s were deeply involved with those problems of form, symbolism, or discourse that were to become the focal points for so much American criticism later in the century. Mencken's generation took it for granted that the cultural and social implications of a work of art were as important as its form or technique. He wanted critics who would help spread ideas, who would champion the new and the unpopular, who would fight for artistic freedom, and who would turn American writers toward material within their own society. It was his pursuit of these goals that made Mencken a major critical force in those years.

A Farewell to Art

It is ironic that Mencken achieved his greatest reputation as a literary critic at the very time that he began thinking of abandoning the arts. As early as 1920 he told Burton Rascoe, "I'll write very little about books hereafter. All my criticism is, at bottom, a criticism of ideas, not of mere books." To poet Louis Untermeyer, Mencken was a bit clearer about the nature of his restlessness. "You will escape from literary criticism, too, as I am trying to do. . . . We live, not in a literary age, but a fiercely political age."[6] In order to understand this shift in Mencken's focus, one must recall that his initial approach to criticism was based on a belief that the artist-iconoclast could make art into a medium for intellectual change, even for social progress. Contrary to his dictum that he never changed his mind, Mencken's faith in the social role of art was beginning to waver, as can be seen in his changing attitude toward his early iconoclastic heroes: Shaw and Ibsen.

Shaw had been one of Mencken's earliest idols and the subject of his first book. But by 1916 Mencken had dismissed the Irish playwright as "an orthodox Scotch Presbyterian of the most cock-sure and bilious sort." Shaw the iconoclast became merely the "Ulster Polonius."[7] Mencken's reaction against Ibsen was less insulting, but he nevertheless denied in 1917 that Ibsen had ever been anything more than a great dramatic craftsman. Ignoring that he himself had once pronounced *A Doll's House* an intellectual breakthrough in drama, Mencken now laughed at those who saw Ibsen as an iconoclast. His ideas were merely "banal."[8]

Mencken was not attacking his former heroes merely to enhance his own stature. Behind his comments on Shaw and Ibsen, lay a general abandonment of the idea that art could be a means for intellectual and social change. For example, although Mencken had once been enthusiastic about the theater of ideas as a vehicle for iconoclastic assaults on society's sacred cows, he insisted in the *Smart Set* of November 1921 that "ideas have no more place in drama than they have in music" (142). The following year, he dismissed drama as the most democratic of art forms—as mere "show for the mob." "The phrase 'drama of ideas' thus becomes a mere phrase. What is actually meant by it is 'drama of platitudes' " (*Prejudices* 3, 300).

Mencken's disillusionment was not limited to drama. In May 1920, he announced in the *Smart Set:* "A work of art with ideas in it is as sorry a monster as a pretty girl full of Latin. The aim of a work of art is not to make one think painfully, but to make one think beautifully" (139). Discussing novelist James Branch Cabell, Mencken insisted that the artist's real aim was "not to suggest improvements in the life about him; it is to escape that life altogether."[9] Mencken even became skeptical about the value of truth seeking. "Nine times out of ten, in the arts as in life, there is actually no truth to be discovered; there is only error to be exposed" (*Prejudices* 3, 93).

Mencken's final break with literature was consummated in a significant manner. By the early 1920s, he was becoming impatient with the idea that the critic existed in the shadow of the artist and his works. In "Criticism of Criticism of Criticism," in the first book of *Prejudices,* he had suggested that the proper role of the critic was that of a catalyst: "He makes the work of art live for the spectator; he makes the spectator live for the work of art. Out of the process comes understanding, appreciation, intelligent enjoyment—and that is precisely what the artist tried to produce" (21). In *Prejudices: Third Series,* Mencken proceeded to destroy his own catalyst theory. There, in "A Footnote on Criticism," he stated that the superior critic was always swallowed up by the creative artist within. Such a critic "moves inevitably from the work of art to life itself, and begins to take on a dignity that he formerly lacked" (87). The critic "usually ends by abandoning the criticism of specific works of art altogether, and [sets] up shop as a general merchant in general ideas, *i.e.,* as an artist working in the materials of life itself" (88). In Mencken's case the literary critic was shown the door by the social critic.

Bit by bit, Mencken had broken the back of his own career. For two decades he had assumed an interconnection between art and society, but he had never really established the nature of that connection. Almost as an act of faith, he had believed that the iconoclastic power of art would somehow alter public opinion by challenging old ideas and institutions. Events shook that faith. From Mencken's point of view, America had moved from the emotional, democratic excesses of Progressivism to the repressive outrages of war-generated hysteria. After the war the quality of art had indeed improved, but American society seemed less enlightened than ever before. Either art had failed, or it could accomplish nothing.

The social and the aesthetic sides of art had never been fully integrated in Mencken's thought. By presenting the individual's heroic but ultimately futile struggle against the essential meaninglessness of the universe, art would lead society to reexamine its basic asumptions and free itself from erroneous and superstitious ideas. The result would be progress. How this process would work, however, was never clear, because it was not the function of art or the artist, having demolished idealism to reveal the tragic core at the heart of existence, to build upon the ruins. As the arts in America freed themselves after World War I, the social benefits of this liberation were not forthcoming. Mencken found his society as unenlightened as ever. Art, for him, then was reduced to its aesthetic function, and because he was primarily interested in society, Mencken bid farewell to art.

The Literary Legacy

As a critic, Mencken unquestionably had his limitations. His ideas, while often sound in themselves, were neither brilliant nor original. He made no real contributions to the theories of literature or criticism, and he had many blind spots. As Burton Rascoe, a fellow critic who had been one of Mencken's early champions, noted in 1922, "The truth is that the literary generation now gaining recognition has progressed beyond the reaches of Mencken's aesthetic equipment."[10] Indeed, Mencken was virtually unaffected by the modernist revolution in writing created by such figures as Ezra Pound, T. S. Elliot, William Butler Yeats, and James Joyce. Although Mencken was on reasonably solid ground when he dealt with realism and naturalism, he was generally unable to appreciate anything avant-garde. He had published excerpts from James Joyce's *Dubliners* at a time when Joyce could have been mistaken for an Irish amalgamation of Henrik Ibsen and Thomas Hardy; however, when Joyce began a revolution in prose with *Ulysses,* Mencken could not comprehend the book's importance or muster much sympathy for those Americans who sought to follow the Irishman's lead. Mencken was limited even in the realm of realism. Although he could appreciate the work of a Dreiser or a Lewis, he was largely unmoved by the subtler style of a Hemingway.

But within his limitations, Mencken's power as a critic lay in his almost intuitive understanding of good writing and in his deep empathy for writers. More than any other critic of the period, Mencken had the ability to make people interested—to get them involved—in the problems facing American literature. He bridged the gap between the writer and the public, bringing into fruitful contact ideas and people. Admittedly, a rather blurred line separates this sort of critic from the skillful popularizer, who passes on to the public a simplified (and often falsified) version of the new and the complex. Mencken certainly crossed that line at times. He was a popularizer when he undertook to explain Nietzsche and Shaw to American readers. Generally, though, he was something much better and more important. When he had a strong sympathy for a writer, as he did for Dreiser, for example, Mencken helped to create an audience for that writer, an audience that was expectant, receptive, and comprehending.

His essays on Dreiser remain unsurpassed for their sympathy and insight. And one still turns to his commentaries on Conrad, Lardner, George Ade, Sinclair Lewis, Cabell, and Fitzgerald for both pleasure and enlightenment. On these authors, and on a number of lesser lights who contributed short stories to the *Smart Set* and later to the *American Mercury,* Mencken's influence was powerful and at times direct. Mark Schorer, in his biography of Sinclair Lewis, suggests that Mencken's concept of Puritanism provided "not only Sinclair Lewis but all the writers of the twenties with a platform from which they could take their literary pot shots at American culture." Schorer's statement also suggests the manner in which Mencken's literary legacy operated; for as he points out, Mencken helped writers like Lewis focus on "the standardization of manners in a business culture and the stultification of morals in middle-class convention."[11]

To understand Mencken's influence, we must bear in mind that the postwar period was, intellectually as well as socially, a very confusing one. The war had destroyed, or at least seriously challenged, many of the old patterns of American thought. Many writers found it difficult to perceive, much less present, the new, emerging America. For those who needed it, Mencken structured the American scene in a convenient series of polarities: the individual versus the masses, the elite versus the mob, the artist versus society, rebellion versus conformity, mediocrity versus excellence, and skepticism versus mindless assent. This structure provided a framework for novelists who might otherwise have been lost amid the chaos of the radically and rapidly changing society around them.

This Menckenized version of America was undoubtedly crippled by the very oversimplifications upon which it was based. One must, for example, question the wisdom of insisting that the artist's natural relationship to society is always one of constant rebellion. For the writers who could not give vitality to these ideas, as Lewis did, or who could not eventually go beyond them, as Fitzgerald did in *The Great Gatsby,* Mencken's polarities could prove a trap, not a liberation. But for those with talent and imagination, Mencken did provide a starting point. He gave writers the means to deal creatively with the postwar American experience.

Mencken also played an important role in helping writers to understand their craft and to see it in terms of a wider literary background. Today, would-be authors may avail themselves of creative writing classes and courses in contemporary literature. As late as the 1920s, however, university courses in modern literature and modern writing were rare. It was quite possible for a college graduate to know more about Edward Taylor than about Walt Whitman, or even more about Oliver Goldsmith than about George Bernard Shaw. Mencken's essays introduced writers to figures like Nietzsche, Shaw, Conrad, Ibsen, Dreiser, and Mark Twain. It was through Mencken, for example, that Fitzgerald came into contact with Conrad's novels, which, according to the author himself, helped him tighten his form and style, thus making *The Great Gatsby* such a significant advance over his earlier novels.[12]

The legacy that Mencken left the writers of the 1920s was a mixed blessing, at once broadening and limiting, combining insight with shallowness. He should, as some of his critics have insisted, share the blame for the intellectual confusion evident in the decade's literature. But when one recalls that the decade witnessed a great blossoming of the American novel, it seems only fair that Mencken should also receive at least some of the credit for this achievement.

Mencken occupied neither the high ground of formal criticism, nor the low ground of the consistent popularizer, but the very important middle ground where new ideas and new writers were introduced to a sympathetic audience prepared to receive them. Without such critics it would have been difficult for a modern American literature to have emerged. Mencken probably did more than any other critic in the two decades following 1908 to bring the new writers into contact with their public. He also helped these writers to gain a productive awareness of each other, and he helped to guide them toward new themes and new material. Finally, during this important period of cultural transition, Mencken was able to interpret for the public the meaning of the literary battles being waged. His views were not always accurate, but he was able to get people interested in cultural questions.

The Sahara of the Bozart

Through Mencken's involvement in the culture of the postwar South, we can trace his shift from literary criticism to a more broadly based social and cultural criticism. Of all of the essays Mencken published during the 1920s, "The Sahara of the Bozart" (*Prejudices: Second Series,* 1920) was the most famous—or infamous, depending on which side of the Mason-Dixon it was read. "Bozart" approximated the American pronunciation of the French *beaux-arts,* or "fine arts." "Sahara" referred to the South: "For all its size and all its wealth and all the 'progress' it babbles of, it is almost as sterile, artistically, intellectually, culturally, as the Sahara Desert" (136). The region, which had once produced almost all of America's political theory, had become a "gargantuan paradise of the fourth-rate," devoid of art, music, theater, literature, and common sense (138). "The vast blood-letting of the Civil War half exterminated and wholly paralyzed the old aristocracy, and so left the land to the harsh mercies of the poor white trash, now its masters" (143). To Mencken, the South was thus a hothouse within which everything wrong with postwar America seemed to flourish: Fundamentalism, Prohibition, intolerance, ignorance, corrupt politics, and democracy.

Elements of "The Sahara of the Bozart" had earlier appeared in Mencken's *Evening Sun* columns and in the *Smart Set* but did not receive much notice. When the revised essay was published in *Prejudices: Second Series,* however, it caused outrage in the South. One suspects that part of the reaction was due to Mencken's claim that southern blacks were culturally more advanced than the whites because the latter were mired in racism.[13] Denunciation rolled in from every corner of the late Confederacy, led by southern newspaper editors, preachers, and politicians. Yet, Mencken's diatribe, indeed the man himself, came to play a major role in the intellectual and artistic rejuvenation of the South. According to Fred Hobson, in his *Serpent in Eden: H. L. Mencken and the South,* much of the debate about the South became "Menckenized"; that is, many young writers and scholars accepted Mencken's diagnosis of southern ills and his proposed cure.

Implicit in the "Bozart" essay was the charge that southern "tradition"—southern values, including white supremacy—had become an intellectual trap. "The south has not only lost its old capacity for producing ideas; it has also taken on the worst intolerance of ignorance and stupidity" (*Prejudices* 2, 150–51). The only escape into the twentieth century lay through an uninhibited rending of the veil of magnolias, southern womanhood, manly chivalry, and the "Lost Cause."

In *The Serpent in Eden,* Hobson suggests that Mencken had not intended to raise the standard of rebellion in the South, and although he was prepared for the vociferous negative reaction that followed on the heels of the "Bozart," he was surprised at the *positive* response from younger southerners. When he realized there was a new generation of writers eager for change, he was prepared to offer leadership. His southern "crusade" began with "The South Begins to Mutter" in the August 1921 issue of the *Smart Set,* in which he hailed the "gathering revolt of the more alert and competent youngsters against the constraints of an ancient, formalized and no longer vital tradition."[13]

Very quickly, Mencken placed himself at the hub of a network linking emerging southern writers: novelists, such as James Branch Cabell (the only writer Mencken praised in "Bozart") and Julia Peterkin; "little magazine" editors, such as Emily Clark of the Richmond *Reviewer* and Basil Thompson and Julius Weis Friend of the New Orleans *Double Dealer;* journalists, such as Frances Newman, Nell Battle Lewis, Julian and Julia Harris, and Gerald W. Johnson; and scholars, such as Howard W. Odum of North Carolina. They all responded in varying ways to Mencken's call for a realistic investigation of the region and a portrayal of the South as it really was. To such people Mencken was generous with his advice. He put them in touch with one another, tried to help them get positions, and praised their works in his reviews. They in turn made him part of the debate about the new South.

Mencken was particularly involved with Emily Clark and her circle around the *Reviewer.* When she first met Mencken in the fall of 1921, he was just entering the period of his greatest popularity, and, in Clark's eyes, he seemed "less a person than a school of thought, a state of mind."[14] They quickly became friends, and, during the four years of her involvement with the *Reviewer,* his almost weekly letters were filled with ideas and advice, as well as the names of the young southern writers he was uncovering. He urged her not to cater to northern writers. "What the South needs, beyond everything, is new growth from within." Often, the advice was more militant in nature. As he wrote to Clark in the early 1920s, "Criticism and progress, to be effective, must be iconoclastic and pugnacious. Before a sound literature can arise in the South, the old nonsense must be knocked down, and from within. It will be useless to attempt compromise. You must arm yourself and take to the highroad, ready to cut throats whenever it is necessary" (Clark, 112).

Mencken's strategy for the cultural rejuvenation of the South was twofold. First, the "civilized" minority had to be liberated from the triple tyrannies of a decayed gentility, the Babbittry of the new South, and the militancy of the Klan and the Fundamentalists. The young writers and intellectuals "must first try to organize and liberate a minority able to differentiate good art from bad, and be eager to lend their aid to the former when it appears" (Hobson 1974, 55–56).

Second, the South had to discover itself. And for this purpose, art was, at best, an imperfect mirror. The enthusiastic response of the young southern literati notwithstanding, "The Sahara of the Bozart" was not about art. True, Mencken ran through the litany of everything southern culture lacked: opera, symphony orchestras, art galleries, first-rate novels, and poetry. The bulk of the article dealt, however, not with southern art, but with southern society. "What is needed down there, before the vexatious public problems of the region may be intelligently approached, is a survey of the population by competent ethnologists and anthropologists" (*Prejudices* 2, 145). In the end, Mencken believed it was social, not literary, criticism that would save the day for the South.

Mencken was therefore particularly interested in finding and helping scholars and journalists who would take a critical look at the new South. He was particularly taken with Howard W. Odum of Chapel Hill, North Carolina, founder of the southern-oriented *Journal of Social Forces* begun in November of 1922. The exterior of the *Journal* might look as drab as a government report, Mencken told readers of the *Chicago Tribune* at the end of 1924. "But inside it is full of dynamite, for what it presumes to do is to upset all assumptions upon which the thinking of North Carolina, and indeed of the whole south, has been grounded since the civil war, and to set up a new theory of the true, the good, and the beautiful upon a foundation of known and provable facts. . . . For the first time the south is getting a whiff of the true scientific spirit" (*Bathtub,* 252–53). Mencken was pleased when the *Reviewer,* under the editorship of Paul Green, moved from Richmond to Chapel Hill in December of 1924. He was also pleased when Gerald W. Johnson, whose journalistic career Mencken encouraged, went to Chapel Hill to teach and collaborate with Odum on the *Journal,* making the University of North Carolina a veritable center of Menckenian social and cultural criticism. Mencken opened the pages of the *American Mercury* to these and other southern writers. During its first year and a half, the magazine published 55 contributions from 23 southerners (Hobson 1974, 108). Much of this material was more "sociological" than literary, corresponding to Mencken's shift from art to social criticism.

During the 1920s and early 1930s, Mencken remained in close contact with southern newspaper editors and journalists who were intent on the critical scrutiny of their region. He was probably instrumental in helping Julian and Julia Harris, of the Columbus (Georgia) *Enquirer,* and Grover C. Hall, of Alabama, win their Pulitzer prizes.[15] He also encouraged the *Sunpapers* to broaden their coverage of the South, first by taking on young, talented correspondents throughout the South; and then by urging Paul Patterson, president of the *Sunpapers,* to go on a "Grand Tour" of the region in 1926 to meet editors and get a better sense of what changes were taking place. Patterson agreed to go if Mencken accompanied him. The purpose behind the trip was serious, and Mencken met many young writers with whom he had been corresponding. During the trip, however, he could not resist opportunities to keep the clowns spinning in the political ring. Interviewed four or five times a day at train stops, he never failed to suggest to reporters that this or that local politico in whichever city he was visiting would certainly be the Democratic nominee in 1928, thus setting off a series of presidential tempests in southern teacups (*Thirty-five Years,* 160).

It was not long before Mencken, scourge of southern magnolias and commercialism, became a booster of a newly awakened South. In "The South Rebels Again," published in the *Chicago Tribune* on December 7, 1924, Mencken reviewed the image of the South as a region mired in "Fundamentalism, Ku Kluxry, revivals, lynchings, hog wallow politics," the very image he had summoned forth in "Sahara of the Bozart." Now, however, he called this the "northern" view of the South. While granting that it was still accurate for much of the late Confederacy, Mencken claimed that the "northerners" were missing "the scattered rebellions that now arise all over the land of cotton—the gallant efforts that small but pertinacious minorities make to break through the cultural fog. . . . The south produced the Klan, but the south was also the first to fall upon the Klan" (*Bathtub,* 249, 250–51).

Throughout the years of his active interest in the South, Mencken's stance shifted from that of the outside critic, a northerner, to that of a friend of the South, even a southerner. In the "Bozart" essay, he had professed admiration for antebellum "civilization" in the South, but he had claimed no kinship with the region. A year later in "The South Begins to Mutter," he announced, "[I]n so far as I am an American at all, I am a Southerner." Elsewhere he wrote, "[A]s one of Southern birth, and of Southerners born . . . I thus qualify as a Southern gentleman."[16] His ties to the region were strengthened in 1930 by his marriage to Alabaman Sara Powell Haardt.

Yet, Mencken's claims of southern lineage were clearly part of his rhetorical strategy; they were seldom made outside of the context of his criticism of the South. During the years of his engagement with southern issues, it was useful to pretend to criticize the South from the inside. Assertions of southern citizenship tended to fade after the mid-1930s, however, by which time he was paying less attention to southern affairs.

His last engagement "on southern ground" revealed the limits of Mencken's understanding of the South. In 1929, a group of critics and writers centered at Vanderbilt University published a collection of essays under the title *I'll Take My Stand: The South and the Agrarian Tradition.* Although Mencken is barely mentioned in the text, the book was to some extent a refutation of the Menckenian school of southern criticism, which, according to Fred Hobson, "viewed culture not as the organic expression of a particular experience of a people but rather as some agent of enlightenment, imposed from without" (Hobson 1974, 118). Rejecting this approach, the 12 southern "agrarians" who contributed to the book insisted that the South should look within its own history and traditions, including its religious values, for the foundations of a true southern civilization. The past, rather than being bankrupt and decayed, would nurture the future in which agrarian values would stave off the cold, crass materialistic society of Yankee industrialism. Predictably, Mencken dismissed this vision as "utopian," without understanding its legitimacy in the cultural debate about the South. At the same time, Mencken (as well as the agrarians themselves) failed to recognize the profound distaste he shared with these southern traditionalists for the kind of society that American industrialization had created. At some level, he too had an organic sense of culture rooted in place and tradition.

Founding the *American Mercury*

As a vehicle for the launching of his new career as a social and cultural critic, Mencken wanted a new magazine. He had begun to tire of the *Smart Set* as early as 1917, and both he and his partner Nathan had been dreaming of a periodical of their own ever since the days of their collaboration with Wright. The model, at least in Mencken's mind, was drawn from H. G. Wells's novel *The New Machiavelli* (1910). Mencken admired the aristocratic views of the novel's hero, an elitist seeking to graft "scientific" socialism onto British Toryism. Wells's protagonist established a magazine, the *Blue Weekly,* which was intended, in Wells's words, to "express and elaborate these conceptions of a new, severer, aristocratic culture"—to make "bold, clever ideas prevail."[17] When Mencken and Nathan began negotiating with Alfred Knopf for the establishment of their new magazine in the early 1920s, the name *Blue Review* was the first one suggested. It was eventually rejected in favor of *The American Mercury* with its famous green cover (Singleton, 33).

The *Mercury* was not merely the product of Mencken's dissatisfaction with the *Smart Set's* low budget and its vaguely tarnished reputation. Mencken wanted a magazine free from literature, so that he could focus directly upon culture, society, and politics. Writing to James Branch Cabell in 1923, Mencken spoke both as an editor and a writer when he described his hopes for the *Mercury.* The magazine would provide "a general survey of the national scene, realistic but never indignant. The field is wide open. To one side the Liberals chase butterflies; to the other side the Otto Kahns, Henry Morgenthaus and other such great patriots sob and moan for endangered capital. Certainly there must be room in the middle for an educated Toryism—the true Disraelian brand. It exists everywhere, but in the United States it has no voice. I want to liberate the young serious writer as the young poet has been liberated" (Bode 1977, 173–74).

Mencken firmly believed that many intelligent Americans were opposed to the forces of mediocrity and materialism, which seemed to dominate the country in the prosperous decade after the war. It was to this audience that he appealed in the *Mercury's* first editorial in January 1924: "There is no middle ground of consolation for men who believe neither in the Socialist fol-de-rol nor in the principal enemies of the Socialist fol-de-rol—and yet it must be obvious that such men constitute the most intelligent and valuable body of citizens that the nation can boast. . . . It will be the design of THE AMERICAN MERCURY to bring, if not alleviation of their lot, then at least some solace to these outcasts of democracy" (29). The reader the magazine sought, Mencken announced, was the type "William Graham Sumner called the Forgotten Man—that is, the normal, educated, well-disposed, unfrenzied, enlightened citizen of the middle minority" (28).

Although the editorial was supposed to speak for both Mencken and Nathan, it soon became clear that there were serious disagreements between the editors as to the real nature and purpose of the *Mercury* venture. Nathan, who could not appreciate fully his partner's growing pre-occupation with politics, remained dedicated to the arts, primarily to the theater. He viewed politics as merely an inferior form of vaudeville. Moreover, Nathan refused to accept the new note of seriousness that characterized Mencken's involvement with the magazine. He once wrote, "[A] magazine, to me—and to my associate, friend, and partner Mencken no less—is a toy, something with which to amuse ourselves" (Singleton, 56 n.6).

Mencken, however, was not toying with the *Mercury.* Nor was he pleased with Nathan's attempt to balance the magazine's social and political orientation with literary material, which, however high its quality, did not take the magazine in the direction of social criticism. Mencken wanted to be free to follow through with the promise, made in the first editorial, that the *Mercury* would "attempt a realistic presenta-tion of the whole gaudy, gorgeous American scene" (30).

Moreover, Mencken was becoming dissatisfied with the editorial arrangements. He had tried to continue the pattern established in the *Smart Set* days, which left the running of the New York editorial office in Nathan's hands while Mencken worked in Baltimore and made brief journeys to New York to help settle each issue. Mencken was soon complaining that Nathan was not carrying the fair share of the editorial burden (*Thirty-five Years,* 134). By October 1924, Mencken had had enough of editorial quarrels. In a long letter to Nathan he unburdened himself of his discontent and pointed to the real issues that divided them. The *Mercury,* he complained, was too casual and trivial; it lacked "solid dignity and influence." "Our interests," he wrote, "are too far apart. We see the world in wholly different colors." The problem had not arisen with the *Smart Set,* "for neither of us took the magazine very seriously." But the *Mercury* was a different matter: "What the magazine needs is a sounder underpinning. It must develop a more coherent body of doctrine, and maintain it with more vigor. It must seek to lead, not a miscellaneous and frivolous rabble, but the class that is serious at bottom, however much it may mock conventional seriousness." Mencken thought it was very significant that one of the most successful articles they had published had been an attack on President Coolidge. "It proved that the civilized minority, after all, *does* take politics seriously." He believed that the *Mercury* could achieve as solid a position among periodicals as that once occu-pied by the *Atlantic Monthly.* "Its chances are not unlike those which confronted the Atlantic in the years directly after the Civil War: it has an opportunity to seize leadership of the genuine civilized minority of Americans" (Forgue 1961, 269, 268–69).

Mencken, as senior editor (with a larger salary than Nathan's), insisted the partnership be dissolved. Knopf, the publisher, who had originally offered the editor's chair to Mencken alone, backed him. By January 1925, the *Mercury* was completely under Mencken's control. Nathan, eventually relegated to a desk in the typing pool, continued to contribute the theater reviews and his column "Clinical Notes" until 1930. There was a price for Nathan's departure as coeditor. Carl Dolmetsch is probably correct when he argues that Nathan had a much better sense than Mencken of what was happening in literature. Without him the *Mercury*'s fiction generally fell short of the best work the editorial team had published in the *Smart Set* (Dolmetsch 1980, 32). This was a price Mencken was probably willing to pay. He now viewed fiction as merely one vehicle for exploring and explaining American society.[18]

Considering that Nathan had been a friend as well as a business partner, Mencken's treatment of him seems callous. Yet Mencken was a firm believer that a newspaper or a periodical needed a clear policy and that an editor had to maintain full control over its contents.[19] Since Mencken was deadly serious about his ambitions for both himself and his magazine, he had determined that the *Mercury* would echo his voice and his alone.

The *Mercury*'s America

Mencken's role as a magazine editor allowed him to extend his criticism of American life beyond the boundaries of his essays and articles. The *American Mercury,* his magazine in every sense of the word, mirrored his passions and prejudices. No other quality periodical was as scathing and as all-pervasive in its criticism of America. If a contribution somehow lacked the necessary bite, the editor was not opposed to sprinkling it with Menckenisms; indeed, half of the magazine's contents sometimes read as if they had come from Mencken's typewriter. The *Mercury* even carried a special department entitled "Americana," intended to provide documentary evidence of the inanities of American life gleaned from the nation's press. One typical piece was an extract from a speech given by a president of the University of Arizona: "We cannot accept European music as the basis of our music, because it is founded on monarchical and aristocratic notions." The cumulative effect of the "Americana" department alone seemed to justify the sentiments that Mencken once expressed in his famous "catechism": "*Q.* If you find so much that is unworthy of reverence in the United States, then why do you live here? *A.* Why do men go to zoos?" (*Prejudices* 5, 304).

Frederick Hoffman noted with some justice, "As comedy, the gestures transcribed from life in 'Americana' mark the worst form of social and intellectual error of which a democratic people are capable. They are grotesque extremes." Extending his criticism to Mencken himself, Hoffman argued that the editor's picture of his country was "a gigantic parody of the social metaphor." Although Mencken "never lied[,] he never actually told the truth" (Hoffman, 313, 314). Hoffman, however, missed two important points. First, Mencken was a satirist, and satire distorts. It seeks to reveal one truth by ridiculing another. Second, Mencken's portrait of America as it appeared in the *Mercury* was not, in fact, executed in a monochrome of hostility and rejection. His mind still juggled with two unresolved, conflicting images of America. This dualism is clearly evident in his magazine. The public was entertained (and outraged) by his continual depiction of America as an oppressive "zoo." Yet, Mencken and the *Mercury* also explored another America, one which was dynamic, exciting, and full of hidden variety—an America in which some values still retained their resilience.

In the December 1928 editorial marking the *Mercury*'s fifth anniversary, Mencken himself claimed that the business of setting forth the absurdities of American life was the least of the *Mercury*'s concerns. "It has given a great deal more space to something quite different, namely, to introduce one kind of American to another" (408). What Mencken had in mind were the many articles about urban immigrant groups, articles often written by children of the ghettos; excellent pieces about blacks written by blacks; autobiographical experiences from Americans of dozens of walks of life. The roster of *Mercury* contributors included hobos, prison inmates, bricklayers, coal-crackers, dock-wallopers, lawyers, generals, Indians, prostitutes, and even a United States senator.

Moreover, Mencken tried to penetrate the surface of the postwar standardized society in order to focus on regional variety. He ran a series of articles on the regional press, on local poets, and on the individual states themselves. Of the 11 states in which 10 or more *Mercury* contributors were born, 8 were Midwestern and southern states. Of the 10 in which 10 or more *Mercury* writers lived, 6 were west of the Monongahela and south of the Mason-Dixon line.[20] Mencken advertised this diversity in the December 1928 *Mercury*: "Despite the ironing-out process, life in America continues to be infinitely various. There are thousands of back-waters that remain to be explored. There are many adventures that have yet to find their bards" (409). The *Mercury*, he claimed, had tried to survey life in America from the vantage points of "visionaries to criminals, from heroes to poor fish. But all of them, writing out of their own lives, have written with that earnest simplicity which is beyond all art" (408).

The magazine also explored the American past. Although the term "debunking" is often associated with Mencken, neither he nor his magazine often submitted historical figures to the superficial iconoclasm popular during the decade. Myths and legends, not real men, suffered at the hands of contributors such as Charles Beard, Bernard De Voto, William E. Dodd, and Louis M. Hacker. The literary past also received sympathetic and responsible attention in essays about writers who had hitherto been neglected, such as Poe, Crane, Melville, and especially Whitman. Mencken also devoted a good deal of attention to that part of the American past in which he himself was rooted. The 1880s and 1890s came alive with articles on the old-time saloons, horsecars, vaudeville, traveling medicine shows, and circuses. Mencken's purpose was to contrast the old, vital America that was passing with the plastic-age America that had come into being. As he noted in a review of Thomas Beer's book about the 1890s, *The Mauve Decade*, "The Americano no longer dances gorgeously with arms and legs. He has become civilized, which is to say, he has joined a country club. His father roared in the stews and saloons" (July 1926, 383).

Mencken no doubt exaggerated when he claimed that "[a]n idea is represented in *The American Mercury* which is wholly new and significant. Through its influence America has been completely rediscovered, from flora and fauna to the inevitable Indians."[21] Nonetheless, this sentiment accurately reflects the reverse side of the *Mercury*'s satirical criticism of America, for it suggests Mencken's own commitment to that *other* America, which he loved. And Mencken could defend as well as attack. His criticisms of conformity and his emphasis on diversity called attention to what was endangered by the new forces in American society, which he himself only partially understood. If he was often grossly unfair and uninformed in his satiric tirades against the boobs and Babbitts, it was because he saw them as the betrayers of a better America, which, for all its faults, was still admirable, still worth defending.

Chapter Seven

The Social Critic in the 1920s

Stirring Up Useful Hatreds: Mencken and the *Sunpapers*

Even as he sought a wider audience through the *American Mercury* and his books, Mencken maintained his base as a newspaperman. When he returned to the *Sunpapers* in 1920, he began a series of weekly articles for the *Evening Sun.* Moreover, he was almost constantly involved in the papers' editorial policy and the company's business affairs. Far from being a sidelight to his career, the *Sunpapers* were an integral part of Mencken's life and identity.

When Paul Patterson became president of the *Sunpapers* in 1919, he asked Mencken and Harry C. Black, the company's chairman, for suggestions for improving the papers. Mencken and Black had been developing ideas for several years, and, now joined by Patterson, they quickly solidified them. They drew up "An Editorial Memorandum," better known around the *Sunpapers* offices as the "White Paper." Black wrote the initial draft and Mencken the final. In it they argued that with money coming in from postwar advertising, it was time to invest in the quality of the newspapers. Since the *Sun,* a morning paper, could reach Washington, D.C., hours ahead of the New York dailies, the Baltimore paper could have a powerful chance to influence national opinion. (As *Sun* men, both Mencken and Black had a low opinion of the Washington papers of the day.) Finally, with both political parties uncertain and cautious about the dawning postwar era, Mencken and Black urged the *Sunpapers* to seize the opportunity to define and articulate the emerging issues. This meant refocusing on the two main ideas that undergirded American politics. The first, according to the "White Paper," "is that the American people, as a people, shall be independent; the second is that, as individuals, they shall be free." It is in stating the latter set of ideas that Mencken's voice comes through most clearly in the paper. "The American citizen, once the freest man in the world, is now rapidly becoming the least free. . . . A multitude of absurd and oppressive laws burden him and the number of laws is steadily being augmented," all in the name of utopian idealism.[1]

The "White Paper" gave Mencken a chance to articulate his dislike of the *Sun*'s wartime editorial policy supporting Wilsonian liberalism. He attacked all moralizing and idealism, claiming that "utopian ideas, economical, political and ethical," had no place in a newspaper that hoped to influence public opinion. Referring to the war years, he announced, "I believed then, as I believe now, that it is the prime function of a really first-rate newspaper to serve as a sort of permanent opposition in politics." As Mencken later recalled, the essential philosophy of the "White Paper" "was the doctrine that public officials, under democracy, were predominantly frauds, and hence did not deserve to be taken seriously" (*Thirty-five Years,* 100, 118).

As the *Sunpapers* began to broaden their coverage, Mencken, whose editorial work brought him in contact with many young writers, helped recruit talented regional correspondents, such as Gerald W. Johnson of Greensboro, North Carolina, who eventually joined the *Sunpapers*. Many of these new correspondents were based in the South, but some were in the Midwest and Far West. He also briefed new reporters and tried to impress upon them what he regarded as the *Sunpapers'* approach to journalism. He also attended weekly editorial conferences whenever he was in town.[2]

Although Mencken found the *Sunpapers* under Patterson's leadership congenial, neither the morning nor evening paper ever came up to his standards. When asked by Patterson to critique the morning paper's editorial page, Mencken complained that the editorials were too "cautious" in tone: "When a scoundrel is on the block he ought to be denounced in plain terms, and without any judicial tenderness." He also felt that the editorials lacked conviction. "In order to carry conviction it is needful to *have* conviction. It is also needful to remember that most men are convinced, not by appeals to their reason, but to appeals to their emotions and prejudices. . . . One of the chief purposes of the *Sun,* as I understand it, is to stir up such useful hatreds." The *Sun's* editor, John Owens, saw things in a rather different light. Responding to Mencken's critique, Owens stated that he wanted editorial vigor based on "facts." "Mr. Mencken wants the kind of vigor which proceeds from single-minded partisanship" (Williams, 173). These two schools of journalistic philosophy did not coexist easily with each other in the *Sunpapers'* offices. When Mencken wrote his scathing obituary on William Jennings Bryan in 1925, Gerald Johnson was assigned the task of writing a more sober and objective companion piece.

As an afternoon paper, the *Evening Sun* could never hope for the authoritative role envisioned for the *Sun*. Nevertheless, it was a more comfortable home for Mencken and his weekly articles. In his memoirs he claimed that the *Evening Sun* "took over not only all the iconoclastic principles of the White Paper, but also all my Free Lance stock company of hobgoblins" (*Thirty-five Years*, 118). Although Mencken's was but one voice on the spritely paper, his was especially loud and sometimes brilliant. Hamilton Owens, the paper's editor, once admitted that his editorial page had a reputation for "being, at worst, smart-alecky and, at its best, witty and pungent. Most of it was due to Mencken" (Williams, 229).

Although involved in helping to guide the *Sunpapers* in business matters and editorial policy, Mencken did not depend upon them for his livelihood. He lived primarily on his magazine editing and his writing. He had always earned less working for the *Sunpapers* than he might have at other papers, but he stayed with them because he liked the atmosphere, had considerable freedom to write what he wanted, and they were in Baltimore (*Thirty-five Years*, 185).

Cracking Heads for Common Decency

Comfortable as he was with the *Sunpapers*, they could not act as the platform on which to broaden and sustain the national reputation Mencken so diligently sought. In 1924, having launched the *American Mercury*, he began a special syndicated series for the *Chicago Tribune*.[3] His brand of satire—boisterous iconoclasm coupled with a bemused aloofness—had not been tolerated during the war and would not prove popular in the crisis years of the 1930s and early 1940s. The 1920s mark the apogee of Mencken's popularity, and his success during this decade was the result of the happy conjunction of a man's talent with his times.

Edmund Wilson, writing for the *New Republic* in 1921, suggested that Mencken had emerged from World War I with a new seriousness that belied the comic mask of his satire. Mencken, who was usually impatient with any interpretations of his motives, confided to Wilson that "you have there told the truth. The brewery cellar, in these days, is as impossible as the ivory tower. For a while the show is simply farce, but inevitably every man feels an irresistible impulse to rush out and crack a head—in other words, to do something positive for common decency."[4]

The postwar decade presented Mencken with a unique opportunity: peace and prosperity produced an atmosphere in which innovation and

confidence papered over the confusion and conflict that seethed beneath
the surface of American society. With the fragmentation of Progressivism and with the ascendancy of retrenchment under the Republicans,
American politics entered a difficult period of transition. There was also
sharp competition between the social, ethnic, and regional groups that
were seeking cultural influence, as well as political and economic power.
The new economics of consumership and the impact of technological
innovations, such as the automobile, the motion picture, and the radio,
produced a cultural environment in which traditional values seemed
threatened and in which new social problems were only dimly perceived.
Amid such confusion, Mencken found wide latitude and many targets
for his satire. The show was good, but Mencken was more than a gleeful
ringmaster. As he told Edmund Wilson, he intended to crack a skull or
two for common decency.

Civil Liberties

Upon returning to the *Sunpapers,* Mencken made the suppression of civil
liberties one of his dominant themes. Even before the war, he had been
sensitive to threats against individual rights and free speech. During the
war, he had been appalled at the wholesale violation of even the most
basic constitutional rights. The Red Scare of 1919–1920 and the continuing crackdown by federal and state agencies against radicals convinced Mencken that civil liberties in America were endangered. In his
first article for his new weekly series in the *Evening Sun,* he denounced
Attorney General A. Mitchell Palmer, the architect of the Red Scare, for
his "medieval attempts to get into the White House by pumping up
the Bolshevik issue." "He has probably done more than any other one
man, save only Mr. Wilson himself, to break down democratic self-
government in America and substitute a Cossack despotism, unintelligent and dishonest" (February 9, 1920).[5] Mencken was convinced that
one of the major issues in the coming presidential campaign would be
personal freedom.

   Mencken maintained his running fire against the Justice Department
throughout most of the decade. He claimed on September 27, 1920,
that under Palmer it had deliberately manufactured evidence and so
constituted "a conspiracy against justice, and what is more, against
common honesty and common decency." Criticizing the deportation of
radicals following the Red Scare, Mencken wrote on April 25, 1921:
"Probably two-thirds of those allegedly Reds were wholly innocent, and

even the guilty ones were not fairly tried." In *Notes on Democracy,* published in 1926, he accused the Department of Justice of having "resorted to perjury in its efforts to undo men guilty of flouting it, and at all times it has labored valiantly to nullify the guarantees of the Bill of Rights."[6]

Mencken was equally critical of the federal courts for having, in his eyes, concurred in the abrogation of civil liberties. Commenting on the late chief justice of the Supreme Court, Edward D. White, Mencken argued on May 23, 1921, that, under White, the court had reached "depths of supineness never before touched in American History. . . . The net effect of its so-powerful cogitation, during the last few years of his service, has been to upset and make a mock of three out of four of the historic rights and liberties of the American citizens." Mencken even accused the Supreme Court of failing to maintain the right to trial by jury. Referring to various rulings that upheld laws that removed certain types of cases involving radicals and Prohibition offenders from juries, Mencken alleged on September 15, 1924, that "[t]he whole system of Federal courts is now engaged . . . upon a deliberate and successful effort to blow [trial by jury] to pieces."

The situation in the individual states was sometimes even worse. Mencken frequently attacked California's combination of rigid antisyndicalist laws with a notorious bias in its courts against accused radicals. "Only in California is it normal for innocent men to be railroaded to prison on perjured testimony, and for public prosecutors to traffic openly with professional perjurers, training them in their lies" (June 19, 1922).

Mencken's interest in civil liberties was based on his strong commitment to individual freedom, as well as on his experience with wartime suppression of opinion. Since his involvement certainly did not spring from any left-wing proclivities, his championing of the rights of radicals was all the more meaningful. Part of Mencken's value as a social critic in the 1920s was that he could occasionally see beyond his own political and economic beliefs and could judge a problem on principle rather than on ideology.

Mencken was especially eloquent on behalf of individuals whose rights had been denied. As late as 1924, he was still the only well-known American writer listed by the Sacco and Vanzetti Defense Committee as having registered a protest with them over the nature of the anarchists' trial. Although he wrote often about this celebrated case, his interest was based entirely on the principle of the right to fair trial. According to one of his biographers, he believed the two men to be guilty.[7] Mencken was more personally involved with the Mooney-Billings case, which concerned two radical labor leaders who had been convicted in 1916 by a highly prejudiced California court and on very questionable evidence of a bombing conspiracy. In October 24, 1921, Mencken wrote in the *Evening Sun* that although most people agreed that Mooney was innocent, he remained in prison, his real "crime" being his radicalism. Perhaps, Mencken mused, if the country had more free speech and fairer trials, it would have fewer bombs. In 1928, he wrote to the imprisoned Mooney, "It is an almost inconceivable outrage that you should be still confined in San Quentin, with the evidence of your innocence known to almost everyone." Mencken frequently lent his name to protests on Mooney's behalf, and in 1932 he wrote a letter to California governor James Rolph Jr. appealing for the radical's release. According to a letter to Mencken from the Mooney Defense Committee in 1931, "Tom [Mooney] instructs [us] to say that if he were making up a list of all his loyal friends, the name of H. L. Mencken would be high upon the roster."[8]

Mencken also sought to focus attention on the Carlo Tresca case in the 1920s. Tresca was the proprietor of *Il Martello,* a small, radical, anti-Fascist New York paper. The paper offended Mussolini's ambassador to the United States, and eventually the American government suppressed it, arresting Tresca for allegedly publishing birth control advertisements. Tresca, an alien, was convicted and was then offered the choice of being deported to Italy or of being jailed. He wisely chose the latter. Mencken corresponded with Elizabeth Gurley Flynn, the famous IWW "Rebel Girl," asking her for material about the case and soliciting an article from her on Tresca for the *Mercury.* In his own account of the case in the *Sun* on January 12, 1925, Mencken stormed, "What becomes of the old notion that the United States is a free country, that it is a refuge for the oppressed of other lands?" Roger Baldwin of the American Civil Liberties Union told Mencken that his was the best statement about Tresca that he had seen.[9]

Not all of Mencken's efforts on behalf of the rights of others were conducted in public. During the 1920s, Mencken struck up a correspondence with Emma Goldman, an anarchist writer who had been deported following the Red Scare. He took articles from her for the *Mercury,* and in 1930 wrote to the Justice Department to urge it to return papers belonging to her that had been seized in a raid on the office of the magazine *Mother Earth* in 1917. He also urged the Bureau of Immigration to allow her to return to America to visit her relatives. In both cases, the responses were negative. "Bless your heart," Goldman wrote to Mencken, "how naive you are to think that you could help to change the law in my direction. It is splendid of you to want to attempt it. . . . The fact that you have tried has done me a world of good."[10] In 1940, he sent the Emma Goldman Recovery Committee a check for 25 dollars. His checkbook often followed his principles as he contributed to various organizations that defended political prisoners and combated censorship.

Mencken's involvement on behalf of individuals like Mooney, Tresca, and Goldman should be seen in its proper light. Protest campaigns serve many functions. They not only organize people's genuine sympathy but are also important in holding political movements together and in disseminating propaganda. Mencken belonged to no political organizations, and he invariably had little sympathy for the liberal or radical goals of those he defended. He was motivated by libertarian principles and basic human sympathy. In 1940, when he passed on to Thurmond Arnold a note received from a man claiming to have been wrongfully imprisoned, Mencken told Arnold that he did not have any idea about the merits of the case, "[b]ut when a man behind the bars asks for help it is hard to resist him."[11]

Marx of the Master Class

Mencken believed that the suppression of radicalism, which had started during the war, was the direct result of business pressure on government. It was "physically dangerous," he insisted in 1923, for a man to so much as hint that a noncapitalistic system would please him. Mencken continually called attention to instances in which he felt that justice had become tainted by economics. He attacked the frequent use of court injunctions to break strikes. In the scramble for such injunctions against union activity, Mencken saw "mill owners eager to get rid of annoying labor leaders, coal operators bent on making slaves of their miners, and so on. The injunction in strike cases has been a stench for years" (October 15, 1923).

Similarly, a Supreme Court ruling against labor's use of the secondary boycott against employers brought forth Mencken's satirical observation that it was "the noblest victory that capitalism has won since the celebrated decision against the child labor laws" (January 17, 1921). The doctrines that the Supreme Court seemed to be following were not those set down by the Founding Fathers "but the doctrine of its current Capi-

talistic masters. . . . It puts maintenance of the *status quo* above everything else" (May 23, 1921). To Mencken, the behavior of the courts was
evidence that America was governed "under democratic forms, by a capitalistic oligarchy, and it is so securely in power that no conceivable
revolt is likely to prevail against it" (September 24, 1923). Satirically, he
announced that the country was approaching a businessman's Utopia:
"Nowhere else in the world, . . . is there such elaborate machinery for
inoculating the proletariat with safe ideas. Every agency of public
information . . . is rigidly controlled, and every agency of counter-
propaganda is under a legal ban. The results are visible in two familiar
phenomena of the past few years: the complete collapse of organized
radicalism . . . and the successful organization of such societies as the
American Legion and the Ku Klux Klan into engines of repression."[12]

Mencken rejected as laughable the idea that postwar "New Era" capitalism had erased the conflict between capital and labor. In the *American Mercury* of March 1929, he claimed that America's economic system
was "inordinately wasteful and inhuman. Labor is still frankly a com-
modity, like iron and coal" (380). Where organized labor survived, it did
so, Mencken insisted, because its leaders cooperated with the bosses. He
singled out the conservative unionism of Samuel Gompers and his suc-
cessors in the American Federation of Labor. "Where else in the world is
there a great union organization that has so long and honorable a record
as a strike-breaker? . . . Practically considered, it [the A. F. of L.] is not a
labor organization at all: it is simply a balloon mattress interposed
between capital and labor to protect the former from the latter" (February 9, 1925).

Considering the times and Mencken's own unswerving adherence to
capitalism, his scattered but trenchant comments on the position of the
working class in America are surprisingly perceptive. Recognizing that
the workers had accepted unquestioningly the precepts of the American
Dream, which promised economic success in return for hard work,
Mencken asserted that "[t]he truth is, perhaps, that nine-tenths of them
[the workers] find it almost impossible to think of themselves as
workingmen, doomed to labor all their lives; in their secret communion
with themselves they still think of themselves as potential capitalists"
(September 24, 1923). "These phenomena hook up;" he wrote,

> the collapse of all the radical movements, and the general sentiment
> against emptying the jails. The United States has never developed a true
> proletariat, which often shows fine generosities and chivalries. Instead, it

has simply developed two bourgeoisies, an upper and a lower. Both are narrow, selfish, corrupt, timorous, docile and ignoble; both fear ideas as they fear the plague; both are in favor of 'law and order,' *i.e.,* of harsh laws, unintelligently administered. . . . There is, on the one hand, none of the fine fury and frenzy, the romantic daring, the gaudy imagination of the true proletarian, and on the other hand, there is none of the tolerance and serenity of the true aristocrat. (November 29, 1920)

Mencken, economic conservative and elitist, could produce a quasi-radical reading of the relationship between government, business, and labor in America because he shared at least one thing in common with Marxists; he saw American society in terms of conflict rather than consensus. He was a bit shrewder than most Marxists, however, because he recognized that conflict in America was cultural as well as economic.

In the end, of course, Mencken's own loyalties lay with the middle class and not with the plutocracy or with the working class. The last thing he wanted was a triumph of radicalism. But he was also convinced that unprincipled suppression of the left would only guarantee the creation of more radicalism. For this reason, he urged voters to reject Coolidge in 1924. "I contend that [the president's reelection] is bound to manufacture radicalism in a wholesale manner, and that this radicalism will be far more dangerous to legitimate business than the mild stuff that Dr. La Follette [Coolidge's Progressive opponent] now has on tap" (October 6, 1924). Big business, as far as Mencken was concerned, lacked any semblance of public spirit. "It is frankly on the make, day in and day out, and hence for the sort of politician who gives it the best chance. In order to get that chance it is willing to make any conceivable sacrifice of common sense and common decencies" (August 4, 1924).

Law and Order in a Dry Decade

Unlike many Americans who have come to think of "law 'n' order" as one word, Mencken distinguished between the two concepts. For order (founded on Menckenian principles, of course), he had the profoundest respect, as a glance at his proposal for a new constitution for the state of Maryland will show. Ideally laws supported order. For Mencken there were either good laws or bad laws. Since bad laws subverted good order, Americans, he insisted, had to choose between law and order. To do so, citizens had to fight laws that threatened their liberties. "Such laws deserve no respect, and deserving no respect, they deserve no obedience." Far from being a criminal, the violator of such laws "is worthy of admiration and imitation" (February 26, 1923). Commenting in *Prejudices: Fifth Series* (1926) on legislation that prohibited people from speaking on behalf of birth control, Mencken stormed: "The way to dispose of such laws is to flout them and make a mock of them. The theory that they can be got rid of by enforcing them is nonsense. Enforcing them simply inspires the sadists who advocate them to fresh excesses. Worse, it accustoms the people to oppression, and so tends to make them bear it uncomplainingly. . . . No, the way to deal with such laws is to defy them, and thus make them ridiculous" (14). True to his word, when the *American Mercury* was banned in Boston in 1926, Mencken personally went to that city, sold copies of the offending issue, and was arrested, tried, and acquitted.[13]

The "bad" law that most often concerned Mencken was the Volstead Act, which had been passed in 1919 to enforce the Prohibition amendment to the Constitution. The Eighteenth Amendment prohibited the manufacture, sale, or transportation of intoxicating liquors. The Volstead Act, which assigned Prohibition enforcement to the Bureau of Internal Revenue, defined "intoxicating liquors" as any beverage containing from one-half to one percent of alcohol—a ban that, strictly applied, could have driven sauerkraut from the market.

From today's point of view, the gap between Mencken's rhetorical defense of individual liberties and the actual threat offered by Prohibition may seem too vast for serious contemplation. During the 1920s, Americans needed no ringing appeals to assert their rights in order to send them out in search of a bootlegger. Yet even Herbert Hoover noted in 1921 that the Volstead Act violated traditional concepts of private property. Nevertheless, the Supreme Court acquiesced in granting the Federal government the power to invade individual privacy through the use of phone taps. As Richard Hofstadter once noted, while Prohibition may seem like "a historical detour," it was indeed *the* major issue of the 1920s.[14]

Prohibition not only seriously affected the nation's politics but was the focal point for various cultural pressures that were building up within the society. As a sincere, if poorly conceived reform, Prohibition marked the conjunction of certain Progressive theories of human engineering with the involvement of evangelical Protestantism in social reforms.[15] It also became a symbolic battleground for various groups and philosophies competing for control of American culture and politics: middle class versus working class, native-born Americans versus immigrants, country versus city, old Progressivism versus new liberalism. Prohibition raised vital questions concerning such issues as governmental power, the proper role of police and government agents, the sanctity of privacy, cultural pluralism, public morality, and individual reformation. In context, there was nothing odd about Mencken's focus on Prohibition.

Appreciative of alcohol in most of its potable forms (he once described himself as being "ombibulous"), Mencken was little inclined to weigh the pros and cons of Prohibition. In *Notes on Democracy,* he charged that the Volstead Act "destroys the constitutional right to a jury trial, and in its administration the constitutional prohibition of unreasonable search and seizures and the rule against double jeopardy are habitually violated" (168). While too biased even to contemplate the dry side of the argument, Mencken did try to focus public attention upon some of the political and social principles involved. Yet as Americans went about their pragmatic way of procuring illegal booze, Mencken occasionally despaired of educating his fellow citizens on the principles at stake. "Even the popular discontent with Prohibition," he lamented in the *Mercury* in May 1926, "is not a discontent with its sneaking and knavishness—its wholesale turning loose of licensed blacklegs and blackmailers, its degradation of the judiciary, its corruption of Congress, its disingenuous invasion of the Bill of Rights. . . . Of any forthright grappling with the underlying indecency there is little show" (35).

The Husbandman

Prohibition was a central issue in Mencken's social criticism during the decade because he sensed in it a double threat. On the one hand, it threatened his libertarian principles; on the other, he perceived it as part of a larger cultural struggle between the countryside and the cities. "What lies under it [Prohibition], and under all the other crazy enactments of its category," he complained in *Prejudices: Fourth Series* (1924), "is no more and no less than the yokel's congenital and incurable hatred of the city man" (54).

Tensions between city and countryside are common to many societies and endemic in American history, hardly unique to the 1920s. By the beginning of the decade, however, events had thrown the perceived differences between the urban and rural areas into unusually sharp relief. Industrialization and immigration, which characterized the urbanizing process in America, had produced an urban cultural environment markedly different from that of the countryside. Urban prosperity and rural depression during the 1920s helped accentuate these differences. Finally, although postwar advances in the mass media and in transportation had brought Americans into closer contact with one another, the resulting familiarity seemed to breed an increased contempt between urbanites and their country cousins.

Mencken took it upon himself to champion the cause of the "beleaguered" cities against the "barbaric yokels" from the hinterland. In a total repudiation of the agrarian myth, he focused his most scathing satire on the image of the farmer. "No more grasping, selfish and dishonest mammal, indeed, is known to students of the Anthropoidea," he wrote in *Prejudices: Fourth Series*. "When the going is good for him he robs the rest of us up to the extreme limit of our endurance; when the going is bad he comes bawling for help out of the public till" (46). Political apportionment and the congressional seniority system gave the rural areas a disproportionate share of power, making them "the reservoir of all the nonsensical legislation which now makes the United States a buffoon among the great nations" (54).

Both sides in the urban-rural conflict had real concerns. Mencken's anti-agrarianism was so one-sided and so extreme, however, that it can be understood only in terms of his general ignorance of rural America. Mencken was almost unique among writers of the 1920s who criticized rural American in that he was an east-coast urbanite. He was, in fact, an urban provincial, lacking deep experience with and even affection for the farms and small towns, those very qualities that created the interesting ambiguity in the writings of Sherwood Anderson, Sinclair Lewis, Edgar Lee Masters, and others. Although Mencken encouraged their work, he was not, strictly speaking, a part of the "Revolt from the Village."[16] For Mencken, rural America was nothing more than a satirical abstraction of all of those forces that he felt were threatening enlightened government and civilized tastes. For this reason, his targets were not so much the small-town citizens of Lewis's or Anderson's novels but the less complex and more easily satirized figure of the farmer, whose image was deeply embedded in the heart of American political and social mythology. Significantly, when Mencken published his most vicious anti-agrarian essay in *Prejudices: Fourth Series,* he entitled it "The Husbandman," using Thomas Jefferson's term for the ideal citizen of the Republic.

The Fundamentalist Crusade

One reason for Mencken's hostility toward rural America was the association in his mind between agrarian politics and evangelical Protestantism. "Once we get rid of campmeeting rule we'll get rid simultaneously of the Klan, the Anti-Saloon League and the Methodist Board of Temperance, Prohibition and Public Morals." During the presidential campaign of 1928, Mencken claimed that the only issues were Prohibition and religion—"or more accurately, only religion, for Prohibition, in the dry areas, has long ceased to be a question of government or even ethics, and has become purely theological" (November 5, 1928).

It was this combination of religion and politics that bothered Mencken, for, although he was a professed agnostic, he was not actually hostile to religion. As long as the faithful did not try to impose their beliefs on nonbelievers, Mencken respected sincere religious beliefs, especially if based on a sound, intellectual grasp of theology. Thus, he counted clergymen, even some Fundamentalists, among his friends and acquaintances.[17]

The Fundamentalist movement, as it was called, had begun prior to the war as a counteroffensive by conservative Protestants against modernist theology. By the middle of the 1920s, Fundamentalism was a large and popular movement, especially in the rural Midwest and South, although it did have its urban adherents. Fundamentalists not only supported moral reforms, such as Prohibition, but also actively lobbied state legislatures for laws against the teaching of the Darwinian theory of evolution, which they believed contradicted the biblical account of Creation.

The anti-Darwin crusade, led by William Jennings Bryan, culminated in the famous "Monkey Trial" in Dayton, Tennessee, in the summer of 1925. After the state legislature passed an antievolution law, a group of Dayton citizens decided to test it. A high school teacher, John T. Scopes, agreed to present the evolutionary theory to his class. His arrest and trial became the most famous court case of a decade that, all too often, saw the ballyhoo of the circus invade the courtroom.

Although sent by the *Sunpapers* to cover the trial, Mencken was not there merely as a reporter. He was a combatant in what he sincerely took to be a struggle of civilization and science against bigotry and superstition. "Let no one mistake it for comedy, farcical though it may be in all its details," he commented about the trial. "It serves notice on the country that Neanderthal man is organizing in these forlorn back-waters of the land, led by a fanatic [Bryan] rid of sense and devoid of conscience. Tennessee, challenging him too timorously and too late, now sees its courts converted into camp meetings and its Bill of Rights made a mock of by its sworn officers of the law. There are other States that had better look to their arsenals before the Hun is at their gates" (July 18, 1925).[18]

Mencken had been instrumental in urging the famous criminal lawyer and libertarian Clarence Darrow to offer his services to the American Civil Liberties Union, which was conducting Scopes's defense. At several pretrial meetings with Darrow and with the ACLU lawyer Dudley Field Malone, Mencken suggested that the defense shape its strategy to discredit Bryan, who was leading the prosecution team.[19] In the end, Bryan was tempted to take the stand as an expert on the Bible and had to endure Darrow's vicious cross-examination. Although the prosecution won at Dayton, Scopes was later acquitted on a technicality. It was an anticlimax to what Mencken had hoped would be a great test case of the Constitution.

As with Prohibition, Mencken was too much of a partisan to appreciate or even recognize that the Fundamentalists' fears, if not always their methods, had a certain legitimacy. The Fundamentalists faced the situation that arises when public schools teach children doctrines to which some parents are deeply opposed. Moreover, as Paul Carter has indicated, the Dayton trial was not, in fact, the battle between liberty and intolerance that Mencken painted. In presenting the Darwinian thesis, the authors of *Civic Biology,* Scopes's textbook, were in their own way just as dogmatic as Bryan, whose authority rested on the Bible. The textbook writers, like Darrow and Mencken, treated science as an unquestioned orthodoxy (Carter, 63–83). There is a certain irony, then, in Mencken's scathing attacks on Bryan, especially in "In Memoriam: W. J. B." in *Prejudices: Fifth Series.* In spite of all the differences between Mencken and Bryan, they both had their orthodoxies, and they both felt uncomfortable with the direction in which postwar America was moving. Bryan fought modernity in terms of education and theology; and Mencken resisted its pressures on the sanctity and the dignity of the individual.

The Flight from Babylon

Although Mencken liked to depict America's "walled cities" as under siege by rural "barbarians," it would be a mistake to take his self-conscious identification with the cities at face value. Just as his rural America was a satirical abstraction of the nation's weaknesses and follies, Mencken made the city into a metaphor for the civilized values he thought were endangered. Neither the abstraction nor the metaphor was soundly based on reality. For example, Mencken claimed: "City rights are worth immensely more than State rights. The city is a genuine community; the State is only too often simply a geographical expression" (November 2, 1925). It is very difficult to think of American cities in the 1920s, with their ever increasing influx of rural migrants (black and white) and their polyglot immigrant populations, as communities, especially when one compares the cities with the more homogeneous small towns such as Dayton, Tennessee. Mencken's ideal city was threatened more by the very nature of the American process of industrialization and urbanization than by the rural pastors and their flocks.

Certainly Mencken was not enthusiastic about the effects of industrialization. In "Libido for the Ugly," in *Prejudices: Sixth Series* (1927), he recounted a train trip through Westmoreland County, an area just east of Pittsburgh, Pennsylvania: "Here was the heart of industrial America, the center of its most lucrative and characteristic activity, the boast and pride of the richest and grandest nation ever seen on earth—and here was a scene so dreadfully hideous, so intolerably bleak and forlorn that it reduced the whole aspiration of man to a macabre and depressing joke" (187). If the industrial landscape was a horror, the industrial cityscape in America was often little better.

The unconscious ambivalence of Mencken's urbanism can also be seen in his essay "On Living in Baltimore," which appeared in *Prejudices: Fifth Series*. The essay is actually a comparison between New York City and Baltimore—a contrast between what Mencken found good and bad in urban life. Admitting that his work took him regularly to New York, Mencken explained why he preferred to live in Baltimore. Gotham, he insisted, was fit only "for the gross business of getting money" and not for living. What made New York so dreadful, in his eyes, was that most of its citizens had no real homes and, therefore, no traditions or sense of community. The average New Yorker was a denizen of flats and apartments: "His quarters are precisely like the quarters of 50,000 other men. The front he presents to the world is simply an anonymous door on a gloomy corridor. Inside, he lives like a sardine in a can. Such habitation, it must be plain, cannot be called a home" (239–40).

What made Baltimore a superior place to live was the strength of its traditions—the rooted feeling it could still impart to its inhabitants.

Because its people lived in real homes, they had permanence and stability in their lives. In Baltimore, a man's "contacts are with men and women who are rooted as he is. They are not moving all the time, and so they are not changing their friends all the time. Thus abiding relationships tend to be built up, and when fortune brings unexpected changes, they survive those changes" (242). In the 1920s, rootless mobility was not an exclusively New York phenomenon. By presenting Baltimore as his ideal city, Mencken was praising a personal urban experience that was becoming less and less characteristic of American cities.

Indeed, even Baltimore was not safe from the threat of destructive change. Mencken insisted that the charms of his city had survived, "despite the frantic efforts of boosters and boomers who, in late years, have replaced all its ancient cobblestones with asphalt, and bedizened it with Great White Ways and suburban boulevards, and surrounded it with stinking steel plants and oil refineries, and increased its population from 400,000 to 800,000" (237); nevertheless, the dangers were present, and Mencken recognized them. He was, in fact, no more at home with the reality of urban America than he was with his distorted image of the rural villages and farms of his imagination. In putting forth his urban ideal, he was, like Bryan, defending certain traditional values that were under increasing pressure from a rapidly changing American society.[20]

The Admass Society

There was a great deal of restless anger in Mencken's writings during the decade, anger that could not be contained within the twin themes of libertarianism and the rural-urban conflict. Beneath Mencken's satire one hears a *cri de coeur* raised against the deterioration of the quality of American life. In an article on his home state of Maryland, he lamented that the state's former charm and color had passed with the days of the old tidewater aristocracy. All the links with the past were broken, he complained. "Maryland was once a state of mind; now it is a machine." In the end, he dismally predicted, his state would, like the rest of America, endure a "complete obliteration of distinction, a wiping out of all the old traditions, a massive triumph of regimentation."[21] It was largely for this reason that Mencken devoted so much space in the *American Mercury* to the survival of regional differences in the United States.

The reasons for Mencken's lamentation over Maryland's future become clearer in light of T. C. Cochran and William Miller's comments about the social impact of "New Era" economics during the 1920s.

Under pressure to put the nation's savings to work in productive enterprises, American businessmen vigorously pushed their sales of automobiles, radios, and moving pictures. And as rapid urbanization and agricultural discontent weakened traditional agrarian individualism, the perfection of these new devices of communications together with the older newspapers and national magazines broke down local insularity. Metropolis and village, city and country, factory town and suburban park came increasingly under identical business influences. Provincial habits and customs crumbled.[22]

What had evolved in the 1920s was the world's first admass society, one in which popular culture is dominated by national (and eventually international) mass media, influenced or controlled by large consumer-oriented industries. The mass media, either directly through advertising or indirectly through the consumer-oriented values promoted by popular entertainment, creates a continuing desire for products, the ownership of which becomes the primary means of defining not only one's class but even one's personality. The economic propaganda for consumption, the prime force in an admass society, is intense, and in the 1920s such pressures, especially in the form of advertising, were relatively new. Edward Bernays noted approvingly in 1928, "As civilization has become more complex, the technical means have been invented and developed by which opinion may be regimented" (Cochran & Miller, 332).

Mencken's understanding of this emerging admass society was rather like the blind man's perception of the elephant: he grasped some of its attributes, but he could never really define the whole. The basis for his social analysis, such as it was, rested on people and principles and not upon the impersonal forces of economics and technological change. Nevertheless, it is against this backdrop of the emerging admass society that Mencken's never-ending stream of satiric abuse aimed at the George F. Babbitts and the Calvin Coolidges must be understood. Richard Hofstadter noted that whereas the businessman in the Progressive Era had been criticized for his economic and political actions, he was ridiculed in the 1920s for his cultural shortcomings: "Where once he had been speculator, exploiter, corrupter and tyrant, he had now become boob and philistine, prude and conformist" (Hofstadter 1960, 287). The tone of such criticism was often snobbish, and Mencken certainly was prepared to indict a Babbitt for being ignorant of Beethoven or a Coolidge for not reading Hauptmann. But the antibusiness sentiment of the decade went much deeper than such self-gratifying elitist exercises. When Mencken complained that the United States was "the first great nation in [the] history of the world to ground its whole national philosophy upon business," he was attacking much more than a shallow business culture (February 9, 1925). As he later argued: "Business is not an end in itself; it is simply a means. Its object is to supply the needs of human beings, not to make slaves of them. . . . [Business] is not the supreme aim of human existence on this earth, and any doctrine that so regards it is ignorant and pernicious" (June 22, 1925).

Mencken's attacks on America's new "business civilization" went beyond intellectual snobbery. He was reacting to the immense pressures upon the individual and upon the community. By personifying the enemy in terms of the businessman and his obedient servant, the politician, Mencken contributed little to the understanding of the underlying forces that were shaping the admass society. But he was eloquent in expressing his anger at the increased conformity and regimentation in American life. As he wrote in the *Mercury* in July 1927, the individual in modern America was being turned into a "Freudian case." "Every one of us has been under the steam-roller; every one of us, in this way or that, conforms unwillingly, and has the corpse of a good impulse below stairs" (290).

American Dream—American Tragedy

Mencken concluded *Prejudices: Third Series* with *"Suite Américane,"* a strange collection of fragments, suggesting the failed lives of Americans enslaved to the American Dream. Mencken lists the following under "Aspiration":

> Police sergeants praying humbly to God that Jews will start poker-rooms on their posts, and so enable them to educate their eldest sons for holy orders . . . [Streetcar] conductors on lonely suburban lines, trying desperately to save up $500 and start a Ford garage . . . Pastors of one-horse little churches in decadent villages, who, whenever they drink two cups of coffee at supper, dream all night that they have been elected bishops . . . Italians who wish they were Irish . . . Ashmen who pull wires to be appointed superintendents of city dumps . . . (320–21)

Under "Virtue" we find this list:

> Women hidden away in damp kitchens of unpainted houses along the railroad tracks, frying tough beefsteaks . . . Watchmen at lonely railroad crossings in Iowa, hoping that they'll be able to get off to hear the United Brethren evangelist preacher . . . Greeks tending all-night coffee-

joints in the suburban wilderness where the trolley-cars stop . . . Women
confined [pregnant] for the ninth or tenth time, wondering helplessly
what it is all about . . . Methodist preachers retired after forty years of
service in the trenches of God, upon pensions of $600 a year . . . Babies
just born to the wives of milk-wagon drivers . . . (321–23)

Finally, there is "Eminence."

The leading Methodist layman of Pottawattamie County, Iowa . . . The
man who owns the best bull in Coosa County, Ala. . . . The author of the
ode read at the unveiling of the monument to General Robert E. Lee at
Valdosta, Ga. . . . The old lady in Wahoo, Neb., who has read the Bible
38 times . . . The youngest murderer awaiting hanging in Chicago . . .
(323–24)

Bits and pieces of Americana such as these could have been culled
from daily newspapers or from scores of novels and short stories in the
1920s. In one sense, they represent the least charming side of Mencken,
as well as one of his more dubious gifts to the Jazz Age—the well-off
sophisticate's easy, snide sneers at the annals of the poor and lowly. Yet
there is something deeper to *Suite Américane.* A satiric depiction of the
hollowness of the American Dream, it is full of irony and, beneath the
surface, not without some sense of pity. As Joseph Epstein has pointed
out, the *Suite* is "a list of the sadness inherent in the lives of Americans."
Undergirding this dark vision is what Epstein calls Mencken's "point of
view," his tragic sense of life. Murray Kempton once noted that Mencken,
for all his "Tory" elitism, carried a "social outrage" that generated within
him, in spite of his harsh philosophy, "a lasting tenderness towards the
victims of life."[23]

For his own age, Mencken's value lay in the passionate indignation
with which he exposed the many threats to America's social and even its
moral values. He was, as Eric Goldman suggested, a latter-day muck-
raker, whose theme was the "shame of the Babbitts" (245). A critic with
a stronger ideological awareness of America's problems might have dug
much deeper into the injustices of the society during the 1920s, but few
would have been more eloquent than Mencken in articulating the basis
for their dissent. He firmly believed, as he wrote in *Prejudices: Sixth
Series,* that "the first aim of civilization is to augment and safeguard the
dignity of man—that it is worth nothing to be a citizen of a commonwealth which holds the humblest citizen cheaply and uses him ill" (77).

Chapter Eight
Democracy and Character

Carnival of Buncombe

On February 9, 1920, Mencken announced his postwar return to the pages of the *Evening Sun* with a column on presidential politics entitled "A Carnival of Buncombe." However wide the net Mencken cast upon the American scene, nothing pleased him more than to drag in a politician, especially of the presidential stripe. Convinced that most politicians were merely job seekers anxious to feed at the public trough, he enjoyed presenting them in the motley of circus clowns, low-comic vaudevillians, Old Testament prophets, revivalists, or, most often, members of the learned professions. The more modest a politician's intellectual gifts, the more honorary degrees Mencken heaped upon him. Presidents usually merited no less than a doctorate. Thus the august procession of Dr. Harding, Dr. Coolidge and Dr. Roosevelt through his columns. (Hoover, however, because of his alleged Anglophilia, was dubbed "Lord Hoover.")

The day-to-day rough-and-tumble of American politics was the delight of Mencken's life. He followed the maneuverings of politicians in the newspapers and in the *Congressional Record* as other men followed baseball standings or the stock market reports. When the summer solstice rolled around on the American presidential leap year, he put aside his personal problems and whatever minor ills were fueling his hypochondria and packed his bags for the party conventions. Nothing could keep him away or dampen his enthusiasm.

Americans today, unless they are of a certain age, have little idea of the combination of high drama and absurdity that used to characterize the nominating conventions. Before television and the primaries reduced them to anachronisms, the nominating conventions were the site of whatever oratory, gaudy demonstrations, and backroom deals it took to choose a candidate. The process was not always edifying, mentally or ethically, which only made the conventions more precious to Mencken. Returning from the Coughlin-Townsend convention in 1936, he told novelist Jim Tully, "There were moments when I almost blew up with delight."[1] What small boys found in circuses and grown women in opera, Mencken found in American politics.

> For there is something about a national convention that makes it as fasci-
> nating as a revival or a hanging. It is vulgar, it is ugly, it is stupid, it is
> tedious, it is hard upon both the higher cerebral centers and the *gluteus
> maximus,* and yet it is somehow charming. One sits through long sessions
> wishing heartily that all the delegates and alternates were dead and in
> hell—and then suddenly there comes a show so gaudy and hilarious, so
> melodramatic and obscene, so unimaginably exhilarating and preposter-
> ous that one lives a gorgeous year in an hour.[2]

As we have seen, Mencken firmly believed that it was the duty of any self-respecting journalist to oppose any reigning politician. Concerning his unrelenting criticism of Coolidge in 1924, Mencken claimed that he had no particular animosity toward the man: "he was simply the sitting President of the United States, and in all my life I don't recall ever writ-ing in praise of a sitting President. Finding virtues in successful politi-cians seemed to me to be the function of their swarms of willing pedicu-lae; it was the business of a journalist, as I conceived it, to stand in a permanent Opposition" (*Thirty-five Years,* 133).

Similarly, Mencken insisted that a first-class newspaper should always criticize, not support, the party in power. The task could not be taken lightly. He insisted to Paul Patterson that most men were convinced, "not by appeals to their reason, but by appeals to their emotions and prejudices. Such emotions and prejudices are not necessarily ignoble. It is just as creditable to hate injustice and dishonesty as it is to love the truth" (Bode 1977, 223–24).[3] He constantly urged Patterson to make the *Sunpapers* into the newspaper of "the Opposition."

Mencken has often been criticized for propagating a cynical view of politics. Anticipating the Democratic convention of 1928, he crowed in the *Evening Sun:* "Thus I look for entertainment of the first calibre, exactly to my taste in all its details, . . . with the advantage of not caring a hoot which side wins. If Al [Smith] wins there will be a four years' cir-cus. And if he loses there will be a circus too" (May 28, 1928). Mencken was not averse to orchestrating some of the fun himself. When he found that some outhern Protestants attending the Democratic national con-vention in 1924 in New York City were convinced that Catholics in the gallery were going to throw bombs at them, Mencken gleefully helped spread rumors that another St. Bartholomew's Day Massacre was at hand (*Thirty-five Years,* 131).

Much of the humor in Mencken's political pieces came from his satiric pose as the bemused observer, above and beyond the fray. After discussing the bitterness between Protestants and Roman Catholics during the campaign of 1928, Mencken observed, "I recite these lamentable facts, not to deplore them, but to say that I do *not* deplore them. Life in America interests me, not as a moral phenomenon, but simply as a gaudy spectacle. I enjoy it most when it is most uproarious, preposterous, inordinate and melodramatic. . . . I'd rather read the *Congressional Record*—or, failing that, any good tabloid—than go see a bishop hanged" (May 28, 1928).

Yet underneath the burlesque, Mencken did take politics seriously; he took sides—on issues and on candidates—and he did so on the basis of principles. In his articles, he discussed issues and candidates; and he always voted. He even found an occasional politician he could support, men such as Governor Albert Ritchie of Maryland, Senator James Reed of Missouri, and, for a time, Al Smith of New York.

Notes on Democracy

Judging from Mencken's daily involvement with politics on the journalistic level and his long-held dissents from the clichés of American democracy, *Notes on Democracy* (1926) should have been his best book. It had been on his mind since the beginning of the 1920s. Unfortunately, the pressure of his work and the raging passion he brought to it produced a weak pastiche of ideas, enlivened only by a series of well-written satirical set pieces. Reviewing the book in the *Saturday Review of Literature* of December 11, 1926, Walter Lippmann found *Notes on Democracy* to be in one sense, "a collection of trite and somewhat confused ideas. To discuss it as one might discuss ideas of a first-rate thinker . . . would be to destroy the book and miss its importance" (413).

Before considering Lippmann's qualification to this otherwise damning statement, we must first understand the failure of *Notes on Democracy* as a *political* work. In the book Mencken does nothing more than follow his well-established pattern of satiric criticism—the inversion of the national myths. "The truth is that the common man's love of liberty, like his love of sense, justice and truth, is almost wholly imaginary. As I have argued, he is not actually happy when free; he is uncomfortable, a bit alarmed, and intolerably lonely. He longs for the warm, reassuring smell of the herd, and is willing to take the herdsman with it" (147). Far from liberating men, Mencken argued that democracy created a tyranny of the mediocre majority over society's intellectual elite. The superior individual, he insisted, "is the chief victim of the democratic process. It not only tries to regulate his acts; it also tries to delimit his thoughts." The aim of democracy was to break all free spirits "to the common harness" (150–51).

Notes on Democracy, then, is a continuation of Mencken's "prejudices," a reiteration of his Nietzschean view that society could be defined as merely the battleground between the superior man and the mob. "The free man is one who has won a small and precarious territory from the great mob of his inferiors, and is prepared and ready to defend it and make it support him. All around him are his enemies, and where he stands there is no friend. He can hope for little help from other men of his own kind, for they have battles of their own to fight. He has made of himself a sort of god in his little world, and he must face the responsibilities of a god, and the dreadful loneliness" (45). In such a barren libertarian landscape, society itself seems to disappear, making any real political or sociological analysis impossible.

The state, on the other hand, loomed to monstrous size. Although any critique of a political system must eventually focus on the institution of the state, Mencken, in his postwar writings, regarded the state a necessary evil, at best. He asserted in the sixth book of *Prejudices* that "[w]hat ails the world mainly, at least in the political sense, is that its governments are too strong. It [government] has been a recurrent pest since the dawn of civilization" (53). In the "Editorial" in the *Mercury* for February 1925, Mencken even managed to see in the widespread disobedience of the Volstead Act the "first glimmers of a revolt that must one day shake the world—a revolt, not against this or that form of government, but against the tyranny at the bottom of *all* governments. Government, today, is growing too strong to be safe. There are no longer any citizens in the world; there are only subjects." Almost 20 years later, he mused in some unpublished notes, "I am convinced . . . that government—*any* government—is a nearly unmixed evil, and that abolishing it altogether would be better for mankind than continuing its development along the path now followed."[4]

Mencken never really analyzed government in political or institutional terms. It is not surprising, therefore, to find that he devoted very little attention in *Notes on Democracy* to his supposed alternative to democracy: aristocracy. Mencken's aristocracy remained nothing more than an abstract ideal that could never cast even the shadow of reality upon American society. Like his view of democracy, it was totally innocent of analysis. *Notes on Democracy,* then, was not a political book in any meaningful sense of the word. If, as Walter Lippmann had suggested, the book did have some importance, one must look for its significance in something other than in the realms of political thought.

Democracy and Character

Lippmann thought that *Notes on Democracy* had captured the antidemocratic mood of the times just as Tom Paine's writings had once set forth the late-eighteenth-century awakening of democracy. Viewing Mencken's book from a different angle, one scholar noted: "There is so much more about Democratic Man than about democracy that this type can be said to be *the* argument of the book. Politics becomes anthropology."[5] Edmund Wilson, seeing *Notes on Democracy* as a prose poem ("the obverse of *Leaves of Grass*"), came closest to perceiving the real focus of the work. Writing in the *New Republic,* Wilson claimed that Mencken's most important achievement was his portrait of democratic man as "super-boob"— the mob-man. Evaluating the average man, Mencken wrote:

> He has changed but little since the earliest recorded time, and that change is for the worse quite as often as it is for the better. He still believes in ghosts, and has only shifted his belief in witches to the political sphere. He is still a slave to priests, and trembles before their preposterous magic. . . . He can imagine nothing beautiful and he can grasp nothing true. Whenever he is confronted by a choice between two ideas, the one sound and the other not, he chooses, almost infallibly, and by a sort of pathological compulsion, the one that is not. Behind all the great tyrants and butchers of history he has marched with loud hosannas, but his hand is eternally against those who seek to liberate the spirit of the race. . . . In two thousand years he has moved an inch: from the sports of the arena to the lynching-party—and another inch: from the obscenities of the Saturnalia to the obscenities of the Methodist revival. So he lives out his life in the image of Jahveh. What is worth knowing he doesn't know and doesn't want to know; what he knows is not true. The cardinal articles of his credo are the inventions of mountebanks; his heroes are mainly scoundrels. (64–65)

This creature, as Wilson remarked in his review, is "an ideal monster, exactly like the Yahoo of Swift, and it has almost the same dreadful reality." The world that Mencken depicted in *Notes on Democracy* was "simply an abstraction from *our* world of all those features of American life that fall short of Mr. Mencken's standards."[6]

These standards—Mencken's system of values applied to human character and society—form the real basis for almost everything he wrote, especially *Notes on Democracy*. In that book, Mencken was concerned with what he regarded as the failure of character under democracy: "Liberty means self-reliance, it means resolution, it means enterprise, it means the capacity for doing without" (45). The average man lacked these qualities because "[l]iberty is unfathomable to him. He can no more comprehend it than he can comprehend honour" (46). Mencken's argument against democracy was based on moral rather than political, economic, or sociological grounds. He simply contrasted two types of human character as he imagined them: the one predisposed toward liberty and the other toward conformity.

This concern with character appeared time and again in Mencken's social and cultural criticism. In the *Mercury* of January 1929, he commented on the University of Pennsylvania's dismissal of economist Scott Nearing because of his radical views. Mencken regarded Nearing's socialism as "hooey," but he greatly admired the man who stood by his convictions. "What our third-rate snivilization fails to estimate at its real worth is the resolute courage and indomitable devotion of such men. His virtues are completely civilized ones; he is brave, independent, unselfish, urbane and enlightened." Mencken commented that if he had a son, he would want him to meet Nearing. "There is something even more valuable to civilization than wisdom, and that is character. Nearing has it" (124).

Even Mencken's attitude toward political candidates was influenced by his estimation of their character. As it became clear that the presidential campaign of 1920 would pit the Republican Warren Gamaliel Harding against Democrat James M. Cox, Mencken complained in the *Evening Sun* on July 26, 1920: "Neither candidate reveals the slightest dignity of conviction. Neither cares a hoot for any discernable principle. Neither, in any intelligible sense, is a man of honor." In the end he voted for Harding but without enthusiasm. "Tomorrow the dirty job," he wrote on November 1, 1920. "I shall be on my knees all night, praying for the strength to vote for Gamaliel. What ass first let loose the doctrine that the suffrage is a high boon and voting a noble privilege."

By the end of the 1924 presidential campaign, Mencken found the candidates of both the Republicans and the Democrats so unpalatable that he urged his readers to vote for Robert M. La Follette, candidate for the Progressive Party. La Follette's ideas, Mencken argued, were so vague as to be incomprehensible. Nevertheless, Mencken admired him "simply and solely because he was the man of honor among the candidates." On the eve of the election Mencken announced, "I shall vote for him [La Follette] unhesitatingly, and for a plain reason; he is the best man running *as a man.* There is no ring in his nose. Nobody owns him. Nobody bosses him" (November 3, 1924). Mencken portrayed La Follette's subsequent defeat as a joke that the American people had played upon themselves. "Mislead by inflammatory and nonsensical issues, alarmed and run amuck by quacks and mountebanks, the people forget the one quality that is worth more in a high officer of state than all the rest. That one quality is character" (August 3, 1925).

Mencken followed the same approach in 1928 when he chose to represent Al Smith, the Democratic candidate, as a man of honor: "But there is more to him than the mere politician. Somewhere on the sidewalks of New York, without benefit of the moral training on tap in Kansas and Mississippi, he picked up the doctrine that it is better, after all, to be honest than to lie" (August 27, 1928). Mencken depicted Al Smith as a gentleman from the aristocratic mold: "He is enlightened, he is high-minded, he is upright and trustworthy. What Frederick the Great said of his officers might well be said of him: he will not lie, and he cannot be bought. Not much more can be said of any man" (October 29, 1928).

Mencken's enthusiasm for Smith may have been largely for public consumption. Among the Mencken-Smith letters in the New York Public Library, there is a note by Mencken to the effect that early on in the campaign he realized that Smith would make an "incredibly bad President." This note is not dated and might have been the product of protective hindsight. If it did reflect Mencken's opinions at the time, however, it suggests that he consciously put Smith forward as a hero and a symbol. For a decade that felt desperately in need of heroes, Mencken was prepared to supply them.

Beneath the surface of his satire, Mencken was a very different figure from the cynical nihilist depicted by so many of his critics. He never denied the importance of values or their necessity in society. He never sought to destroy those values in which he believed. He did attack, sometimes ignorantly and intolerantly, ideals that seemed to him hypocritical or false. Even then he usually produced his condemnation by juxtaposing the qualities he admired against those he rejected. Throughout his writings, certain key words constantly reoccur: "dignity," "decency," "honesty," "courage," and, most often, "honor." "Every man has feelings," he once wrote to Fanny Butcher. "Mine chiefly revolve around a concept of honor."[7]

Ultimately, Mencken's deepest interest lay not with politics, as it is usually defined, but with character and human conduct. Ethics, not ideologies and institutions, was his principal concern. He was in his own way a moralist, angrily decrying the erosion of those values necessary to a humane and civilized society. Beneath the surface of his satire and social criticism there thundered a constant jeremiad delivered to a wayward people who had wandered from the paths of the good and the honorable.

In Defense of the Forgotten Man

Mencken could pass off his polemics on character as a critique of democracy because he appeared to champion the virtues of the gentleman and aristocrat against the elemental appetites and fears of the craven, venal mob. Mencken's values were not, of course, derived from either a real or an imagined aristocracy. When he hailed the Forgotten Man as his ideal citizen in the first issue of the *American Mercury,* he underscored the source of his own code of conduct. He described the Forgotten Man as "the normal, educated, well-disposed, unfrenzied, enlightened citizen of the middle minority"—in other words, as an intelligent and responsible member of the middle class (28). And what Mencken celebrated and defended were the values of this class. As Douglas C. Stenerson has suggested, "Mencken cultivated the virtues associated with the Protestant ethic, and for him, as frequently as for the Forgotten Man, these virtues had lost all traces of religious feeling. He exhibited, and admired in others, individual initiative, hard work, punctuality, thrift and prompt payment of debts."[8] If one adds honor, dignity, integrity, and character to the list, one is still not very far from the core of traditional American middle-class values, as a glance at any McGuffey reader will quickly show. Mencken's supposed aristocratic values were formed, not out of some remote and romantic Germany of the imagination or from the old Maryland tidewater estates, which he never knew, but in the middle class, whose loyal if sometimes errant and eccentric son he remained.

Through Mencken's defense of middle-class values (via a defense of the Forgotten Man), an aspect of his role in the 1920s that has seldom been recognized can be glimpsed. Mencken assumed that his Forgotten

Man, although civilized and superior, was also culturally and politically isolated, because neither his tastes nor his values seemed to prevail. The very term "forgotten" suggests that Mencken's ideal citizen was alienated to some degree from the prevailing tendencies of American life. Consider the situation in which many middle-class Americans found themselves during the decade. Normally law-abiding, they broke the law if they drank, used contraceptives, or read certain magazines or books. Yet, they did not feel themselves to be antisocial. They still believed in individualism, honesty, and hard work. They were still attracted to the verities of home and community, stability and tradition. Such values were under increasing pressure in the 1920s, however. Postwar changes in American society challenged these values at almost every level. F. Scott Fitzgerald indulged in a bit of romantic exaggeration when he proclaimed all gods dead and all faiths shaken. Nevertheless, the decade was a time of insidious moral crisis, as Fitzgerald and most of the best writers of the period were well aware.[9]

For sophisticated, urban Americans, traditional values often seemed devalued, rendered ridiculous and old-fashioned by such self-appointed defenders as Bryan. In such hands middle-class values not only appeared trite, they were often used to bolster such dubious crusades as Fundamentalism and Prohibition or to hammer home demands for political and cultural conformity. Mencken's Forgotten Man still believed in most of the old verities but found it difficult to express them without sounding like the preachers, the superpatriots, and the politicians from whom he recoiled. Mencken appeared to provide a solution. By positing these values as the code of an aristocracy of character—the "civilized minority"— Mencken enabled both the Forgotten Man and himself to cling to a traditional value structure while making it seem superior, even advanced.

The mantle of the "civilized minority" that Mencken offered to the Forgotten Man had originally been reserved for those whose superiority had been based on intellect and aesthetics, not status. Status, however, never very cleanly defined in America, had become even more blurred by the new consumer economics of the postwar era. New occupations and modes of consumption were challenging the more traditional methods of defining and identifying social position. For example, a new white-collar middle class, caught between the corporate plutocracy and the working class, was anxious to clarify its own place on the socioeconomic ladder. Since membership in Mencken's "civilized minority" was self-selective (would any readers would have classified themselves under the suborder *homo boobiens?*), Mencken offered some easy assurances to the Forgotten Man about his intrinsic worth and place in the society. This affectation stood as the sole defiant gesture of many of those alienated from the culture of boobery and Babbittry.

During the 1920s, Mencken used the terms "civilized minority" and "Forgotten Man" almost interchangeably. They symbolized, however, two rather different sides of Mencken's rhetorical appeal. The concept of the "civilized minority" came out of his earlier enthusiasm for art and iconoclasm, when he had hoped that a talented cultural elite could transform society. The Forgotten Man was the product of Mencken's more defensive postwar mood, when he realized the need to locate his elite within the enlightened portion of the middle class.[10]

By fusing these images of the civilized minority and the Forgotten Man, Mencken failed to see that he was altering his position as a satirist and abandoning the aggressive figure of the artist-iconoclast. His Forgotten Man was a defensive image, more victim than hero, more threatened than threatening. Although his satire was as vigorous as ever and although his public image remained irresponsibly brash, Mencken's main role in the 1920s was that of the conserver. His headlong assaults on presidents and Prohibitionists were, in effect, sallies from behind the walls where he and the Forgotten Man were defending a vision of American life that was passing into a disturbing and uncharted future.

The Libertarian

The political implications of Mencken's appeal to the Forgotten Man are harder to pin down but are, nonetheless, suggestive. For all of his satiric attacks on Harding and Coolidge, Mencken never supported any policies that would have been detrimental to the interests of the middle class. His defense of Socialist Eugene Debs and his praise of La Follette were political only to the extent that he believed that a narrow, ruthless suppression of radical opinion would only beget more and worse radicalism in the future.

In previous periods of American history, middle-class discontent and frustration had sometimes found outlets in movements such as Abolitionism and Progressivism. But what sort of reform movement could have been mounted against the dullness and mediocrity that characterized so much of American politics in the 1920s? In Mencken's first editorial in the *Mercury,* he pictured the Forgotten Man faced with an irrelevant choice between a Progressivism that no longer seemed credible and a form of conservatism that was narrow, mean, and self-serving.

Although Mencken promised nothing more than solace for those caught in this dilemma, he was, in fact, groping toward some new political response. He was urged on in this pursuit by no less a figure than Senator James Reed of Missouri. Wishing Mencken luck with his new magazine, the *Mercury,* Reed was confident that Mencken would succeed "because what is needed is a man who does not fly off at a tangent . . . neither committing himself to new fancies of reform or [so] anchoring himself to the rock of conservatism that he is incapable of movement. We are living in an age of transition. The thing today is to develop a philosophy which will meet new conditions without doing violence to old and sound principles."[11]

This search for a new political stance based on "old and sound principles" is exactly what Mencken himself intended, as can be seen in his letter to Nathan (quoted in chapter 6) in which he claimed that the *Mercury* could provide leadership for the enlightened minority. Mencken even entertained a vague hope that some sort of third party movement would fill the vacuum. In the early 1920s, he had urged the *Sunpapers* to run an editorial calling for the formation of a new party (Bode 1969, 195).[12] In *Notes on Democracy* he wrote: "For what democracy needs most of all is a party that will separate the good that is in it theoretically from the evils that beset it practically, and then try to erect that good into a workable system. What it needs beyond everything is a party of liberty" (205–6).

What made Mencken's love of liberty refreshingly free from clichés and hypocrisy, with which it is all too often embalmed by American political rhetoric, was the rigorous, almost Fundamentalist type of logic with which he pursued it. "By liberty I mean the utmost freedom possible under an orderly society," he explained in his "Autobiographical Notes" in 1925 (165). This idea was sometimes difficult for even his friends to comprehend. When Mencken was asked in 1931 by the Pittsburgh *Courier,* a black newspaper, to support a campaign against the popular *Amos an' Andy* radio program because of its racist nature, Mencken expressed sympathy but could not go along with the protest. As he told George Schuyler, the paper's leading columnist, "[A]ll such crusades seem to me ill-advised and dangerous. . . . I am unalterably opposed to all efforts to put down free speech, whatever the excuse" (Forgue 1961, 330). To Benjamin de Casseres he wrote in 1935: "I insist that if we had free speech argument against free speech should be permitted also, for it is part of my doctrine that free speech itself may be an error. I don't believe it is, but neither do I think my conviction should choke off any man who disagrees." De Casseres apparently balked at this attitude, for a few days later Mencken angrily responded, "You talk foolishness. If I am in favor of free speech I should be in favor of it up to the last limit of endurance. Thus, I argue that even those who are against it ought to be heard. It is you who make the compromise, not I."[13]

In the 1920s, Mencken's libertarianism was aimed largely at conservative opinion. With radicalism weak and on the defensive and with liberalism in a state of transition, momentary alliances with those on the left on specific issues presented no difficulties for him. He never confused their aims with his own, however. He was convinced that liberals did not really believe in free speech, for he felt they would not oppose the suppression of illiberal attitudes. "I believe that I am more liberal than they are," he wrote in "Autobiographical Notes" in 1925. "I am against Socialism in all its forms, but I have always done all I could to help the Socialists when their rights were denied them" (169).

In the 1930s, liberalism was transformed into the image of the New Deal, and Communism, although far from popular, for a time appeared to wield influence among writers and intellectuals. In these changed circumstances Mencken became increasingly disturbed by this revival of radicalism. When John Dos Passos wrote in 1947 to ask him to be part of a committee being organized to defend Edmund Wilson's *Memoirs of Hecate County* against the censors, Mencken complained that the Communists would invariably take over the protest. It was better for authors to fight their own battles. Nevertheless, he joined the committee.[14]

Although politics for Mencken was a battleground of personalities and values rather than of political parties or institutions, he did have a rudimentary political philosophy that provided power and some meaning to his social criticism and undergirded the real unity to his career. Writing to his German publisher in 1923, Mencken explained himself: "My literary theory, like my politics, is based chiefly upon one idea, to whit, the idea of freedom. I am, in brief, a libertarian of the most extreme variety, and can imagine no human right that is half as valuable as the simple right to pursue the truth at discretion and utter it when found."[15]

Chapter Nine

The Depression and the War Years

The Passing of an Era and an Editor

The December 1933 issue of the *American Mercury* was the last one to be published under Mencken's name. Ten years after he founded the magazine, he resigned as its editor for a variety of reasons. Having edited magazines for two decades, the 53-year-old Mencken was getting tired of the pressures and the constant trips to New York. Moreover, he was now much more involved in his domestic life. In 1930 he had finally relinquished his position as one of America's most famous bachelors by marrying Sara Powell Haardt from Alabama in 1930.

There were, of course, other factors behind Mencken's decision to leave the *Mercury*. The magazine had been losing readers since it had reached its peak of popularity in 1927. By 1929, the readership was down to 67,420, almost 10,000 below the 1927 figure, and the drop in circulation continued (Singleton, 214). The decline of the *Mercury* was but one reflection of a gradual weakening of Mencken's popularity. His *Prejudices* series had ended with the sixth book in 1927, as there was no longer enough interest to continue it. By the following year, both the quantity and the quality of critical comment about Mencken had also perceptively declined. Intellectuals, bored with what they considered Mencken's obsessions with Methodists and Prohibition, and with his failure to cultivate new ground, regarded him as a spent force. Although many of their criticisms were valid, few critics understood or appreciated what Mencken had been trying to say. Only a few observers, such as Walter Lippmann, Edmund Wilson, and Joseph Wood Krutch, had glimpsed the serious intent beneath Mencken's now repetitious satire.

The fault, of course, was largely Mencken's. He had so successfully exploited the situation as he found it in the early 1920s that he had failed to develop as the decade continued. He assumed, apparently, that the political vacuum of the 1920s would, along with the decade's prosperity, last forever. Moreover, having imaginatively, if not always accurately, interpreted the forces at work in the decade, he had failed to reconsider his own judgments. The rigidity of his views, the reiteration of set themes, and the satiric pretense of uninvolvement, all of which had helped to make him popular, now began to work against him. Vincent Starrett, an early admirer, summarized the problem in 1927: "What he has been saying is stock in trade—it is expected, looked for. . . . He must continue as he began. . . . He cannot go back; he dare not now go ahead. To do either would be to cease to be Mr. Mencken, an institution."[1]

By the end of the decade, Mencken was aware of his declining popularity and was seeking to solidify his hold on what he considered his essential, "serious" audience. He put great effort into two books in which he sought to make a realistic appraisal of religion and ethics. *Treatise on the Gods* and *Treatise on Right and Wrong* were published in 1930 and 1934, respectively. Although he considered the former his best work, its sales were disappointing.

By the early 1930s, the crash of the stock market and the Depression had brought a rude end to the Mencken era. In fact, the Great Depression exposed the serious weakness of Mencken's social criticism. Mencken's satire had worked during the 1920s because the decade had been full of ambiguities following the collapse of Progressive idealism and the emergence of unfamiliar economic and social forces. Mencken had peopled the political and cultural landscape with heroes and villains, but he had also imposed some pattern on the otherwise confusing events of the decade. He had continually depicted the sensitive, talented, honest, free spirits of America as engaged in an unequal combat against a society of ignorant, timorous conformists who had been constantly misled and swindled by their political, religious, and financial masters.

The Depression inaugurated for Mencken and America a dramatically different atmosphere. Complicated as the underlying economic problems were, the plight facing millions of Americans was certainly not ambiguous. Its everyday effect on their lives was all too clear. The cataclysm was far too massive to allow Mencken's pose of disinterestedness to retain its satiric cutting edge. Also, although the Depression brought politics back into the foreground of American life, Mencken's brand of satiric demonology was no longer effective. Finally, the financial collapse posed a stark threat to Mencken's economic conservatism. He had been willing to belabor the excesses of capitalism when the system seemed impregnable, but when it appeared to totter, he rallied to its support. In the 1920s, his defense of values had been covert. His defense of capitalism, limited government, and individual self-reliance in the 1930s was overt. The days of his iconoclasm had passed.

Mencken acknowledged this in the series of private memoirs he wrote in the 1940s. Looking back on the early days of the New Deal, he bemoaned the *Evening Sun*'s flirtation with Franklin Roosevelt's first administration. He had protested "every day and with violent earnestness" against the *Sun*'s position but to no avail. Yet, under the circumstances, it was hardly possible, he admitted, "to adapt the methods of the old merry wars on Prohibition, Ku Kluxry, the Coolidge Prosperity and the Hoover New Economics to what was essentially a serious fight" (*Thirty-five Years,* 231).

The Depression had robbed Mencken of his old issues and, for a time, had presented him with new ones, which he was totally unable to handle. Consequently, he tried to ignore the situation, hoping, as did so many Americans, that it would go away. It was not until 1932 that he tried to deal with the Depression editorially in the *Mercury* and then only to admit an almost pathetic impotence. In January 1932, in a column entitled "What's Going On in the World," Mencken wrote that he had once believed that democracy was endurable because it supported capitalism. The politicians had followed the bankers, but the bankers now were calling upon the politicians for help. "No wonder I am upset! All my natural prejudices have been outraged. Temperamentally incapable of Socialism, ... I find myself hanging upon a precarious branch, trying unhappily to figure out what is going to happen next" (6). Although Mencken was soon echoing the Hooverian line of belt-tightening and predicting imminent recovery (all the while despising Hoover), the editor of the *American Mercury* clearly had nothing more to offer.

As the readers began to turn away, Mencken tried to find ways to revamp the magazine and to halt its decline. Changes in the magazine's cover and alterations in its format—the telltale signs of sickness in the magazine trade—were about all he could accomplish. Growing clashes of personality and ideology between him and his assistant editor, Charles Angoff, plunged the *Mercury* into additional confusion. By the time he left the magazine in December 1933, Mencken and the *Mercury* had declined together.

In the Days of Roosevelt II

Mencken retired from the *Mercury* but not from the American scene. He published several books during the 1930s, revised and extended *The*

American Language, and wrote widely for magazines. He still gloried in the presidential nominating conventions. He continued his weekly articles for the *Evening Sun,* and he was involved in regular editorial conferences, in which he struggled to turn the papers against the New Deal and away from Anglophilia in foreign policy. Indeed, as a member of the papers' board of directors, his involvement with the *Sunpapers* was greater than ever. He negotiated, unsuccessfully, on behalf of the *Sunpapers* to purchase one of the Hearst publications and represented the publishers in their negotiations with the Newspaper Guild. His correspondence remained as voluminous as ever, and, although there were fewer literary figures among his acquaintances now, there were more politicians and public figures, even a few New Dealers. He exchanged letters with Congressman Emanuel Sellers on a proposed antilynching law, with Maury Maverick of Texas on a law to enforce the Bill of Rights, with Justice Felix Frankfurter on the rights of privacy (the justice in turn cited Mencken on journalistic ethics in one of his opinions), and with Thurmond Arnold on everything from language to the New Deal.

It was Franklin Roosevelt's New Deal that, by giving Mencken a target, helped to alleviate somewhat his own personal depression of the mid-1930s. Following his own dictum to "throw the reigning rascals out," he voted for Roosevelt (and an end to Prohibition) in 1932. As the New Deal began to assume its protean shapes, he fired, almost by reflex action, broadsides at the burgeoning bureaucracy and at the "wizards" of the Brain Trust. Franklin Roosevelt, however, seems to have confused Mencken for a time. He was unnerved by the powers that the new president assumed but, as late as January 2, 1934, he could tell his readers in the *Evening Sun* that Roosevelt was "shrewd, candid and bold." He also felt that the president was at least a "gentleman" and that, as such, "[h]e will fight longer, and he can be trusted farther."

On the whole, however, Mencken was already a consistent critic of the New Deal. In the halcyon days of 1934, before the political lines against Roosevelt had hardened, Mencken enjoyed a rather unique position as one of the few senior, well-known journalists opposed to the administration. Therefore, in December of that year, when the time came for the annual Gridiron Banquet in Washington D.C., where journalists and the administration confront each other over cocktails and gibes, Mencken was asked to give the after-dinner speech. Although his remarks were barbed, they were in keeping with the evening's high jinx. "In the early days of the New Deal I used to do a great deal of worrying about the Constitution. . . . But the other day I had a postcard from a judge saying that the Constitution was really very well taken care of. He said it was in the National Museum here in Washington, stuffed with excelsior, and waiting for Judgment Day. No doubt there are many Republicans there too, but what they are waiting for I don't know."[2]

Then came the president's opportunity to reply to the evening's good-humored critique of his administration. To everyone's surprise and initial shock, the usually urbane Roosevelt launched into a vitriolic attack on the press. He called journalists lackeys of the plutocrats and accused them of being generally ignorant and uncultured imbeciles. Gradually, shock gave way to laughter as the assembled pressmen recognized that Franklin Roosevelt was reading them one of Mencken's essays, "Journalism in America," from *Prejudices: Sixth Series*. Only Mencken was not amused. According to one biographer, he began scribbling notes for a furious rebuttal. As soon as FDR was finished, however, he was wheeled out, pausing to shake hands with his outmaneuvered adversary. Mencken's own account of the evening displays only a hint of anger. He felt the president had employed a "fair device, and he carried it off very well. Despite his wide smile and insistence that I was a friend, it was plain enough that he had a grudge and was trying to get revenge. He has had plenty of grounds for wanting to do so, and he will have even more grounds hereafter."[3] Mencken now roasted "King Roosevelt II," and his New Deal court in the *Sunpapers* and in magazine pieces. In the *Sunpapers* offices, Mencken helped swing the editorials into the anti-New Deal camp and worked hard to offset the influence of some of the younger "radicals" on the staff.

In the spring of 1938, Mencken was asked to take over a three-month stint as editor of the *Evening Sun*. Paul Patterson wanted to revitalize the editorial policy and hoped that Mencken, working on a daily basis with the editorial writers, would come up some suggestions. It had been years since Mencken had edited a newspaper, and at the age of 58 he found it hard going. But he plunged in and made the most of his opportunity to inject some of his old gusto into the staid paper by turning the editorial page into an anti-New Deal circus. One editorial was nothing but a mass of Benday dots, each one representing one of the million or so federal officeholders. On March 4, on the fifth anniversary of the New Deal, Mencken produced a six-and-one-half column editorial (the longest ever published, he claimed), which was a massive blast at Roosevelt and his policies. True to form, he invited one of the liberals on the staff, Gerald W. Johnson (whom Mencken had brought up from the

South in the 1920s to work for the paper) to write a defense of the New Deal. (*Thirty-five Years*, 303–4).[4]

Liberals and even radicals, who had known Mencken in the 1920s as a libertarian and sharp critic of New Era capitalism, were shocked by what appeared to be a sellout to conservatism. In 1936, one correspondent in the Communist *New Masses* had to remind the readers that there had been a time when "[y]ou couldn't throw a stone into a Communist Party mass meeting without hitting someone who, one time in the past, heartily agreed with Mr. Mencken's bitter assault on everything that was typically bourgeois."[5] Many readers who had admired him during the 1920s thought he had changed. The problem was, however, that Mencken had *not* changed; his libertarianism, built upon the foundations of social Darwinism and a dedication to laissez-faire philosophy, had never been aimed at capitalism itself. And although he heaved many a dead cat into the sanctums of Americanism, he never threw one at the Constitution, which he fretted over with an almost Federalist concern. The man who could accuse the Republican administrations of Harding, Coolidge, and Hoover of having increased the power of the state and who could conjure up in 1926, as he did in *Notes on Democracy,* the horror of the welfare state, was not likely to view the New Deal with even a modicum of equanimity.

On March 13, 1933, a week of so after the new president's inauguration, Mencken previewed his opposition to Roosevelt and the New Deal in an article in the *Evening Sun*. The country, he noted, had had two dictatorships in the past—those of Lincoln and Wilson. It now seemed about to embark on a third. Roosevelt had, so far, carried out his dictatorship with restraint. "But it is always well, when anything of the sort is set up in a presumably free country, to scrutinize it very carefully and even biliously, lest it get out of hand." Concluding, he commented: "If the American people really tire of democracy and want to make a trial of Fascism, I shall be the last person to object. But if that is their mood, then they had better proceed toward their aim by changing the Constitution and not by forgetting it. And they had better remember that Fascism means not only rough usage for crooked bankers but also rough usage for multitudes of far better men."

Mencken soon decided the specter of radicalism, rather than that of Fascism, stalked Washington. It was not just Mencken's own capitalistic bias, which caused him to be disturbed by the leftward shift within the ranks of the intellectuals and writers in the 1930s. He suspected and resented what he considered the hypocritical stand by left-wing ideologues who supported Stalinism in Russia and demanded free speech for Communists in America. In 1938, he wrote an article for the October issue of the *Mercury* in which he argued that Communists had no place in the top ranks of the American Civil Liberties Union, because they maintained a dual standard. For a time, a lawsuit was threatened. Arthur Garfield Hayes, an American Civil Liberties Union lawyer and an acquaintance of Mencken, complained to him that his article amounted to a rejection of Communists simply for their political beliefs. Mencken certainly did not like Communism, but, as a longtime supporter of the American Civil Liberties Union, he was chiefly concerned that the appearance of Communists in the organization's leadership would weaken its usefulness.[6] Although he obviously rejected the philosophy of the Popular Front, Mencken did not repudiate his libertarianism: he did not deny the right of people to be Communists. Less flexible than he had been in the past, he was, nevertheless, simply following the logic of his own views. Liberty, for him, was an end in itself, and commitment to it had to be absolute.

Mencken's libertarianism, thus, remained unchanged. In the end, it at least kept him from joining with the most hysterical of the hues and cries raised against the New Deal. In 1936, when playwright Channing Pollock invited him to join the American Liberty League, Mencken expressed sympathy with the concerns of the league but refused to join.[7] Although Mencken was by now a respected member of Baltimore's conservative business community, his libertarianism remained a sharp contrast to the repressive tendencies that have sometimes accompanied conservatism in America. He continued to defend free speech by attacking loyalty oaths for teachers. He dismissed Congressman Martin Dies and his Un-American Activities Committee as "goons." He testified before a Senate committee in favor of an antilynching bill, and the last article he wrote in 1948 ridiculed the racial segregation of Baltimore's sporting facilities.[8]

In the end, it is not Mencken's hostility to the New Deal that surprises—given his philosophy, it was natural and inevitable—but rather his failure to make his satire hit home. There was certainly much to satirize about the New Deal, for Roosevelt often pursued conflicting and sometimes incompatible policies simultaneously. A satirist on the left could have been damaging. But Mencken's brand of economic conservatism was so hopelessly out of date, his adherence to laissez-faire principles so negative, that what could have been a biting critique often degenerated into an impotent, angry roar.

Germany

In his private memoirs written in the 1930s and 1940s, Mencken stated that his interest in Germany had developed only a few years before the outbreak of World War I.

> But it remained for the shock of World War I to carry me all the way. Even in its preliminary rumblings I saw the beginnings of an inevitable struggle to the death between the German *Weltanschauung* and the Anglo-Saxon *Weltanschauung,* and it was quickly apparent which side I was to take myself. I, too, like the leaders of Germany, had grave doubts about democracy. I, too, felt an instinctive antipathy to the whole Puritan scheme of things, with its gross and nauseating hypocrisies, its idiotic theologies, its moral obsessions, its pervasive Philistinism. It suddenly dawned on me, somewhat to my surprise, that the whole body of doctrine that I had been preaching was fundamentally anti-Anglo-Saxon, and that if I had any spiritual home at all it must be in the land of my ancestors. (*My Life,* 173–74)

Mencken made several trips to Germany during the 1920s and 1930s. On each trip he delved deeper into his German background. He found the books, the portraits, and the graves of his learned ancestors. He found living relatives with whom he entered into correspondence. In 1938, he took his last trip to Germany because, as he wrote, "I wanted to see it again before the next war began" (*Thirty-five Years,* 308–9). Although no more prescient than most journalists, Mencken had never believed that the Versailles peace would last.

Through his acquaintances and relations in Germany, Mencken came to understand many of the frustrations and grievances of the Germans and sympathized with most of them, including some of their attitudes toward Jews. "Though I believe thoroughly that many innocent Jews have been badly used, I am also convinced that there are plenty of Jews in Germany who deserve to be set down," he wrote to George Sylvester Viereck in October of 1933. To a German relation, "Tante Anna," he stated in 1935 that although he disapproved of Hitler's tactics, "I agree with him that [Jews] ought to be kept within bounds" (Hobson 1994, 409).

Yet when he was asked in May 1933 to join the Friends of Germany, he refused. Although sympathetic to the German people, he responded that he could see no way to defend them "so long as the chief officer of the German state continues to make speeches worthy of an Imperial Wizard of the Ku Klux Klan, and his followers imitate, plainly with his

connivance, the monkey-shines of the American Legion at its worst."
True friends of Germany, Mencken insisted, should try to dissuade
"Hitler and company" from their present course. "My sympathy for the
German people is not diminished in the slightest. I believe today, as I
have always believed, that the right was on their side in the war, and I
am distressed beyond measure to see them exposed once more to their
enemies, many of whom are obviously not honest. But I see no way to
give them any effective help so long as their official spokesmen are such
blatant and preposterous damned fools" (Bode 1977, 287). In responding in 1936 to a German correspondent who was concerned about a
report that Mencken was a Jew, he denied the report but took the
opportunity to state his position on Hitler.

> I should add that I am entirely out of sympathy with the method used by
> Hitler to handle the Jewish question. It seems to me that the gross bru-
> tality to harmless individuals must needs revolt every decent man. I am
> well aware that reports from Germany have been exaggerated, but am
> also well aware that intolerable brutalities have been practiced. I don't
> know a single man of any reputation in America who is in favor of the
> Nazi scheme. As it stands, Germany has completely lost the sympathy it
> had during the years following 1920. (Bode 1977, 370)

At the same time, he retained his old, sentimental attachment to
Germany, which even the violence of Hitler's anti-Semitism (exaggerated, thought Mencken) could not shake. Moreover, Mencken was so
convinced that democracy was on its way out that he professed to see
little intrinsic difference between what he called the New Deal in Berlin
and the New Deal in Washington. Liberty was doomed. Writing to a
friend in 1940, he predicted that "the New Dealers will try to put down
free speech under cover of the war and that we'll probably be a long
while regaining it, if, indeed, we ever do."[9] His vision of the future was
basically grim, no matter which direction the events took. Early in
1941, he wrote to Albert G. Keller, an old associate of William Graham
Sumner, that if Roosevelt was successful in taking America into the war,
"the country will have on its hands the policing of the whole civilized
world. It will have to maintain enormous armies, not only in Europe but
also in Asia."[10]

Mencken severed his connections with the *Sunpapers* in February
1941, months before Pearl Harbor, and withdrew to Hollins Street. An
aging man, he was plagued by fears of declining health; he was nursing

the memory of his dead wife; and he was disappointed and disgusted with the violent drift of events. As he had during World War I, he sought solace in work.

Sunset and Darkness

Mencken retained an uncanny ability to shift his interests and seek new audiences. In his semiretirement, he continued his work on *The American Language* (by now four volumes) and then began a series of boyhood reminiscences. He had started writing these pieces for the *New Yorker* in 1939, and, during the early 1940s, he published three volumes of sketches of his youth, of his early newspaper days, and of some of his later experiences in the 1920s. The memoirs were well received. The satire was now gentler, the writing style was simple, the humor, genuine and pleasant. Nonetheless, the *Days of H. L. Mencken* constitutes an ingenious footnote to his long battle against modern America. The pre–World War I America depicted in the first two volumes, *Happy Days* and *Newspaper Days,* was presented as a golden age of simplicity, vitality, and individualism. He avoided sentimentality, but he gave way to nostalgia as he tried to show Americans what had been lost.

After the war, Mencken did not return to the *Sunpapers* until 1948. He covered the nominating conventions that year, rediscovering for a brief moment in the Henry Wallace campaign the old, zany world of the "carnival of buncombe." By this time, however, Mencken's health, so long a subject of hypochondriacal speculation, was seriously deteriorating. He had had a slight stroke in 1939, and then he began having trouble with his eyesight and his memory. Shortly after the election in November 1948, he suffered a severe stroke, which impaired his speech and left him unable to read or write—a terrible, ironic end for a man who had spent a lifetime dedicated to language. Only the devotion of his bachelor brother, August, with whom he had lived since his wife's death, pulled Mencken out of the suicidal despair that followed. He regained comparatively good physical health, but his career, one of the most extraordinary in American letters, had come to an end. Death finally relieved him of his fate on January 29, 1956.

Chapter Ten

The Posthumous Mencken

Deliverance from Anonymity

No American writer labored more intensively to make sure that his name would live on after his death than Henry Mencken. In the 1940s, he not only spent months organizing his voluminous correspondence and his manuscripts for deposit at the Pratt Library in Baltimore and the New York Public Library, but he also prepared two large collections of memoirs of his careers as a newspaperman, a magazine editor, and a writer. During these decades, Mencken also kept a diary. The diary and the memoirs were sealed until 1981, when they were made available to researchers. Generous selections from all of this autobiographical material appeared in book form, starting with *The Diary of H. L. Mencken* in 1990, quickly followed by *My Life as Author and Editor* in 1993, and *Thirty-five Years of Newspaper Work* in 1994.[1]

Mencken began his diary in 1930, a year he may have hoped would be a turning point for him. His marriage to Sara Haardt began happily enough, although he knew that she was incurably ill with tuberculous. In the same year, he published *Treatise on the Gods,* a book intended to draw the curtain on his old image as the wild iconoclast and to reveal to the public the real, more serious Mencken.

Since the late 1920s, Mencken had been seeking a new direction. There are hints in his letters to Theodore Dreiser that he was plagued by depressions during the decade. He had become famous but had discovered the hollowness that lies at the heart of fame. The empathy he revealed in his account of a meeting with film actor Rudolph Valentino suggests the depth of Mencken's own feelings. Valentino, at the height of his extraordinary popularity, felt insulted and humiliated by the press. As Valentino talked, Mencken discovered the "gentleman" beneath the actor and something else besides: "Valentino's agony was the agony of a man of relatively civilized feelings thrown into a situation of intolerable vulgarity, destructive alike to his peace and to his dignity" (*Prejudices* 6, 309).[2]

Mencken had scaled nothing like the pinnacle of notoriety occupied by Valentino. He was, nonetheless, a celebrity during the 1920s. Newspapers covered his trips to Hollywood and to the South and reported speculations of imminent marriage to this or that film actress or society matron. The hollowness of it all came home to Mencken when, in 1926, he was arrested for selling a banned copy of the *American Mercury* in Boston Common. Mencken had seriously intended the gesture as another battle in his campaign against censorship. The newspapers, however, portrayed the whole effort as a bid for publicity (Hobson 1994, 269).

In early 1927, Mencken wrote to film actress Aileen Pringle: "I have practiced a trade that uses men up, and leaves them empty. It looks easy now, when I have (at least transiently) an audience, but getting that audience was a violent and exhausting business, and now I have no respect for it."[3] Around the same time, he admitted that, as a young man, he had been "interested in the gaudy spectacle of life, i.e., the superficial effects of ideas." In the future, he would focus on what he called "the immemorial instincts and emotions that lie under them [ideas]. . . . The show is not over, I hope, but there is a climax and a new beginning" (Hobson 1994, 290–91).

Mencken had always taken his career and his ambitions with a seriousness that stares out from the various photographic portraits (as opposed to snapshots) of the period. As part of the attempt to exchange notoriety for solidity of reputation, he spent several years in the late 1920s researching *Treatise on the Gods,* a popular history of religious thought. Published in 1930, the book that was to launch the new Mencken was not particularly well received, and its companion piece, *Treatise on Right and Wrong* (1934), fared even worse. To make matters worse, Sara's illnesses became more frequent and more severe, leading to her death in 1935. As a result, Mencken's diary became an increasingly grim and bitter record of disappointment instead of the new triumphs he might have originally anticipated.[4]

The autobiographical material and especially the diary present the reader with several problems. First, it is the product of the latter part of Mencken's life. He began the diary in 1930, his 50th year, and the memoirs of his newspaper and literary days were written a decade later, in the 1940s. The diary especially reflects the situation of the aging Mencken: the illnesses and the eventual death of his wife, the decline in his popularity, the deterioration of his health, his growing dissatisfaction with the *Sunpapers,* his anger at the New Deal, and his despair at the impending war. All of this may explain the mordant cast of much of the diary, which contrasts sharply with the vibrant personality that shines through his earlier works. Louis D. Rubin Jr. has called Mencken's diary "one of the saddest, most melancholy books ever published by an important American author."[5]

Although he certainly wanted his papers made available to scholars, there is no clear evidence that Mencken ever intended them for publication. This is certainly the case of the "Diary." The keeper of the manuscript and Mencken's literary executor, the Enoch Pratt Free Library in Baltimore, sought the opinion of the Maryland attorney general before deciding on publication (*Diary,* xxii–xxiii). Whatever his intentions for the memoirs, Mencken placed a lock on this material to ensure that it would be not be read until virtually everyone to whom he referred was dead. Even so, his apparent no-holds-barred views on people, some of whom had considered themselves his friends, surprised some readers. Others were shocked at the harsh comments he sometimes made about certain ethnic groups. It would appear, then, that here at last was the "real" H. L. Mencken, with no humorous, satiric mask to hide his prejudices and his egotism.

Yet, what constitutes the "real" Mencken, or the "real" anyone for that matter? Was the Mencken of 60, a widower deeply concerned about his health, more "real" than the feisty young journalist of the "Free Lance" days or the confident social critic at the height of his powers in the 1920s? There are no easy answers to such questions, but they should warn the reader against assuming too quickly that with the diary and autobiographical works we finally have the whole of H. L. Mencken.

Despite what would appear to be a frank record of his life and opinions, revealing the "plain truth, regardless of tender feelings," large areas of his life remain unexplored, some barely even hinted at. Even as he entered the last stage of his life, Mencken was not prepared to reveal much about his private life. With few exceptions, the inner man is silent. For example, we get only hints about intermittent depressions, which he had apparently struggled with for most of his life. As he wrote to a distant relative in 1935: "I have had the blues steadily for thirty-five years. They are somewhat uncontrollable but . . . they don't seem to be fatal" (Hobson 1994, 283).[6]

Mencken guarded his emotions closely. For example, except for his wife, Sara Haardt, there is virtually nothing in his diary or the vast autobiographical notes about the various women in his life, not even those whom he was seeing on a social basis during the 1930s and 1940s. Of his long, very serious love affair with Marion Bloom, not a word! Indeed, when in the early 1920s he received news that Marion, on a rebound, had married someone else he burned all of her letters.[7] In a diary entry for February 5, 1942, he wrote: "There will be very little about my private life [in the memoirs], and next to nothing about women. Such things, it seems to me, are nobody's business—and I must always remember that what I write may be read by others after I am gone. They are, in fact, not even the author's business. The women a man sleeps with make charming episodes in his life, but it is seldom that they influence the main course of it." Marriage was different, he admitted, but he was married so late in life and for such a short time that he claimed it had little "effect" on him (*Diary*, 191).

Here we approach the essence of Mencken's myth of Mencken. He saw himself—and he wanted to present himself in his diary and memoirs—as someone who was *sui generis,* a complete individualist who had sprung full blown from the nurturing womb of his family and class. As far as he was concerned, his opinions (or "prejudices") were fixed early, deriving from the laissez-faire ideology of his father, the Darwinism of Huxley, and the egoism of Nietzsche. He had always claimed as a matter of pride that he never changed his ideas, and the aging Mencken we meet in the autobiographical material was not about to depart from that lifelong position. As he noted in the diary, "My belief is that every really rational man preserves his major opinions unchanged from his youth onward. When he vacillates it is simply a sign that he is stupid." Commenting on how little the opinions of others influenced him, he wrote that he lived "in a sort of vacuum," as he imagined most writers did (*Diary*, 133).

Throughout the memoirs Mencken seems at pains to show how he carefully plotted and guided his career. Also, in both his diary and memoirs, he seems anxious to prove to posterity that his prejudices had been well founded, consistently held, and, in matters great and small, had generally proved correct. Yet, there are hints that he was willing to tailor the record of his opinions in order to demonstrate that he had always been a hardheaded, no-nonsense realist. For example, as noted in chapter 8, Mencken had urged his readers to support Robert La Follette, the only "man of honor" running in the presidential election in 1924. Mencken even announced that he would vote for the Progressive candidate himself. Yet, in his account of the presidential campaign of 1924 in *Thirty-five Years of Newspaper Work* he makes no mention of La Follette, although he refers to the very article in which he had endorsed the Wisconsin Progressive. Instead, he claimed, "If I remember rightly, I voted for Davis, but I was certainly under no illusions about him" (133). It seems unlikely that Mencken's memory, which was able to recall meals eaten and drinks taken decades earlier, would have failed him on this occasion, especially when he had his own *Evening Sun* articles in front of him as he wrote. Perhaps, as a staunch defender of economic conservatism under pressure from the New Deal, Mencken did not want to call attention to his earlier defense of individual radicals. Perhaps he was embarrassed at his support of a suicide (La Follette killed himself shortly after the election). Or, was the aging Mencken embarrassed about evidence of his highly idealistic public championing of a man he had considered honorable? Whatever the reason, we find him here quietly tidying up the image he wished to pass on to posterity. The real Mencken remains hidden.

The diary and the autobiographical notes provide us with the world according to Mencken, and what a very small world it turns out to have been toward the end of his career. One can hardly fault a diarist and autobiographer for focusing on himself. Yet, a leading journalist and commentator of the American scene might have tried to present some perspective on the larger events of his times, or at least his reactions to them. With few exceptions those events—the Depression, the deteriorating international situation, and then the war—appear in the diary only to the degree that they affected Mencken directly. Franklin Roosevelt and the New Deal were always good for a volley or two, but his comments on the war were minimal. In a diary entry for October 30, 1944, Mencken noted that it was "astonishing" how little the war impinged on him, apart from higher taxes and the loss of certain foodstuffs. "I am hardly affected by the great effort to save humanity and ruin the United States. So far, no one that I know has been killed in the war, or even injured" (*Diary,* 334).[8]

The memoirs of his editorial and journalistic activities are more expansive than the diary, dealing as they do with the personalities and events of earlier decades. Both collections provide some important insights into Mencken's roles in a variety of events, and they are full of his personal observations on many important figures, mostly literary, of the prewar and postwar decades. Both memoirs are disappointing, however, especially the unfinished *My Life as an Editor,* which has more than its share of inconsequential literary gossip (who drank what, who slept with whom), as well as Mencken's often disapproving judgments on the characters of his associates. In fact, much of the diary and memoirs is given over to such judgments, as well as explanations and self-justifications regarding his opinions of his associates and friends. Few individuals survive intact. The closer he was to someone, the more assiduous Mencken seems to have been in pointing out his or her shortcomings and offenses.

It was apparently extremely important to Mencken that the record of his opinions and his judgments demonstrate that he was a superior individual whose opinions had been usually correct. For example, *Thirty-five Years of Newspaper Work* contains many detailed accounts of his conversations with Paul Patterson, president of the *Sunpapers*, in which Mencken presents himself as having been quite free not only with his criticisms of the newspapers but of Patterson himself, whom he seems to have continually upbraided for having compromised the ideals set forth in the old "White Paper" of 1919.[9]

Mencken was so intent on handing his self-myth down to posterity that he took elaborate and expensive measures to ensure the survival of his papers. A diary entry for July 15, 1945, finds him wondering if they will survive catastrophes, such as a bombing. He notes he has taken precautions by sending duplicate copies to two different libraries. A few years earlier, contemplating the great effort involved in arranging his manuscripts and the high cost of binding them, he stated: "Not many American authors will ever leave a more complete record." Perhaps, he mused, no one would want to see them. "In the end every man of my limited capacities must be forgotten utterly. The best he can hope for is a transient and temporary postponement of the inevitable" (*Diary,* 376, 207).[10] For this materialist who believed in the absolute finality of death, the diary and the memoirs were the instruments through which "inevitable" obliteration was to be postponed as long as possible. Once, in what was a relatively optimistic tone for him, Mencken noted with satisfaction, "I have delivered myself from anonymity" (Hobson 1994, 493). Most of the time, however, he was not so sure.

Racism

The dairy and autobiographical material, timed to be released several decades after his death, certainly helped to keep the name of Mencken in the public eye. Ordinarily, interest in a writer's diaries and autobiography would be confined to students of literature and history. True, 30-plus years after his death and almost a half century after his stroke, Mencken was better known than many of his contemporaries. Enough biographies, studies, and collections of his works had been published to keep him alive in the public mind. Unfortunately, it was not his ability as a critic or writer but the charge of racism that launched Mencken into posthumous prominence on the front pages and in the op-ed pieces of leading newspapers in the early 1990s. The *Diary* in particular seemed to offer evidence that Mencken had been a racist in general and an anti-Semite in particular, charges that threatened to ruin his reputation as America neared the end of the twentieth century. It was a controversy of a magnitude seldom bestowed upon dead authors.

Allegations of racism had hung around Mencken's name since the 1930s. With only a few exceptions, however, those who wrote about Mencken after his death, although critical of certain of his ideas, had a high regard for the man and his work. His surviving friends (including his Jewish friends) were adamant in rejecting the label of racism.[11] The available evidence, such as it was, was scattered thinly throughout letters and occasional paragraphs in his later writings. Moreover, after World War II, the charge of racism, especially anti-Semitism, became a very serious one to level against anyone, living or dead. In fact, by the time the diary and autobiographical material began to appear in the early 1990s, "racism" had taken on an absolute, all-devouring quality. Either one was a racist or one was not. Shades of difference did not exist. Racism subsumed the person charged with harboring it. It became his one, defining characteristic. Under the aegis of what was called (derisively) "political correctness," ideological purity was demanded in all things regarding race, gender, gender preference, and minority status. Here, indeed, was a new puritanism Mencken would have relished, even as he became its target of the moment.

It was within this strident intellectual atmosphere that Mencken's posthumous works had their stormy resurrection. Charles A. Fecher, the editor of the *Diary*, had defended Mencken against the charge of anti-Semitism in his 1978 book *Mencken: A Study of His Thought*.[12] Several years later, having seen material that previously had been closed to him, Fecher, perhaps embarrassed by his earlier defense of Mencken, felt incumbent upon making amends. "Let it be said once, clearly, unequivocally," Fecher wrote in the introduction to the *Diary*, "Mencken was an anti-Semite." Although Fecher quickly pointed out that Mencken was no Nazi, in an age of instant headlines and skimmers rather than readers, a very ugly cat seemed to have been let out of the bag (*Diary*, xix).

Caught up in the furor over Mencken's posthumous publications (a very minor aspect of the "cultural wars" of the 1990s) was the question of how Americans could balance a democratic ideology with an understanding of the past. The diary and memoirs opened the door not only to Mencken's closet but also to a relatively recent past that many Americans had forgotten or wished to forget. The post–Civil War America, into which Mencken was born and in which he grew up, was an intensely race-conscious society. Between the end of the Civil War and the onset of World War I, immigrants arrived on American shores in unprecedented numbers. During the two world wars, vast shifts in populations sent blacks out of the South, and Appalachians out of the mountains. During these decades, many Americans were strangers to one another, and they commonly attached ethnic and regional labels to one other. Often, the labels reflected the underlying fears, hostility, and prejudices that few groups were free from harboring: "kike," "sheeny," "wop," "bohunk," "mick," "harp," "nigger," "okie," "linthead," "ofay," "chink," "spic," "hun." Thus, Mencken's references to a person's ethnicity and his occasional use of such terms in private, although in no way admirable or clever, were hardly unusual for an American of his generation. According to satirist and fellow Baltimorean Russell Baker, who grew up a few blocks from Hollins Street, "[I]n the 1930s and 1940s, we were all racists and anti-Semites, and much more that now seems just as unsavory."[13] "In short," as Hobson suggests in his biography of Mencken, "in a pre-Holocaust world in which a certain amount of anti-Semitism was nearly assumed among most non-Jewish Americans and Western Europeans, it may be somewhat remarkable that, to this point [late 1930s], Mencken was no more culpable than he was" (Hobson 1994, 411).

Mencken was probably more aware than most white, American Gentiles of the tensions within America's multiethnic society. His own group, the German Americans, had been attacked during the World War I. After the war, Mencken unceasingly called attention to examples of intolerance. The Ku Klux Klan had always been a favorite target, and, during the 1930s, Mencken brought the fury of Maryland's Eastern Shore down upon himself and the *Sunpapers* for his scathing remarks about the lynchings that took place in that area. As late as 1947 he warned his Jewish friend and business colleague Alfred Knopf about publishing a book critical of the Catholic church. "The Catholics, as you probably know, are already showing signs of violent anti-Semitism, and the book might only give them a chance to perform in the grand manner" (Bode 1977, 581).

As a satirist, Mencken sometimes invoked the language of racial prejudice to try to help his readers recognize certain realities that might lay beyond the narrow horizon of their own racism. Rather than attacking a racial stereotype, Mencken would typically present it and then in a sense say, "But . . ." For example, there is a passage in the original 1930 edition of *Treatise on the Gods* that in any time and place could be considered anti-Semitic: "As commonly encountered, they [the Jews] lack many of the qualities that mark the civilized man: courage, dignity, incorruptibility, ease, confidence. They have vanity without pride, voluptuousness without taste, and learning without wisdom. Their fortitude, such as it is, is wasted on puerile objects, and their charity is mainly only a form of display." The passage continues: "Yet these same Jews, from time immemorial, have been the chief dreamers of the human race, and beyond all comparison its greatest poets."[14]

Or consider Mencken's way of warning his fellow citizens about the growing power of Japan in 1939. He began with the average American's stereotype of the Japanese: "They look, talking one with another, like Boy Scouts with buck teeth, wearing horn-rimmed spectacles." Mencken quickly makes his main point, however: "They are a people of considerable talents, and will have to be reckoned with in the future history of the human race." They are no longer content to learn from the West that has despised them: "In all fields of human endeavor save theology, politics and swine justice they are showing the way to their ofay mentors."[15] In this piece, Mencken began by describing the Japanese as he knew many of readers saw them and then blasted his readers with something that they may not have wanted to hear.

To take a final example, during the 1920s, Mencken wrote several articles about African Americans containing words such as "niggero," "blackamoor," and "coon." One was in fact titled "A Coon Age." The gist of these pieces, however, was that southern blacks were moving ahead of whites in the region and that black culture permeated every aspect of American arts and speech.[16]

It is not hard to see the problems Mencken's satiric style created for late-twentieth-century Americans, when even a satirist had to take into account the pain his remarks might cause a group, whatever his ultimate intentions. As Joseph Epstein noted: in deciding to publish the *Diary,* Mencken's executors "fed a man known for his candor into the maw of an age wishing to be known for its spirit of caring" (Epstein 1990, 34).

Nevertheless, we cannot set down the racist elements in Mencken's diary and memoirs as simply the results of his times and literary style. His satire was based, after all, on a moral vision that measured the world against a set of ideals founded on freedom, honor, and decency. How could a man such as Mencken allow racist comments to creep into his correspondence and proliferate in his private memoirs? It is not the extent of Mencken's racism that shocks. Given the period in which he lived and wrote, his comments are hardly unusual for the time. The problem is that the very presence of racism seems to contradict what the man appeared to stand for.

The first thing to recognize is that race was incorporated into the very foundations of Mencken's thought. The late-nineteenth-century social Darwinism, on which he based many of his ideas, made some form of racism almost inevitable. To this he added a worldview based on a simplistic division between the few individualists of talent and honor, and an abstract, inferior "mob." As far as he was concerned, the majority of any ethnic group or race was bound to be inferior, whether they were Jew or Gentile, black or white. He was not even fond of Germans as a group. In 1940, in response to the then editor of *American Mercury,* he rejected the suggestion he write an article about Germans, saying that although he admired them, he did not like them. "They have all of the unpleasantness of really efficient people. I am, in a way, one of them myself, but I have become Americanized enough to dislike their cock-sureness" (Bode 1977, 465). For those groups he did not admire, his remarks could be brutal. In July of 1944, Mencken complained in his diary about the Appalachians who flooded into Baltimore during the war. "They are so filthy and destructive that the Jews who own the houses have begun to turn them out and put in blackamoors." Mencken regarded the blacks as more "civilized" than the Appalachians because they grew flowers in their yards and painted their houses, such as the one behind Hollins Street. "The same little house is well painted—obviously at the cost of the tenants, for the Jew who owns it never spends a cent on decorations. The colors used are garish, but they are at least characteristically niggerish, and the occupants plainly take some pride in the appearance of their house. No linthead or mountaineer ever shows any feeling for beauty. They all live like animals, and are next door to animals in their habits and ideas" (*Diary,* 325–26).

Mencken did not believe in the equality of races but rather in the equality of superior individuals. Mencken had no problem seeking out black writers and championing them or entertaining them in his house in Baltimore. He did not do these things as someone who was color blind, but rather as a person who was very conscious of ethnic differences. Of the Pittsburgh journalist George S. Schuyler, he wrote: "He

has a white wife, but is very dark himself, with plainly negroid features."
Yet Mencken admired him greatly because he was a superior person.
"When I compare him with any of the dunderheads now roaring on the
Sun, I am sharply conscious of his enormous superiority. He is not only
much more intelligent than they are; he is vastly more honest" (*Diary,*
383). Concerning the arrest of a black artist (who had once painted his
portrait) for attempting to eat at a restaurant in New York City,
Mencken protested, "So few men are really worth knowing that it seems
a shameful waste to let an anthropoid prejudice stand in the way of free
association with one who is" (Hobson 1994, 455).[17]

Mencken's relations with Jews represent the classic case of "some of
his best friends are . . ." Mencken had many Jewish friends and associ-
ates, some of very long standing, such as Alfred Knopf, his publisher;
Louis Cheslock, a Baltimore musician; and George Jean Nathan.
Although he had split with Nathan in the mid-1920s, they renewed their
friendship and were meeting socially in the 1940s, when Mencken's anti-
Semitism was supposedly at it most intense. Interviewed in 1990,
Lawrence Spivak, who had followed Mencken in editing the *American
Mercury,* suggested that Mencken was around Jews so much that if "he
was anti-Semitic, then he went out of his way to punish himself." Spivak
felt the charge of anti-Semitism was "nonsense." "He always talked with
his tongue in his cheek, but he always felt comfortable with Jews. He
talked about Jews the way Jews talked about Jews."[18]

Mencken's was the first generation of American Gentiles to come
into close and frequent contact with Jews. It was during his lifetime that
Jews not only arrived in America in unprecedented numbers, but they
made their presence felt in many fields, especially on the east coast. As
an editor, Mencken encountered many Jewish writers, published some
of them, and hired one, Charles Angoff, as his assistant on the *American
Mercury.* Unfortunately, like many Gentiles, Mencken could not accept
the increased Jewish presence in American society with equanimity. In
his diary, Mencken invariably noted if a man or woman he had met was
a Jew, whereas he only occasionally took note of an Irish or German ethnicity among Gentiles. That he had Jewish friends and associates probably allowed him to hide from the knowledge that he was moved by the
same prejudices that, in others, he tended to disparage.[19]

By the late 1930s, Mencken seems to have become increasingly
antagonistic toward Jews as a group.[20] Whenever he looked at those
subjects that concerned him the most—the growing negativity about
Germany under Hitler, Franklin Roosevelt's New Deal, militant trade

unionism, and what appeared to be the growing strength of radicalism in all aspects of American life—in all these areas Mencken thought he saw Jews. As a result, he succumbed to the same error that ensnared so many other twentieth-century European and American Gentiles: associating Jews with the confusing and disturbing changes taking place in the world around them.[21]

Yet, as Sheldon Richman has pointed out, "Nowhere does he [Mencken] blame 'the Jews' for anything. One would expect this of a virulent anti-Semite" (408). In fact, Mencken rarely lent his public voice (as opposed to his private correspondence) to criticisms of, much less attacks on, Jews. In his letters, he often rejected the anti-Semitic views of others. More interesting are his efforts to help individual European Jews escape to America: acting as a sponsor, signing immigrant affidavits, and pleading cases with the State Department (Hobson 1994, 422–23). In November 1938, he wrote a piece attacking the Roosevelt administration for being unwilling to take Jews trying to leave Germany. "Why shouldn't the United States take in a couple of hundred thousand . . . or even all of them?" (Hobson 1994, 423). In January 1, 1939, he again argued that America could easily absorb the refugees, and condemned "the political mountebanks who fill the air with hollow denunciations of Hitler, and yet never lift a hand to help an actual Jew" (Owens, 10).[22] Why then, did Mencken not speak out more forcefully and frequently against Nazi treatment of the Jews? Why did he retreat again into journalistic silence during World War II?

Germany

Part of the answer lies in recognizing how deep were the unhealed wounds from World War I. Mencken had bitterly resented the attacks on German Americans and on himself. He was convinced that Germany had been in the right in 1914, and that it had been badly treated by the Versailles treaty (a view many in America came to share). On his trips to Europe he saw the Germany and met the Germans he wanted to find, and he listened sympathetically to the complaints of his German acquaintances and relatives. Unfortunately, he initially mistook Hitler for just another zany demagogue thrown up by democracy.

During his visits there, Mencken became aware of the rising anti-Semitism in Germany. As early as 1922, he wrote to Paul Patterson that although everything seemed calm on the surface in Germany, "every intelligent man looks for a catastrophe. If it comes, there will be a colossal massacre of Jews" (Hobson 1994, 224). Yet although Mencken wrote several articles condemning Hitler and the Nazis, he refused to lend his voice in attacking Germany. In his memoirs of his journalistic career, Mencken commented: "The only consequence I could see [at the time] in the rise of the Nazis was a revival of anti-German agitation all over the world. But it was one thing to feel thus, and quite another thing to help the Jews foment that agitation." Indeed, the more he was pressured to denounce Germany, the more stubborn his refusal. To individuals who privately sought his opinions on the subject, Mencken's rejection of Nazism was clear. "If they [the Jews] had let me alone I might have said in print substantially what I had already said in my letter [to the Friends of Germany], but in the face of their attempt to browbeat me I could only refuse to write a line" (*Thirty-five Years,* 226).

Mencken was apparently anxious that his Jewish acquaintances understood his position. For example, he sent a copy of his letter rejecting overtures from the Friends of Germany to Isaac Goldberg, one of his early biographers, saying that its criticism of Germany was for his eyes only and not for circulation. "Many Jews have beset me to make a public statement on the subject, but I have invited them to go to Hell." To James Rosenberg, another Jewish acquaintance, he expressed his belief in 1934 that American Jewish agitation would make Jews "look like the most extreme hyphenates ever heard of and so the way is open for professional patriots to whoop up an anti-Semitic movement" (Bode 1977, 288, 310).

As Mencken maintained his public silence, he became embittered over the criticism he received for not being more outspoken in his comments on Nazi Germany. In a letter to Paul Patterson, Mencken said that if he did respond to Jewish demands ("none from any Jew I know, or from any of any apparent dignity"), he would have to discuss the causes of anti-Semitism "and that would only provide a field day for all the professional kikes." So that Patterson would know how he felt about Hitler, he enclosed his letter to the Friends of Germany. Mencken claimed that Patterson supported him in his stubborn silence and the only result of the Jewish pressure was a "sharp rise" in the anti-Semitism in the *Sun* offices (*Thirty-five Years,* 226–27).[23]

There was more to all of this than simple stiff-necked pride. Although pained and embarrassed by Hitler, Mencken could not bring himself to attack Germany publicly. He continued to insist in letters that while the treatment of the Jews in Germany was bad, the reports were no doubt exaggerated. Yet he turned down offers from the *Sunpa-*

pers to go to Germany and file firsthand reports. As he told a friend, he suspected that "the situation there is really very bad and I hesitate to be the one to have to report it." When he did take a final trip to Germany in 1938, it was a sentimental journey. He sent home no dispatches and wrote no articles. He was aware of the problems facing the Jews, and he wrote to Paul Patterson that "[a]ll decent Germans seem to be ashamed of the business" (Hobson 1994, 399, 416). But he did not delve into the situation. His much-vaunted dedication to truth telling deserted him. Instead, he toured Germany's countryside and the haunts of his ancestors, confident that war was coming and that he would never see Germany again.[24]

Under intense criticism in Baltimore for not being more vociferous in condemning Hitler and Nazi Germany, Mencken continued to be scornful about such attacks, although seeing to it that those whose opinions mattered to him saw copies of his letter to the Friends of Germany. Privately, however, he must have been confused, perhaps even hurt by the criticism. He once asked John Owens, editor of the *Sun,* if Owens believed he was a Nazi or anti-Semite. When Owens said no, Mencken suddenly produced a justification for his position. "I believe in only one thing," Owens remembers him saying, "and that is human liberty. If ever a man is to achieve anything like dignity, it can happen only if superior men are given absolute freedom to think what they want to think and say what they want to say. I am against any man and any organization which seeks to limit or deny that freedom." When Owens asked him if he limited such freedom to only "superior men," Mencken responded that for the superior man to be free, all men had to be free (Forgue 1994, xiii). This was Mencken's credo—the credo of a "superior" man.

Chapter Eleven

Conclusion

Contradictions

In trying to draw some conclusions concerning Mencken and his position within American cultural history, we immediately encounter a maze of contradictions. A very American writer in both his style and choice of subjects, Mencken cultivated the image of the outsider, one who lived in America but was not of it. Although deeply committed to a wide variety of causes, he often pretended to a total lack of involvement with his society. A self-proclaimed iconoclast, he nevertheless used his talents for idol smashing to defend values that, far from being Nietzschean transvaluations, were simply solid bourgeois principles in good repute at the hearthside, in the countinghouse, and even in the rectory. He was a friend of Jews and a sharp critic of Jews. Conservative and even reactionary in some matters, he was almost radical in others. An iconoclast, he abhorred disorder in himself and others.

These contradictions were not merely the product of the writer's desire to camouflage the private man from public gaze. They tend to increase, not decrease, as one penetrates into Mencken's private world through his letters and memoirs. The contradictions seem to lie within Mencken's personality. He appears so deeply divided in many of his attitudes that Louis D. Rubin Jr. has suggested a sort of "willed schizophrenia, an apparent denial of any connection between what he thought and did on a day-to-day basis and certain ingrained emotions and beliefs" (Rubin, *1991,* 449). The resulting ambiguities found expression rather than resolution in his writing.

The Immense Indifference of Things

It is significant that the writers who stirred Mencken to produce some of his best criticism were those who, in his own words, depicted the "immense indifference of things . . . the profound meaninglessness of life" (*Prefaces,* 11). Reviewing Theodore Dreiser's *Jennie Gerhardt* in the November 1911 issue of the *Smart Set,* Mencken tried to unravel the philosophy behind the novel: "What else have Moore and Conrad and Hardy been telling us these many years? What else does all the new knowledge of a century teach us? One by one the old ready answers have been disposed of. Today the one intelligible answer to the riddle of aspiration and sacrifice is that there is no answer at all" (153).

Mencken's reaction to his own conclusion that life was an impenetrable mystery was itself ambiguous. Sometimes he rejoiced in it, as in this passage from *Men versus the Man* (1910): "Life impresses me, most of all, by its appalling complexity. It is not static but dynamic; not a being, but an eternal becoming. The constant reaction of diversified individuals upon a fluent environment produces a series of phenomena which seems to me, at times, to be beyond all ordering and ticketing" (230). Life in the Menckenian universe could be complex, diversified, dynamic, and, in a peculiarly special way, free. Man was bound by natural laws but free from any supernatural order or intervention. There was nothing outside or beyond the discoveries of science that was guiding, shaping, and directing mankind. Life had no ontological meaning—no God, no History with its Hegelian or its Marxian capital "H."

For a while Mencken believed that this absence of ontological meaning freed man to realize his ultimate potentiality, his own human dignity. In an exchange of letters with Theodore Dreiser, Mencken defined what he considered the scientific as opposed to the religious approach to the problems of life: "The efficient man does not cry out 'Save me, O God.' On the contrary, he makes diligent efforts to save himself. But suppose he fails? . . . He accepts his fate with philosophy, buoyed up by the consciousness that he has done his best. Irreligion, in a word, teaches men how to die with dignity, just as it teaches them how to live with dignity" (Forgue 1961, 9).

Ultimately, however, the meaninglessness of life was not a benign concept for Mencken. It was the "*intolerable* meaninglessness" that fascinated and, in spite of himself, so often shocked and haunted him. Nietzsche had brought Mencken to the threshold of existentialism, but the critic did not have the philosophical equipment to enable him to cross it. His empirical, rationalistic turn of mind, his innate demand for things to make sense, made him frequently cry out against the *non*sense of the blind, clockwork universe in which he felt obliged to believe. Time and again his stoical pose slipped from him, as when he found the death of a promising young novelist "a fate too cruel for understanding." When his wife died, he burst out in a letter to Ellery Sedgwick, "What a cruel and idiotic world we live in!" (Forgue 1961, 392).

On occasion he could bluster, as once he did to Burton Rascoe: "My notion is that all the larger human problems are insoluble, and that life is quite meaningless—a spectacle without purpose or moral. I detest all efforts to read a moral into it" (Forgue 1961, 188). Yet what else was he doing when he tried to illuminate the meaningless void with the light of human dignity? It was as if, having triumphantly proclaimed his meaningless universe, Mencken then issued one caveat after another against its lack of meaning. As he himself once observed, "Man is never honestly the fatalist, nor even the stoic. He fights fate, often desperately. He is forever entering bold exceptions to the rulings of the bench of gods. This fighting makes for beauty, for man tries to escape from a hopeless and intolerable world by creating a more lovely one of his own."[1]

The creation of this lovelier world was, however, an artistic and, ultimately, an emotional impulse based, according to Mencken, on a denial of reality. For this reason, Mencken believed that poetry, as he explained in *Prejudices: Third Series,* was essentially "a series of ideas, false in themselves, that offer a means of emotional and imaginative escape from the harsh realities of everyday." Man's mind turned to poetry only when inflicted with "the mood of revolt against the insoluble riddle of existence" (151, 169).

The Head versus the Heart

"The taste for romance," Mencken once noted, "like the taste for impropriety, is inborn in all normal human beings. . . . The day comes when we turn inevitably from Zola to Dumas, just as the day comes when we turn from Richard Strauss to Johann. . . . [A man's] head may rule his heart for a week, a month or a year—but on some fatal day or other that head of his will succumb to sorrow, weariness, alcohol, an unbalanced ration, the coo of a baby or the perfume of a women's hair, and that heart of his will go upon a debauch straightway."[2] The emotions themselves, therefore, could never be trusted. Emotional impulses, no matter how alluring, were only traps for the unwary. The only path to truth lay through empirical reason. For Mencken, the head was eternally at war with the heart. This dichotomy lies at the very basis of Mencken's personality, for he could not conceive of the possibility of integrating the intellect with the emotions, of achieving a balance between rationality and feeling.

This problem would not have been quite so acute for Mencken had he not been a very emotional, indeed, sentimental person. As writer Elizabeth Shepley Sergeant noted after her first conversation with Mencken in the 1920s, "I had expected to meet an artist and an epicure, but I was hardly prepared for the sentimentalist—the solid, Germanic sentimentalist."[3] Since Mencken considered the emotions a constant threat to the intellect, he tried to protect himself by accentuating the hard, tough-minded side of his nature. The result was a dualism that became obvious to almost everyone who came to know him. Sara Mayfield, an intimate friend of both Mencken and his wife, recalled: "The carapace of H. L. Mencken, the hardboiled critic, we soon discovered, had been developed as a defensive mechanism by an extremely sensitive man" (Mayfield, 115). Marion Bloom, who at one point was almost engaged to Mencken, once accused him of hiding his real tenderness beneath a cover of hard cruelty (Bode 1969, 153).[4] As critic Burton Rascoe put it, "It is not that [Mencken] does not feel deeply, but that his emotions are primarily sentimental and not aesthetic, and, being a sentimental fellow, he has built up a defense mechanism of gay cynicism which stands between him and a free expression of the emotions felt and recorded" (Hensley, 73).

Only in music did Mencken seem to resolve the tensions between head and heart. For one thing, music obviously demanded great intellect and talent. "More than any other art, perhaps," he commented in *Prejudices: Sixth Series,* "music demands brains. It is full of technical complexities" (167). Yet, at the same time, it has deep emotional appeal. Mencken could thus give himself over to sentiments that in another art form might have been embarrassing. To critic Fanny Butcher, he confessed in 1921: "I can't think of any books that I'd like to have written. . . . Words are veils. It is hard enough to put into them what one thinks; it is a sheer impossibility to put into them what one feels." He would rather, he said, have written a symphony by Brahms than a play by Ibsen: "In music a man can let himself go. In words he always remains a bit stiff and unconvincing" (Forgue 1961, 219, 220).

It is significant that one of the few organizations to which Mencken belonged was a music group, the Saturday Night Club, which met for years in Baltimore. Mencken played the bass line in four-handed piano arrangements for the club, an assignment that he carried out with gusto, if not always total expertise. Those weekly meetings of music and beer were an important, central part of his life. Unfortunately, without formal training in music, the one art form in which the dichotomy of intellect and emotion could disappear, was closed to Mencken's creativity. "I shall die an inarticulate man," he wrote wistfully in *Happy Days,* "for my best ideas have beset me in a language I know only vaguely and speak only like a child" (198).

The Hidden Idealist

Unable to resolve the emotional and the sentimental parts of his nature with his rationalist principles, Mencken therefore sought to protect the more vulnerable side of his personality by throwing around it a hard shell of mannerisms and attitudes. His brave embrace of the meaningless universe, his harsh attempts to repress sentimentality, his rigid insistence on the primacy of intellect, and even his tough, masculine pose seem to have been intended to ward off, or at least alleviate, the inevitable pain that emotional involvement might produce. As a result, Mencken could sometimes appear to be callous and uncaring when he was, in fact, suffering greatly. Although his wife's death was a serious blow to him, on the weekend after the funeral he insisted on standing his turn as host to the Saturday Night Club. There was no joy in the occasion for anyone, least of all Mencken, but what seems an insensitive gesture on the surface was Mencken's way of trying to close the door against grief. He turned to work and retreated within the carapace of stoic toughness beneath which the intolerable meaninglessness of life could be met with a resigned shrug instead of with a painful shudder.[5]

There was more at stake, however, than seeking protection from emotional pain. Mencken was a very egotistical man who, for most of his life, was prone to committing himself enthusiastically to both men and ideas. Such commitments, of course, threatened to make him vulnerable to disappointment. Worse, if his commitment proved wrongly placed, it meant that he had been guilty of allowing his enthusiasms (and emotions) to run ahead of his rational judgment. His desire to avoid such embarrassments explains two very basic characteristics of the man: his pretense of noninvolvement and his often bitter rejection of those who disappointed him. Thus, he went out of his way to ridicule his early hero George Bernard Shaw, when he decided that the playwright was not an iconoclast of the heroic mold. Even the failure of an ideal could result in a dramatic rejection. When his concept of art and iconoclasm failed to have its expected impact upon society, Mencken completely abandoned literary criticism.

This pattern of behavior can be clearly seen in his relationships with those writers to whom he had lent friendship and support. Many of Mencken's literary friendships experienced deep rifts when his strict codes, both personal and professional, were somehow offended. Willard Huntington Wright, James Gibbons Huneker, Theodore Dreiser, George Jean Nathan, Sinclair Lewis and F. Scott Fitzgerald all came under varying degrees of the Menckenian ban. As Dreiser himself told him in 1920, "The truth is that you are an idealist in things literary or where character is concerned and expect men to ring centre 100 times out of 100." After reminding Mencken of some of his misjudgments in the past, Dreiser predicted, "You will probably continue for years to come to bring in tin cans from the street and set them on the mantel. But in view of past flops—you might be careful—& not too hard on your idols once they are out in the street again" (Forgue 1961, 198, 199).

In a clumsy way, Dreiser had put his finger on one of the most important aspects of Mencken's character. For, despite his lifelong attempt to play the skeptic, Mencken was an idealist. At least he believed that life should be governed by standards of perfection rather than by convention or convenience. His adherence to these standards was so rigid that he sometimes took a Fundamentalist approach to concepts such as free speech and honor.[6] That Mencken sought to hide this idealism, even from himself, was the result of his need to shield his ego from the pain of disappointment and the chagrin of a misjudgment or error. This is one of the reasons why he was attracted to iconoclasm. His original concept of the artist-iconoclast was itself highly idealistic. Yet the iconoclast's methods could conceal that idealism. Mencken could champion one writer by denouncing another; he could defend a virtue by exposing a vice. His commitment to an ideal was not lessened by these methods, but it could be hidden. The mask of satire completed the iconoclast's disguise.

The Mask of Satire

Mencken wrote little about the art of satire. Once, however, in a *Smart Set* review in April 1918, he provided a brief glimpse into the satirist's way of looking at life. In commenting on the discrepancy between the American's professed idealism and his intense business practicality, Mencken concluded that the American had to master two distinct sets of politics, economics, and ethics: "the one that meets his complex and elegant notion of propriety, and the one that works." Although

Mencken did not actually say so, this dualism was in fact the starting point for much of his own satiric approach to American society. He exploited instinctively the disparity between what is officially approved and what is privately done.

In his study of satirists, Leonard Feinberg contends that satire is grounded upon such dualisms: the contradiction between reality and pretense, between what is and what society piously claims ought to be. Most people, Feinberg claims, adjust themselves to such discrepancies and become largely oblivious to them. The personality of the satirist, however, makes him acutely aware of such incongruities. His talent enables him to evolve an artistic vision from this awareness. What would be a useless and immature crankiness in others becomes, in the hands of the satirist, "a logical search for artistic material which is suitable for his particular kind of art."[7]

Mencken's sensitivity to this central dualism of life came from his own failure to resolve the various dichotomies within himself. He was eternally pulled between individualism and determinism, meaninglessness and meaning, intellect and emotion, aloofness and commitment, love and loneliness. In a sense, satire may have been his salvation. As David Worcester has suggested in *The Art of Satire,* irony, one of the modes of satire, tends to offer an escape from conflicting emotional responses to life. The ironist escapes a possible paralysis of mind and spirit by focusing on the tragic-comic results of the eternal clash between the ideal and the actual. By exploiting the duality of his own vision, he maintains his own equilibrium.[8]

In Mencken's case, satire enabled him to give vent to the idealistic streak in his nature, while at the same time assuming the stance of the hardheaded, tough-minded, self-centered egotist. In a letter to Burton Rascoe in 1920, he asserted: "Few doctrines seem to me worth fighting for. I can't understand the martyr. Far from going to the stake for a Great Truth, I wouldn't even miss a meal for it. . . . I do not write because I want to make converts. . . . I write because the business amuses me. It is the best of sports" (Forgue 1961, 188).

In Feinberg's opinion, this is the whole story. To him the vehemence in Mencken was aesthetic, not moral: "Mencken's is an aesthetic choice [of material], not a moral one, any more than the choice of colors by Van Gogh is a moral choice" (Feinberg, 39). To take this view, however, is to fall into the error of positing a monistic concept of man. Feinberg's artistic man is no more real than the Marxist's economic man or the hagiographer's spiritualized saint. Mencken's artistic instincts doubtlessly helped to determine the *way* he handled his material, but his inclination toward satire was hardly the sole arbiter of his choice of material and his basic reaction to it. Mencken's battle for the liberation of American letters, his stand on free speech and minority rights, his defense of the values of individualism, and his tireless protest in the name of "common decency" were not the results of a purely aesthetic impulse. Mencken was genuinely committed to these things.

Nor did his use of satire conflict with this commitment. As Worcester suggests, "Satire . . . is the most rhetorical of all the kinds of literature. . . . It has an aim, a preconceived purpose: to instill a given set of emotions or opinions into its reader" (Worcester, 8). Mencken did not expect to make converts in the sense of turning a Bryan into an agnostic or a Coolidge Republican into a libertarian. But such people did not comprise his audience: Mencken wrote for the Forgotten Man—the responsible but politically uncommitted reader, who could be swung into opposition against the Red Scare, Fundamentalism, and Prohibition.

In order to remain an effective satirist, however, Mencken had to adopt a persona that seemed to stand back bemused and above the battle. To have done otherwise would have ruined the effectiveness of the rhetorical appeal of his satire. For satire distorts. Instead of investigating complexities it often tries to make the complex appear simple. The satirist is not initiating a dialogue in hopes of discovering the truth; he already has the truth and seeks to propagandize his version of it.

According to Worcester, the satirist "secretly aims at exposing a discrepancy in the strongest possible light. Once he has exposed it, the fewer words the better, for his insistence on pointing the moral will rob the reader of his share in the game. So long as he abstains from sermonizing, he has the reader with him" (Worcester, 42). At times, Mencken came close to giving the game away. Sometimes his real feelings broke through the humor of an essay with an almost Swiftian passion. At the end of such passages, it was vitally necessary for him to pull back and to disclaim any real interest or involvement in the subject under discussion. In fact, the discrepancy between Mencken's supposed aloofness and his genuine outrage thundering through so many of his essays was sometimes so great that only total mastery of his style kept his satiric persona intact.

The effectiveness of this persona depended, in part, on Mencken's ability to personalize the values upon which he based his satire. Since most humor is founded upon fixed moral standards and values, the average humorist derives his comedy from the contrast between society's stated ideals and its actual behavior. Satisfied in catching society in the act of tripping over its own ideals, he does not need to question their validity. The satirist, however, may go one step farther. He may intrude his own moral vision, or he may at least make it appear that the moral standard he is using is his own. The bite of his satire comes, then, not merely from the contrast between what society says and what it does, but from the demolition of *both* society's practices *and* its pretenses. In such a case, the satirist does not wish to pose as society's inner conscience but as its external accuser. By so doing, he makes the satiric absurdity of a situation lie in the implication that society cannot act correctly or intelligently because its very ideals and motives are corrupted.

Mencken went out of his way to appear the outsider when criticizing American society, supposedly applying the private values of the iconoclast, the aristocrat, or the Forgotten Man. As we have seen, these values were for the most part the common stock of middle-class America. Had Mencken made this clear, however, the moralistic jeremiad rumbling beneath the surface of his satire would have been exposed. The disguise would have fallen away, and Mencken would have appeared in his true light: the spokesman for the old, bourgeois, individualistic America that was passing away before the pressures of the twentieth century.

The American Mencken

Satire, then, was the natural, almost inevitable, artistic form for Mencken. It was perfectly adapted to meeting those twin needs of his divided mind: commitment and protection. As a disguise, it fooled no one so successfully as the mummer himself. As a consequence Mencken was never fully aware of the complexity of the relationship between himself and his country. As suggested earlier, Mencken dealt with two conflicting images of America: that of the visible land of follies—Babbittland—and that of an internalized vision of an America to which he was secretly but deeply attached. By taking the drastic step of making the word "American" stand for folly, he made it difficult, if not impossible, to identify himself with his country. The values that he preached were made to seem private ones in conflict with a supposedly degraded national character.

Mencken, therefore, found it hard to present a clear, positive image of America that could be seen as an alternative to the negative paradise of fools and knaves that he had created in his satire. The best he could do was to present fragments of the other America he loved, as when he belatedly discovered an iconoclastic tradition in American literature.

Occasionally, he contrasted superior men of the past, such as John Adams, Jefferson, and Lincoln, with the Hardings and the Coolidges of his own day. He celebrated what he remembered as the vital individualism of the 1880s and 1890s, and, as a magazine editor, he diligently sought to uncover and publicize the diversity and vitality that still survived in the United States. His knowledge of and interest in the American past was too limited, however, and his egotistical desire to stand aloof from the sordidness of his times was too strong, to allow him to follow writers like Sherwood Anderson and Sinclair Lewis into the Depression-era rediscovery of a more promising image of America. The alienation that had begun as a satiric pose eventually took on a certain reality in Mencken's mind.

His constant criticism of democracy suggested to some critics that Mencken was sympathetic to the antidemocratic ideologies that rampaged abroad and the right-wing extremism that flourished at home in the 1920s and 1930s. Mencken was not a Fascist, however, nor was he a part of the reactionary tendencies in literary and cultural criticism during the 1920s and 1930s. His cultural radicalism, which questioned all standards in art, remains in sharp contrast to the views of Yeats, Pound, Eliot, and Wyndham Lewis—those critics on the right who sought in art, if not always in politics, the imposition of order amid chaos.[9] Mencken's commitment to cultural pluralism and his libertarian demand for complete freedom of thought and speech do not fit comfortably within the twentieth-century conservative tradition. As Walter Lippmann recognized in 1926, Mencken's cultural attitudes warred with his supposedly antidemocratic opinions. "If Mr. Mencken really wishes an aristocracy he will have to give up liberty as he understands it; and if he wishes liberty he will have to resign himself to hearing *homo boobiens* speak his mind." Lippmann was "amazed" that Mencken did not recognize "how fundamentally the spiritual disorder he fights against is the effect of the régime of liberty he fights for."[10] Here again, Mencken was caught up in the muddle of his inability to reconcile conflicting impulses. He wanted all the positive benefits provided by an well-ordered society but was too much the rebel to accept the sort of authoritarianism that could impose such an order. He thoroughly distrusted the political power of the masses, but he required a totally free society for the emergence of the creative individual.

Mencken's failure to sketch even the bare bones of his aristocracy throws into question the seriousness of his search for an alternative to democracy. In *Notes on Democracy,* Mencken insisted that he was not maintaining that "democracy is too full of evils to be further borne. . . .

All I argue is that its manifest defects, if they are ever to be got rid of at all, must be got rid of by examining them realistically" (200). A decade later, in his introduction to a new edition of James Fenimore Cooper's *American Democrat,* Mencken admitted that, within the "false dogma" of equality, democracy did, nonetheless, contain a conception of human dignity: "I incline to think that that modicum of dignity is the chief and perhaps the only gift of democracy to mankind." And although careful as always to reject the democratic label for himself, he did quote Cooper to the effect that the true democrat, "recognizing the right of all to participate in power, . . . will proudly maintain his own independence of vulgar domination."[11]

In the end, Mencken was much closer to the tradition of the squire of Cooperstown than to that of the reactionary intellectuals of his own day. He was a critic rather than a dedicated opponent of democracy. When one remembers that he did not criticize democracy as a political theorist but as a social moralist and as a cultural liberator, his position within the American cultural tradition begins to emerge. Emerson and Thoreau, for example, were also critics of democracy; both men believed in what they called the "majority of one." And nowhere in Mencken's writings is there so thorough a repudiation of the moral authority of democracy as there is in Thoreau's essay "On the Duty of Civil Disobedience." Although Mencken shared little else with the transcendentalists, he too was concerned with the moral freedom of the individual to pursue his own vision of what was just and right. The aesthetic counterpart of this vision, for him no less than for Emerson and Thoreau, was what Joseph Wood Krutch dubbed Mencken's "worship of excellence"—a response to the special imperative that a democratic society, although dedicated to equality and the rule of the majority, must nevertheless allow individual intellectual and artistic creativity to follow a different path.[12] It is to this tradition of moral and cultural dissent that Mencken ultimately belongs.

Mencken's unyielding commitment to the freedom of the individual gave his criticism its power and even occasional flashes of vision. Yet this commitment proved an obstacle to understanding and analyzing American society. His libertarian landscape was too barren to sustain any form of individualism that went beyond mere self-interest. Mencken had a sense of community, just as he had a sense of human sympathy. He had no means, however, of integrating them with his extreme libertarianism. The Menckenian individual remains an isolated, lonely figure.

Perhaps this is why, toward the end of his career, Mencken indulged in a nostalgic look at his own boyhood in *Happy Days* and *Newspaper*

Days. America in the 1880s and 1890s had been, as far as he was concerned, a good place in which to grow up. It represented the last moments of a golden age in which Mencken's individualistic value systems had seemed to flourish. In the twentieth century America had changed; and although Maxwell Geismar was wrong when he claimed that Mencken's role in the 1920s was that of the nihilist, he was correct when he noted, "it is change in America which is the true villain of the piece, and Mencken's is in many ways the most illuminating of all these chronicles of change."[13] Mencken was, in fact, one of the chief victims of change among the writers of his generation. He lived to see what William Graham Sumner had dreaded—the passing of laissez-faire society. What was left of the once confident, late-nineteenth-century bourgeois liberal values of individual competition and limited government had found in Mencken one of their most articulate literary spokesman—and their chief mourner. His reiteration of those values in the 1920s represents, in retrospect, one of his most important contributions to the cultural debates of the decade. After the Depression, however, he was no more convincing than Herbert Hoover in attempting to revitalize them. His retreat into the nostalgia of *Happy Days* and *Newspaper Days,* charming as those books are, represents a tacit admission of failure—a lamentation disguised as a celebration.

Mencken never really admitted, perhaps never quite realized, how much his nostalgia for the late nineteenth century represented his love not only for the days of his childhood but also for those aspects of life in America that he valued and fought to preserve. Much of his career actually consisted of contrasting the individualistic verities of this older America with the new, strange, and disturbing society that had emerged in the twentieth century. But for such a large part of his adult life he had been like a guerrilla fighter in a country so long dominated by forces alien to him that he had forgotten that it was really *his* country he was defending. In the end, he came to believe that it was he who was an alien in America; as he wrote in an unpublished autobiographical fragment from 1941: "Thus I have lived in the United States all my life without becoming, in any deep sense, an American" ("Notes" 1941). In an entry for August 27, 1942, in the *Diary,* he claimed that his grandfather had made a mistake in coming to America. "I have spent all of my 62 years here, but I still feel it impossible to fit myself into the accepted patterns of American life and thought. After all these years I remain a foreigner" (215). There is more than a touch of tragedy in this statement; for no man has ever been more thoroughly American than Henry Louis Mencken.

Notes and References

Preface

1. Richard Wright, *Black Boy: A Record of Childhood and Youth* (New York: Harper & Brothers, 1937), 217–18; see also Charles W. Scruggs, "Finding Out about This Mencken: The Impact of *A Book of Prefaces* on Richard Wright," *Menckeniana,* no. 95 (Fall 1985): 1–11; James J. Kilpatrick, "The Writer Mencken," *Menckeniana,* no. 79 (Fall 1981): 2; Joseph Epstein, "H. L. Mencken: The Art of the Point of View," *Menckeniana,* no. 71 (Fall 1979): 3.

Chapter One

1. H. L. Mencken, "On Living in Baltimore," *Prejudices: Fifth Series* (New York: Knopf, 1926), 240, 241. There are five other books in the *Prejudices* series (all published by Knopf): *First Series* (1919), *Second Series* (1920), *Third Series* (1922), *Fourth Series* (1924), and *Sixth Series* (1927); hereafter they are cited in text as *Prejudices* followed by the appropriate number.

2. H. L. Mencken, "Good Old Baltimore," *Smart Set* (May 1913): 113.

3. In Fred Hobson's *Mencken: A Life* (New York: Random House, 1994), 45–48, more stress is placed on Mencken as a southerner; hereafter cited in text. See also D. C. Stenerson, *H. L. Mencken: Iconoclast from Baltimore* (Chicago: University Chicago Press, 1971), 47–56; hereafter cited in text.

4. In later life Mencken wrote of German Americans, "My opinion of [them] was always very low. The plain fact is that the majority of German-Americans are of the lower and more backward classes, culturally speaking" (Hobson 1994, 44).

5. H. L. Mencken, *My Life as Author and Editor,* ed. Jonathan Yardley (New York: Knopf, 1993), 34; hereafter cited in the text as *My Life.* "The point of view that was to color all my writings probably came, in its essence, from my father, for he was a natural skeptic, and hence had a low opinion of the prevailing American scheme of things" (*My Life,* 172).

6. Letter from H. L. Mencken to A. G. Keller, December 15, 1939, Mencken Collection, New York Public Library.

7. Of the four Mencken children, only Henry's brother Charlie left the nest and married while his mother was alive. Neither brother August nor sister Gertrude ever married.

8. H. L. Mencken, *Thirty-five Years of Newspaper Work: A Memoir,* ed. Fred Hobson, Vincent Fitzpatrick, and Bradford Jacobs (Baltimore: The Johns

Hopkins University Press, 1994), 154–55; hereafter cited in text as *Thirty-five Years*.

9. Hobson 1994, 28. Considering that Mencken was a person who internalized a tremendous amount of discipline, this early application of an external physical restraint must have had some influence upon him. The Mencken quotation is from H. L. Mencken, *Happy Days, 1880–1892* (New York: Knopf, 1940), vii; hereafter cited in text as *Happy Days*.

10. H. L. Mencken, "Autobiographical Notes: 1925," p. 73, bound typescript, Enoch Pratt Free Library, Baltimore; hereafter cited in text as "Notes" 1925.

11. To the very end of his life, Mencken continued to acknowledge the influence of Huxley; see H. L. Mencken, *Minority Report* (New York: Knopf, 1956), 292–93; hereafter cited in text as *Minority*. See also Alistair Cooke, "Mencken and the English Language," in John Dorsey, ed., *On Mencken* (New York: Knopf, 1980), 112–13; book hereafter cited in text as Dorsey.

12. As early as 1905, Mencken wrote in the November 29 Baltimore *Morning Herald:* "He [Mark Twain] is the premier American humorist, but he is also the premier American novelist"; Miscellaneous Clippings, Mencken Room, Enoch Pratt Free Library, Baltimore.

13. H. L. Mencken, quoted in Carl Bode, *Mencken* (Carbondale: Southern Illinois University Press, 1969), 23; hereafter cited in text.

14. H. L. Mencken, *Newspaper Days, 1899–1906* (New York: Knopf, 1941), 3; hereafter cited in text as *Newspaper Days*.

15. David Graham Phillips, quoted in Larzer Ziff, *The American 1890s: The Life and Times of a Lost Generation* (New York: Viking, 1966), 150.

16. For Mencken's comments on Ade, see *Prejudices* 1, 121–22.

17. Richard Bridgeman, *The Colloquial Style in America* (New York: Oxford University Press, 1966), 136.

18. Henry F. May, *The End of American Innocence: A Study of the First Years of Our Own Time, 1912–1917* (New York: Knopf, 1959), 201–2; hereafter cited in text.

Chapter Two

1. Not only does Mencken's humor reflect the broad parodies of the vaudeville stage, but he frequently referred to specific features of the old vaudeville and burlesque shows, such as "slapstick," "bladder," and "Krausmeyer's Alley." For Downer quotation, see Alan S. Downer, *Fifty Years of American Drama, 1900–1950* (Chicago: Regnery, 1957), 39.

2. H. L. Mencken, "Mere Opinion," Baltimore *Morning Herald,* December 24, 1905. Clipping, Enoch Pratt Free Library.

3. H. L. Mencken, "The Last Round," Baltimore *Evening Sun,* April 6, 1911.

4. H. L. Mencken, *George Bernard Shaw: His Plays* (Boston: Luce, 1905), x, xi, ix–x; hereafter cited in text as *Shaw*. Shaw would not have appreci-

ated Mencken's attempt to place him within a Darwinist framework. He rejected Darwinism and adhered, instead, to some form of "vitalism." See Harry Gershenowitz, "Mencken's Misinterpretation of Shaw's Position on Evolution," *Menckeniana,* no. 93 (Spring 1985): 7–10.

5. H. L. Mencken, introduction to *A Doll's House,* by Henrik Ibsen (Boston: Luce, 1909), vi, xii.

6. H. L. Mencken, "The Literary Olio," *Smart Set* (February 1909): 155.

7. H. L. Mencken, "George Bernard Shaw as 'A Hero,' " *Smart Set* (January 1910): 154.

8. *Vanity Fair's* "Hall of Fame," quoted in Frederick J. Hoffman, *The Twenties: American Writing in the Postwar Decade* (New York: Viking, 1955), 304; hereafter cited in text.

9. For a brief but excellent discussion of Nietzsche's influence in prewar America, see May, 206–10.

10. Guy Jean Forgue has suggested that the movement from Darwin and Spencer to Nietzsche was natural for Mencken because of certain affiliations between Darwinism and the German's philosophy. Since Nietzsche himself had decried the influence of Darwin's teachings, it seems unlikely that the philosopher was already "Darwinized" when Mencken read him. As Forgue himself points out, the mechanistic materialism in Mencken's American form of social Darwinism warred with the central core of Nietzsche's existentialism. See Forgue's *H. L. Mencken, l'homme, l'oeuvre, l'influence* (Monaco, 1967), 92; hereafter cited in text as Forgue 1967.

In a letter to Fielding H. Garrison dated August 9, 1919, Mencken admitted that he had tried to make Nietzsche comprehensible to Americans, and so he "tried to translate the thing into terms of [Nietzsche's] common concerns." See Carl Bode, "Mencken in His Letters," in Dorsey, 257.

11. Writing in the 1930s to A. G. Keller (who had succeeded to Sumner's chair at Yale), Mencken commented, "The books of your old chief, Dr. Sumner, made a powerful impression on me when I was young, and their influence has survived." The letter, dated January 5, 1932, is reprinted in Guy Jean Forgue, ed., *Letters of H. L. Mencken* (New York: Knopf, 1961), 337; hereafter cited in text. For the influence of Sumner on Mencken, see Stenerson 1971, 21–30.

12. R. R. LaMonte and H. L. Mencken, *Men versus the Man: A Correspondence between Rives La Monte, Socialist, and H. L. Mencken, Individualist* (New York: Holt, 1910), 25; hereafter cited in text as *Men.*

13. H. L. Mencken, *The Philosophy of Friedrich Nietzsche,* rev. ed. (Boston: Luce, 1913), 105; hereafter cited in the text as *Nietzsche* 1913. References to the 1908 edition will be cited in text as *Nietzsche* 1908.

14. Nietzsche, quoted in George Allen Morgan, *What Nietzsche Means* (Cambridge, Mass.: Harvard University Press, 1941), 212.

15. H. L. Mencken, "The Prophet of the Superman," *Smart Set* (August 1913): 154. Guy Forgue rightly points out that Mencken had trouble con-

necting his scientism, with its assumption that truth could be empirically established, to Nietzsche's more instinctive and passionate intuition of truth. Forgue goes too far, however, in suggesting that Mencken forces on Nietzsche a form of bourgeois utility of the kind epitomized by Henry Ford; see Forgue 1967, 97.

16. See Richard Hofstadter, *Social Darwinism in American Thought, 1860–1915* (Boston: Beacon, 1955), 104; and Eric F. Goldman, *Rendezvous with Destiny: A History of Modern American Reform* (New York: Vintage, 1977), 73–76.

17. H. L. Mencken to Fielding H. Garrison, August 9, 1919, quoted in Carl Bode, "Mencken in His Letters," in Dorsey, 257.

Chapter Three

1. H. L. Mencken, quoted in Betty Adler, comp., with the assistance of Jane Wilhelm, *H. L. M.: The Mencken Bibliography,* (Baltimore: The Johns Hopkins University Press, 1961), 49; hereafter cited in text. For Mencken's role as Sunday editor, see Harold Williams, *The Baltimore Sunpapers, 1837–1987* (Baltimore: The Johns Hopkins University Press, 1987), 119; hereafter cited in text.

2. Mencken also claimed that it was around this time that he began to pick up a following among the younger writers and critics on the east coast.

3. Untitled and unsigned editorial in Baltimore *Sun,* dated 1911, Miscellaneous Clippings, Mencken Room, Enoch Pratt Free Library. Mencken never quite gave up some of these ideas. See his "A Proposed Constitution for Maryland," *Menckeniana,* no. 100 (Winter 1986): 1–14.

4. H. L. Mencken,"Roosevelt in Europe," bound in "Editorials and Other Articles, Baltimore *Evening Sun,* 1910–1912," 6:14, Mencken Room, Enoch Pratt Free Library.

5. Except in the section "The American," unless otherwise noted, all dates enclosed in parentheses in this chapter refer to "Free Lance" articles printed in the Baltimore *Evening Sun.*

6. H. L. Mencken, Baltimore *Sun,* 1911, pencil-dated miscellaneous clipping, Mencken Room, Enoch Pratt Free Library.

7. See Peter G. Filene, "An Obituary for 'The Progressive Movement,' " *American Quarterly* 22 (Spring 1970): 20–34.

8. For Mencken's claim to have voted for Roosevelt in 1912, see "The Last Gasp," Baltimore *Evening Sun,* November 1, 1920.

9. Clyde Griffen, "The Progressive Ethos," in *The Development of an American Culture,* ed. Stanley Coben and Lorman Ratner (Englewood Cliffs, N. J.: Prentice-Hall, 1970), 130.

10. See Mencken's preface and the chapter entitled "Munich," in H. L. Mencken, George Jean Nathan, and Willard Huntington Wright, *Europe after 8:15* (New York: Lane, 1914).

11.   H. L. Mencken, "The American," *Smart Set* (June 1913): 87–94; "The American: His Morals," (July 1913): 83–91; "The American: His Language," (August 1913:, 89–96; "The American: His Ideas of Beauty," (September 1913): 91–98; "The American: His Freedom," (October 1913): 81–88; "The American: His New Puritanism," (February 1914): 87–94. All page numbers in parentheses in this section refer to those of the *Smart Set* issue mentioned by date in text.

12.   For the idea of puritanism as a cultural force in early-twentieth-century America, see Randolph S. Bourne, "The Puritan's Will to Power," in *War and the Intellectuals: Collected Essays, 1915–1919,* ed. Carl Resek (New York: Harper & Row, 1964), 156–61; hereafter cited in text; and Richard Ruland, *The Rediscovery of American Literature: Premises of Critical Taste, 1900–1940* (Cambridge, Mass.: Harvard University Press, 1967), 34–42; hereafter cited in text. See also May, 33, 42–43.

Chapter Four

1.   For the history of the *Smart Set,* see Carl R. Dolmetsch, *The* Smart Set*: A History and Anthology* (New York: Dial, 1966); hereafter cited in text; Andy Logan, *The Man Who Robbed the Robber Barons* (New York: Norton, 1965); Frank Luther Mott, *The History of the American Magazines,* vol. 5, *Sketches of 21 Magazines, 1905–1930* (Cambridge, Mass.: Harvard University Press, 1968).

2.   James Collins and Charles Moore quotations from Howard Mumford Jones, *The Theory of American Literature* (Ithaca, N.Y.: Cornell University Press, 1965), 122. *Forum* quotation from Grant C. Knight, *The Strenuous Age in American Literature* (Chapel Hill: University of North Carolina Press, 1954), 127.

3.   Unless otherwise noted, all page numbers in parentheses in this chapter refer to the issue of the *Smart Set* mentioned by date in the text.

4.   Percy Boynton, quoted in Ruland, vii.

5.   H. L. Mencken, quoted in William H. Nolte, ed., *H. L. Mencken's* Smart Set *Criticism* (Ithaca N.Y.: Cornell University Press, 1968), 25; hereafter cited in text as Nolte *Smart Set.*

6.   H. L. Mencken, "A Novel of the First Rank," *Smart Set* (November 1911): 153. At least one writer agreed with Mencken's idea about the European quality of good writing in America. Willa Cather, after reading his essay "The National Letters," wrote to Mencken on February 6, 1922: "I've often had a deep inner tooth ache of the soul, wondering whether I was unconsciously copying some 'foreign' writer. When Oh Pioneers was written, it was a terribly lonesome book; I couldn't find any other that left out our usual story machinery. I wondered then . . . whether my mind had got a kink put in it by the four shorter novels by Tolstoi. . . . I used to wonder if they had so 'marked' me that I could not see the American scene as it looked to other Americans"; letter in the Mencken Collection, New York Public Library.

7. H. L. Mencken, "The Folk Song," Baltimore (Sunday) *Sun,* 1909, bound in "Editorials and Dramatic Reviews, Baltimore *Sun,* 1906–1910," 127, Mencken Room, Enoch Pratt Free Library.

8. H. L. Mencken, "On American Stage Plays," Baltimore *Evening Sun,* bound in "Editorials and Other Articles, Baltimore *Sun,* 1910–1912," 227, Mencken Room, Enoch Pratt Free Library.

9. H. L. Mencken, in William Nolte, *H. L. Mencken, Literary Critic* (Middletown, Conn.: Wesleyan University Press, 1968), quotations on Howells, 6, 178; on James, 13; hereafter cited in text as Nolte *Mencken.*

10. H. L. Mencken, "The Vernal Bards," Baltimore *Evening Sun,* April 14, 1911.

11. H. L. Mencken, *A Book of Prefaces* (New York: Knopf, 1917), 15; hereafter cited in text as *Prefaces.*

12. H. L. Mencken, ed., introduction to *We Moderns: Enigmas and Guesses,* by Edwin Muir (New York: Knopf, 1920), 14, 15.

13. H. L. Mencken to Marion Bloom, December 11 [1920?], *The New Mencken Letters,* ed. Carl Bode (New York: Dial Press, 1977), 137; hereafter cited in text.

14. Thomas P. Riggio, "Dreiser and Mencken in the Literary Trenches," *American Scholar* 54 (Spring 1985): 234. For the Mencken quotation, see William A. Swanberg, *Dreiser* (New York: Scribner's 1965), 174.

15. Some of Mencken's biographers tend to see Wright as little more than Mencken's protégé. Burton Rascoe and Groff Conklin, however, depict Wright's editorship of the *Smart Set* as the high point in the magazine's history and denigrate the later efforts of Mencken and Nathan. See Burton Rascoe and Groff Conklin, eds., *The* Smart Set *Anthology* (New York: Reynal, 1934), xxxi–xliv. Carl Dolmetsch gives a balanced view of the merits of all parties involved. For the history of the *Smart Set* and Mencken's involvement with the magazine, see Carl R. Dolmetsch, "A History of the *Smart Set* Magazine, 1914–1923" (Ph.D. diss., University of Chicago, 1957); hereafter cited in text.

16. In later years, Mencken insisted that the *Smart Set* had discovered few writers. Writing to Isaac Goldberg in 1935, he stated: "Most of the authors we were supposed to have 'discovered' were being printed before we heard of them. . . . The most that can be said for us is that we recognized the good ones when they popped up" (Bode 1977, 340–41).

17. Mencken to T. Dreiser, December 16, 1916, *Letters of Theodore Dreiser,* vol. 1, ed. Robert Elias (Philadelphia: University of Pennsylvania Press, 1959), 239. "My dissents" (Mencken) quotation in Sara Mayfield, *The Constant Circle: H. L. Mencken and His Friends* (New York: Delacorte, 1968), 167; hereafter cited in text.

Chapter Five

1. H. L. Mencken, "The Mailed Fist and Its Prophet," *Atlantic Monthly* 114 (November 1914): 601, 607.

2. Mencken claimed that there were other considerations in giving up the "Free Lance" besides the likelihood of America's entry into the war. He found himself increasingly involved with his editorial duties in New York; he had been on the *Sunpapers'* staff for 10 years and needed a change; and he was afraid that, if he somehow continued to write on local affairs, he would degenerate into "a mere columnist . . . a town celebrity, a local worthy," something [he had] always tried "most diligently to avoid." Looking back on the "Free Lance," from the vantage point of several decades, Mencken claimed that it had been useful to him, "if only in the way of clarifying my ideas" (*Thirty-five Years,* 59).

3. See Robert E. Spiller et al., *Literary History of the United States,* rev. ed. (New York: Macmillan, 1953), 1135–56, 1358–60.

4. Walter Lippmann, *Drift and Mastery: An Attempt to Diagnose the Current Unrest* (New York: M. Kennerley, 1914), xviii.

5. With *Prefaces,* Mencken set the pattern which he would follow for many of his subsequent books, particularly the *Prejudices* series. "First I used an idea in a newspaper article, then I developed it in a magazine article, and finally I put it into a book" (*My Life,* 194).

6. Dreiser came from Terre Haute, Indiana, not Warsaw. Mencken probably knew this because he had been very close to Dreiser. But for the purposes of satire, Warsaw, invoking perhaps images of the millions of Polish peasants who had streamed into America in recent decades, was more effective.

7. See Ernest Earnest, *The Single Vision: The Alienation of American Intellectuals* (New York: New York University Press, 1970), 3–21.

8. For a detailed discussion of Humanism and Mencken's controversy with the Humanists, see chapters 1 through 4 of Ruland.

9. Stuart Pratt Sherman, review of *The Genius,* by Theodore Dreiser, *Nation* 101 (December 2, 1915): 648. For the key role that Dreiser's reputation played in the literary debates of this period, see May, 189–91, 389–91.

10. Stuart Pratt Sherman, "Beautifying American Letters," review of *Prefaces,* by Mencken, *Nation* 105 (November 29, 1917): 594.

11. For Mencken's attitude toward Sherman, see Menken's letter to Carl Van Doren, September 1, 1936, in Forgue 1961, 408.

12. Stuart Pratt Sherman, *Americans* (New York: Scribner's, 1922), 11; hereafter cited in text.

13. Charles Scruggs, *The Sage of Harlem: H. L. Mencken and the Black Writers of the 1920s* (Baltimore: The Johns Hopkins University Press, 1984), 52, 53; hereafter cited in text.

14. Between 1924 and 1933, the years of Mencken's editorship, the *American Mercury* published 54 articles about blacks, half by African-American authors. See Fenwick Anderson, "Black Perspectives in Mencken's *Mercury,*" *Menckeniana,* no. 70 (Summer 1979): 2.

15. Mencken quoted in Charles Scruggs, "H. L. Mencken and James Weldon Johnson: Two Men Who Helped Shape a Renaissance," in Douglas C.

Stenerson, ed., *Critical Essays on H. L. Mencken* (Boston: G. K. Hall, 1987), 187; Scruggs essay hereafter cited in text; Stenerson also cited hereafter in text.

16. Scruggs 1984, 117–18, 199 n. 2; White's own novel *Fire in the Flint,* which Mencken helped him publish, was inspired by Mencken's essays on the South (118).

17. For example, see George Schuyler, "View and Reviews," *Pittsburgh Courier,* July 30, 1927; reprinted in Stenerson 1987, 76–77.

18. Stuart Pratt Sherman, *The Genius of America* (New York: Scribner's, 1923), 28.

19. The statement is from the introduction to Mencken's unpublished anthology of short stories, "Modern American Short Stories" (1921), p. 6, bound typescript, Mencken Collection, Enoch Pratt Free Library.

20. Mencken, "My Dear Walpole. An Open Letter from H. L. Mencken," *Bookman* 62 (December 1925): 438, 439. For Walpole's letter see the November 1925 issue of the same journal, 62: 246–48. For an earlier exchange of open letters between the two men, see the *Bookman* 55 (May 1922): 225–28; 55 (June 1922): 364.

21. H. L. Mencken, *The American Language: A Preliminary Inquiry into the Development of English in the United States* (New York: Knopf, 1919), 321.

22. For an updated, one-volume version of Mencken's classic work, see Raven I. McDavid's *The American Language: An Inquiry into the Development of English in the United States,* 4th ed., and the two supplements, abridged with annotations and new material (New York: Knopf, 1963).

23. See Owen Dudley Edward's article on Mencken in *Encyclopedia of Language and Linguistics,* ed. R. E. Ashur, vol. 5 (New York: Pergamon Press, 1994), 2448.

24. Stuart Pratt Sherman, *Critical Woodcuts* (New York: Scribner's, 1926), 240.

Chapter Six

1. Letter from T. Dreiser to Mencken, April 26, 1915, Forgue 1961, 69. For Pound's comment, see Pound to Mencken, September 27, 1916, *The Letters of Ezra Pound, 1907–1941,* ed. D. D. Paige (New York: Harcourt, Brace, 1950), 98; hereafter cited in text as Pound.

2. See, for example, letter from Mencken to E. Boyd, March 13, [1919], Forgue 1961, 142.

3. For "aesthete" reactions to Boyd's article and the publishing of *Aesthete: 1925* (a copy of which is in the University of Pennsylvania library), see Malcolm Cowley, *Exile's Return: A Literary Odyssey of the 1920's* (New York: Viking, 1951), 190–93; Matthew Josephson, *Life among the Surrealists: A Memoir* (New York: Holt, Rinehart, Winston, 1962), 267–69, 289–91; M. K. Singleton, *H. L. Mencken and the* American Mercury *Adventure*

(Durham, N.C.: Duke University Press, 1962), 49–52; hereafter cited in text.

4. H. L. Mencken, *A Bathtub Hoax and Other Blasts and Bravos from the Chicago Tribune*, ed. Robert McHugh (New York: Knopf, 1958), 109; hereafter cited in text as *Bathtub*.

5. For a well-balanced evaluation of Mencken's comments on poetry, see Carl R. Dolmetsch, "H. L. Mencken as a Critic of Poetry," *Jahrbuch für Amerikastudien* 19 (1966): 83–95.

6. Letter from Mencken to Burton Rascoe [Summer 1920?]; letter from Mencken to L. Untermeyer, November 25, [1920]; Forgue 1961, 189–90, 210–11.

7. "The Ulster Polonius," *Smart Set* (August 1916): 140; reprinted in *Prejudices: First Series,* 181–90. Mencken probably knew that Shaw, of a Protestant background, had been born in Dublin; however, the Ulster Protestants were very much in the news at this time, and Mencken may have wanted to associate Shaw with their fanaticism. For interpretations on Mencken's turning against Shaw, see Edgar Kemler, *The Irreverent Mr. Mencken* (Boston: Little, Brown, 1950), 114–16; Stanley Weintraub, *Shaw's People: Victoria to Churchill* (University Park: Pennsylvania State University Press, 1996), 73–85.

8. "Ibsen, Journeyman Dramatist," *Dial* (October 11, 1917): 323; see also "More Notes on Books—2," *Smart Set* (November 1921): 141.

9. See H. L. Mencken, *James Branch Cabell* (New York: McBride, 1927), 12.

10. Burton Rascoe, quoted in Donald M. Hensley, *Burton Rascoe,* Twayne United States Authors Series (New York: G. K. Hall,. 1970), 71; hereafter cited in text.

11. Mark Schorer, *Sinclair Lewis: An American Life* (New York: McGraw, 1961), 290–91. In a similar vein, William F. Goldhurst suggests that "Mencken deepened Fitzgerald's understanding of American society"; see his *F. Scott Fitzgerald and His Contemporaries* (Cleveland, Ohio: World Publishing, 1961), 90.

12. Henry Dan Piper, *F. Scott Fitzgerald: A Critical Portrait* (New York: Holt, Rinehart, Winston, 1966), 130.

13. Fred C. Hobson Jr., *Serpent in Eden: H. L. Mencken and the South* (Chapel Hill: University of North Carolina Press, 1974), 28, 34, 35; hereafter cited in the text. Charles Scruggs points out that this comparison had been absent in the original newspaper version of "Sahara" and suggests that, in revising the essay, Mencken was influenced by James Weldon Johnson, who had suggested in a piece on Mencken that it was racism that debilitated southern culture (Scruggs 1987, 193–94).

14. Emily Clark, *Innocence Abroad* (New York: Knopf, 1931), 109; hereafter cited in text.

15. Hobson 1974, 84; and *Thirty-five Years,* 158.

16. *Smart Set* (August 1921): 138; and Hobson 1994, 45.

17. For Wells's quotations, see H. G. Wells, *The New Machiavelli* (New York: Duffield, 1910), 23, 24.

18. For accounts of the dispute between Mencken and Nathan, see Carl Dolmetsch, " 'HLM' and 'GJN': The Editorial Partnership Reexamined," *Menckeniana,* no. 75 (Fall 1980): 29–39; hereafter cited in text as Dolmetsch 1980; Alfred Knopf, "H. L. Mencken, George Jean Nathan, and the *American Mercury* Venture," *Menckeniana,* no. 78 (Summer 1981): 1–10.

19. As a writer for the *Sunpapers,* Mencken never argued with his editors whenever prudence suggested changes in his copy. If an editor proposed altering his material, Mencken once wrote, "I invariably invited him to do his damndest, and usually refused to listen to his reasons. He was the editor, not I" (*Thirty-five Years,* 123).

20. Anonymous, "Editorial Notes," *American Mercury,* December 1927, xcii–xciii; Mencken Room, Enoch Pratt Free Library.

21. [H. L. Mencken], preface to *Three Years, 1924–1927: The Story of a New Idea and Its Successful Adaptation* (New York: Knopf, 1927), unsigned, Mencken Room, Enoch Pratt Free Library.

Chapter Seven

1. For the "White Paper," see *Thirty-five Years,* 76–77, 355–65; for quotations, see 362, 364. See also Williams, 164–68.

2. *Thirty-five Years,* 118, 121–22; see also Williams, 230.

3. The *Tribune* series ran until 1928. For it, Mencken produced some of his best pieces of the decade. See *The Bathtub Hoax* for reprints some of these pieces.

4. Letter from Mencken to E. Wilson, May 26, 1921, Forgue 1961, 225. See also Edmund Wilson, "H. L. Mencken," *New Republic* 27 (June 1, 1921): 10–13.

5. All dates in this chapter refer to articles in the Baltimore *Evening Sun,* unless otherwise noted.

6. H. L. Mencken, *Notes on Democracy* (New York: Knopf, 1926), 183; hereafter cited in text as *Notes on Democracy..*

7. William Manchester, *Disturber of the Peace: The Life of H. L. Mencken* (New York: Harper, 1950), 177.

8. Letter from Mencken to T. Mooney, July 11, 1928; letter from Tom Mooney Defense Committee to Mencken, July 9, 1931; both in the Mencken Collection, New York Public Library.

9. "The Land of the Free," January 12, 1925, Baltimore *Evening Sun;* letter from R. Baldwin to Mencken, January 16, 1925, Mencken Collection, New York Public Library.

10. Letter from E. Goldman to Mencken, May 20, 1930, Mencken Collection, New York Public Library.

11. Letter from Mencken to T. Arnold, March 29, 1940, Mencken Collection, New York Public Library.

12. H. L. Mencken, "Americanism: Exterior View," *Smart Set* (April 1923): 140.

13. The banning of the *Mercury* and the subsequent trial, better known as the "Hatrack Case," are discussed in all the Mencken biographies and in Singleton, 167–81. For background to Boston censorship during the 1920s, see Paul S. Boyer, "Boston Book Censorship in the Twenties," *American Quarterly* 15 (Spring 1963): 3–24.

14. For Hoover's comments and for information on phone taps, see Paul Carter, *Another Part of the Twenties* (New York: Columbia University Press, 1977), 102; hereafter cited in text; Richard Hofstadter, *The Age of Reform* (N.Y.: Vintage, 1960), 289; hereafter cited in text.

15. For more on Prohibition, see James H. Timberlake, *Prohibition and the Progressive Movement* (Cambridge, Mass.: Harvard University Press, 1963); Kenneth K. Baily, *Southern White Protestantism in the Twentieth Century* (Gloucester, N.Y.: Harper & Row, 1968); see also Paul Carter's discussion of Prohibition, 85–102.

16. Anthony Channel Hilfer nevertheless included Mencken among the "Village Rebels" in his study *The Revolt from the Village, 1915–1930* (Chapel Hill: University of North Carolina Press, 1969).

17. For Mencken's respect for evangelist Billy Sunday and especially for fundamentalist theologian Gresham Machen, see D. G. Hart, "Mencken and Fundamentalism: Another Perspective," *Menckeniana*, no. 107 (Fall 1988): 1–8. Mencken even managed to maintain friendly relations with some of the religious supporters of Prohibition, such as Methodist bishop James Cannon; see Hobson 1994, 345, 386, 482; see also Mencken, *The Diary of H. L. Mencken*, ed. Charles A. Fecher (New York: Knopf, 1990), 39–40, 63–64, 69–70, 128–30; hereafter cited in text as *Diary*.

18. Mencken made it clear, in an article in the *Nation* of July 1, 1925, that the issue was not one of academic freedom for public school teachers. "When a pedagogue takes his oath of office he renounces the right to free speech quite as certainly as a bishop does, as a colonel in the army, or an editorial writer on a newspaper" (*Thirty-five Years,* 139). Mencken's whole aim was to expose the "imbecility" of the Tennessee Fundamentalists and, especially, of Bryan.

19. See Mencken, *Thirty-five Years,* 137; Hobson 1994, 265. See also letter from Mencken to E. L. Masters, May 27, 1925, Mencken Collection, New York Public Library. For Mencken's articles on the trial and reminiscences by some of the participants in the trial, see *D-Day at Dayton: Reflections of the Scopes Trial,* ed. Jerry R. Tompkins (Baton Rouge: Louisiana State University, 1965).

20. In truth, Mencken liked Baltimore because the city gave him ample privacy. In his memoirs he confessed, "I had no desire to degenerate into a local worthy, and always resisted efforts to draw me into Baltimore activities." With the exception of his colleagues of the *Sunpapers* and his fellow musicians of the

Saturday Night Club, he saw few Baltimoreans socially. Although he knew many people in the city, he reserved his social life during his editing days for his frequent trips to New York (*Thirty-five Years,* 121).

21.   H. L. Mencken, "Maryland: Apex of Normalcy," *Nation* 114 (May 3, 1922): 518, 519.

22.   T. C. Cochran and William Miller, *The Age of Enterprise: A Social History of Industrial America* (New York: Harper Torchbooks, 1961), 324; hereafter cited in text.

23.   Joseph Epstein, "H. L. Mencken: The Art of the Point of View," *Menckeniana,* no. 71 (Fall 1979): 10; Murry Kempton, "A Very Great Whale Indeed," *Menckeniana,* no. 83 (Fall 1982): 4, 5.

Chapter Eight

1.   Letter from Mencken to J. Tully, August 20, 1936, Mencken Collection, New York Public Library.

2.   H. L. Mencken, "Post-Mortem," Baltimore *Evening Sun,* July 14, 1924. In this chapter all in-text citations consisting of dates, unless otherwise noted, will refer to articles from the *Evening Sun.*

3.   For all of his partisanship and satire, Mencken could be a first-class reporter. He took on the reporter's role when he covered the presidential nominating conventions, international disarmament conferences, and "big stories" such as the Scopes trial. Mark Sullivan, a fellow journalist, once urged the *Sunpapers* to nominate Mencken for a Pulitzer prize for his reporting of one the Democratic conventions. Mencken had a strong dislike of all professional and honorary organizations and their awards. He refused to have his name put forward (*Thirty-five Years,* 298).

4.   "Autobiographical Notes: 1941," unpublished, unbound typescript, Enoch Pratt Free Library; hereafter cited as "Notes" 1941.

5.   Anders Iversen, "Democratic Man, The Superior Man and the Forgotten Man in H. L. Mencken's *Notes on Democracy,*" *English Studies* 50 (1969): 354.

6.   Edmund Wilson, "Mencken's Democratic Man," review of *Notes on Democracy, New Republic* 47 (December 15, 1926): 110.

7.   Letter from Mencken to F. Butcher, February 20, [1921], Forgue 1961, 219. Writing to novelist Percy Marks on December 2, [1922], Mencken promised that he would write a book he had been thinking about for a long while, "to wit, 'Advice to Young Men,' a frank, realistic, unsentimental treatise . . . revolving around the doctrine that the most precious possession of man is *honor*" (239). "Advice" evolved into *A Treatise on Right and Wrong* (1934).

8.   D. C. Stenerson, "The 'Forgotten Man' of H. L. Mencken," *American Quarterly* 18 (Winter 1966): 687.

9.   See Irving Howe's essay, "American Moderns," in *Paths of American Thought,* ed. Arthur Schlesinger Jr., and Morton M. White (Boston: Houghton, Mifflin, 1970), 314.

10. Certainly, by the end of the decade, some portion of Mencken's readership was solidly placed in the upper middle class. According to a readership survey dated May 1, 1931, 39.2 percent of the *American Mercury*'s readers had an annual income of 10,000 dollars or more. Thirty-five percent of subscribers were bankers, corporation officials, or business executives. Thirty-one percent were professional men. (This survey is bound in "Mercury Miscellany" in the Mencken Room of the Enoch Pratt Free Library.) Yet the *Mercury*'s audience was not necessarily ultraconservative. In December 2, 1932, Mencken wrote to Knopf, his publisher, stating that the liberal *Nation* duplicated more of the *Mercury*'s subscription list than either *Harper's* or the *Atlantic Monthly* (Forgue 1961, 353).

11. Letter from J. Reed to Mencken, September 3, 1923, Mencken Collection, New York Public Library.

12. Mencken put the *Mercury* on the same tact of political independence from the established parties he had urged on the Baltimore *Sunpapers* in the "White Paper" of 1920. See *Thirty-five Years,* 359–61.

13. Letter from Mencken to B. de Casseres, March 2 and March 5, 1935, Mencken Collection, New York Public Library.

14. Letter from Mencken to J. Dos Passos, January 27, 1947, Mencken Collection, New York Public Library.

15. Letter from Mencken to Georg Müller, 1923, Mencken Room, Enoch Pratt Free Library.

Chapter Nine

1. Vincent Starrett, *Haldeman-Julius Monthly,* December 1927, 123–25.

2. Mencken's speech and his account of the evening are in the F. D. Roosevelt folio in the Mencken Collection of the New York Public Library. A slightly different version may be found in appendix B of *Thirty-five Years,* 368–70.

3. Quotation from Mencken's comments in the F. D. Roosevelt folio in the Mencken Collection of the New York Public Library. Fecher notes that Mencken's diary entry for the evening breaks off, although it is not clear if some pages are missing (76–77 n. 6). Hobson says that although biographer Edgar Kemler reported that HLM was furious with Roosevelt, Hobson has found no such evidence in Mencken's correspondence or notes. Hobson does note, however, that Mencken subsequently did shift the focus of his attack from the New Deal to FDR (Hobson 1994, 384).

4. Although Johnson remained an admirer and defender of Mencken for years after his death, Mencken's memoirs are full of depreciating, sometimes scathing remarks about Johnson, based primarily on the younger man's liberalism.

5. Quoted in Daniel Aaron, *Writers on the Left: Episodes in American Literary Communism* (New York: Harcourt, Brace, and World, 1961), 412 n. 26.

6. Letter from A. G. Hayes to Mencken, April 25, 1938, Mencken Collection, New York Public Library. The American Civil Liberties Union had apparently read the article before it was to be published. Mencken did rewrite it slightly and the controversy never spilled into the courtroom.

7. Letter from C. Pollock to Mencken, December 27, 1935; Mencken to Pollock, January 9, 1936, both in the Mencken Collection, New York Public Library.

8. For the latter piece, see "Mencken's Last Stand," in *The Vintage Mencken,* ed. Alistair Cooke (New York: Vintage, 1955), 227–30.

9. Letter from Mencken to Mrs. Olga Ross, June 3, 1940, Herman Schapiro folder, Mencken Room, Enoch Pratt Free Library.

10. Letter from Mencken to A. G. Keller, February 17, 1941, Mencken Collection, New York Public Library.

Chapter Ten

1. The diary contains between 500,000 and 600,000 words on about 2,100 double-spaced, typed pages. Charles A. Fecher, its editor, selected about one-third of the diary for publication (*Diary,* xxiii). The manuscript of the unfinished memoirs of Mencken's experiences as a magazine editor and author consist of well over 1,000 pages of text and notes, 717 pages of appendixes, and an index. About 60 percent of this material is published in *My Life as Author and Editor* (*My Life,* xiv). The memoirs of his newspaper career, begun in 1941 and completed in 1942, runs to 1,391 typewritten pages, with an additional 257 pages in 30 appendixes; approximately 520,000 words. About 45 percent of the manuscript was published in *Thirty-five Years of Newspaper Work.*

These manuscripts were deposited with the Enoch Pratt Free Library in Baltimore. Mencken also gave the library bound copies of all of his previous manuscripts, complete sets of the *Smart Set* and *American Mercury* magazines, letters, plus over 100 bound volumes housing newspaper clippings about himself, which Mencken had amassed and assembled from the gleanings of the clipping service to which he had subscribed since the early 1920s.

2. For more on Mencken's depression, see Thomas P. Riggio, ed., *The Dreiser-Mencken Letters: The Correspondence between Theodore Dreiser and H. L. Mencken, 1907–1945,* 2 vols. (Philadelphia: University of Pennsylvania Press, 1986), 2:324.

3. Letter from Mencken to A. Pringle, quoted in Edward A. Martin, ed., *In Defense of Marion: The Love of Marion Bloom and H. L. Mencken* (Athens: University of Georgia Press, 1996), 178–79; hereafter cited in text.

4. Concerning his own attempt to produce a more serious, dignified public image, Mencken may have been more prescient in his essay of Valentino than he knew. He speculated that if Valentino had lived, he would have tried to become a great actor rather than a film celebrity. Under such circumstances, Mencken believed that he would have achieved only "increasing pretension . . . solemn artiness . . . deceptive only to himself" (*Prejudices* 6, 310). Toward the

end of the 1920s, some of Mencken's friends and associates noted with amusement and some dismay his growing air of gravitas. He himself never realized that the *Treatise*s on which he labored so diligently were little more than superficial glosses on old scholarship.

5. Louis D. Rubin Jr., "The Mencken Mystery," *Sewanee Review* 99 (Summer 1991): 459; hereafter cited in text.

6. The letter suggests that the depressions began around 1900, a few years after the conflict with his father that ended with August's sudden death in 1898.

7. When Marion's sister, Estelle Bloom Kubitz, later sent Mencken a collection of her sister's correspondence, including his letters to Marion, Mencken did preserve them, depositing them in the New York Public Library, along with the rest of his correspondence, without appending any comment.

8. Mencken's distancing himself from the war can be seen in his correspondence with P. E. Cleator who was living in London during the blitz. Although the two men kept up a lively correspondence, with Mencken commiserating on the loss of Cleator's parents in a bombing raid and sending him books and shirts, Mencken never commented on the political aspects of the conflict. P. E. Cleator, ed., *Letters from Baltimore: The Mencken-Cleator Correspondence* (Rutherford, Madison, and Teaneck, N.J.: Fairleigh Dickenson University Press, 1982).

9. In 1934, when Mencken retired from magazine editing, Patterson offered him the vice presidency of the A. S. Abell company with responsibility for editorial matters. Mencken declined, for he wanted no more of routine jobs. Moreover, he saw problems if a split in editorial policy developed between himself and Patterson (*Diary,* 148–49). Mencken seems to have become increasingly bitter over the failure of the *Sunpapers* to adhere to the vision he had set forth for them in the "White Paper." See *Diary,* 307, 311, 389–90.

10. Occasionally, Mencken provides a glimpse of the gap between his ambitions and his sense of what he accomplished. In 1922, in a letter to Marion Bloom, he claimed: "I really have no false idea about my work. It is basically trivial and will die. But what you must understand is that trivial or not, I can't escape trying to do it. To take it away from me would leave me the worst wreck you ever saw" (Martin, 187).

11. The most obvious exception is Charles Angoff, Mencken's assistant editor and successor at the *American Mercury.* Angoff's book on Mencken contained many examples of what its author regarded as Mencken's anti-Semitism, as well as his general vulgarity. Although the accuracy of Angoff's "quotations from memory" of Mencken's conversation is certainly questionable, one does hear echoes of Angoff's Mencken in the diary and some of his correspondence. See Charles Angoff, *H. L. Mencken: A Portrait from Memory* (New York: Yoseloff, 1956).

12. Charles A. Fecher, *Mencken: A Study of His Thought* (New York: Knopf, 1978), 99.

13. Russell Baker, quoted in Joseph Epstein, "Mencken on Trial," *Commentary* 89.4 (1990): 32; hereafter cited in text. Gwinn Owens who grew up in Baltimore noted in 1980, "I still occasionally meet elderly Baltimoreans usually in their eighties, who quite casually speak of 'the Jews' in that monolithic sense [used by Mencken]. . . . these offenders are not anti-Semitic so much as vestigial remnants of an earlier social climate" (Gwinn Owens, "Mencken and the Jews, Revisited," *Menckeniana*, no. 74 [Summer 1980]: 7; hereafter cited in text).

14. H. L. Mencken, *Treatise on the Gods* (New York: Knopf, 1930), 345–46. See Mary Miller Vass and James L. W. West III, "The Composition and Revision of the *Treatise on the Gods*," in *The Papers of the Bibliographical Society of America* 77.4 (1983): 447–61. They point out that Mencken did revise the offensive passage for the 1936 edition of the book.

15. H. L. Mencken, quoted in Gore Vidal, "The Essential Mencken," *Nation* 253 (August 26 / September 9, 1991): 232–33; hereafter cited in text.

16. In "A Coon Age," which appeared in the *Mercury,* sought to educate whites about black contributions to America. Beginning with an apparent show of prejudice, Mencken went on to argue that black culture interpenetrated white. The African-American paper the *Pittsburgh Courier* approved of "A Coon Age," concluding that Mencken was "performing a great service for us [African Americans] in banishing bigotry, prejudice and ignorance so effectively. America would unquestionably be a much more lively place for the Aframerican if there were a lot more intelligent people like Mencken" (Scruggs 1984, 28). In an earlier *Smart Set* piece, "Si Mutare Potest Aethiops Pellum Suarm" (Can the Ethiop change his skin?), Mencken began by assuming the persona of a southern redneck only to announce by the end of the article that blacks were demonstrating "more progress than southern whites." W. E. B. DuBois called the article a "delicious" piece of writing and found in it evidence that Mencken had seen a "vision" (Scruggs 1984, 49–50).

17. Hobson points out that George Schuyler shared most of Mencken's views and was one of the few intellectuals who did not abandon Mencken in the 1930s (Hobson 1994, 455). Hobson also contends that while Mencken showed a "humane" respect for African Americans of his acquaintance, including his cook and housekeeper, it was mixed with a certain amount of paternalism (456).

18. Lawrence Spivak, quoted in Sheldon L. Richman, "Mr. Mencken and the Jews," *American Scholar* 59 (Summer 1990): 410; hereafter cited in text.

19. See Hobson 1994, 407. Only in rare moments did Mencken seem to acknowledge an irrational prejudice regarding Jews. In a letter to Benjamin De Casseres, dated August 3, 1935, Mencken called for a "really scientific book" on anti-Semitism. Those written by anti-Semites, he claimed, were idiotic and those by Jews sentimental. "My belief, often expressed, is that the Jews probably deserve their troubles, but if you ask me to say categorically *why* they

deserve them I can't answer you. Go into prayer on the subject and let me hear what your own theory is" (Forgue 1961, 393).

20. See Hobson 1994, 413, 454. Also, Hobson notes that although Mencken always seems to have been highly *conscious* of Jews (412), there is little evidence of anti-Semitism during the 1920s (169).

21. For Mencken's tendency to identify Jews with radicalism, see *Diary,* 71, 336, 399.

22. Hobson also argues, however, that Mencken urged helping German Jews, not those from eastern Europe, who tended to be too "radical" (Hobson 1994, 423).

23. Mencken noted what he considered the extreme anti-Semitism of William E. Moore, managing editor of the *Sun,* who refused to hire a Jewish reporter (*Thirty-five Years,* 227).

24. Mencken did talk to various people in Germany and gathered a clear sense that the country was preparing for war against Poland. However, he wrote nothing about this (*Thirty-five Years,* 115).

Chapter Eleven

1. H. L. Mencken,"Editorial," *American Mercury* (July 1927): 288.

2. H. L. Mencken,"Novels—The Spring Crop," *Smart Set* (May 1911): 165.

3. Elizabeth Shepley Sergeant, *Fire under the Andes* (New York: Knopf, 1927), 241.

4. Marion Bloom experienced the full impact of both sides of Mencken's nature during their long, off-again, on-again relationship. In a letter to Mencken, she once complained: "You infuriate me by hiding a tenderness behind your cruelty. Why then, be either? Why be so ungracious and irritated because you find that you can care for someone besides yourself?" (Martin, 44).

5. See Hobson 1994, 357–59.

6. D. G. Hart suggests that Mencken's objection to the Christian fundamentalists was based, not on their theology, but on their militant attempts to translate it into law. As a nonbeliever, Mencken had no time for liberal Christianity that was merely "an excuse and an evasion." According to Hart, "his conception of Christianity was as literal and dogmatic as that of fundamentalism. . . . The Bible and Christianity had to be either accepted or rejected at face value." Mencken rejected it, but he applied a similar type of fundamentalism to his belief in free speech. See Hart, 4, 5.

7. Leonard Feinberg, *The Satirist: His Temperament, Motivation and Influence* (Ames: Iowa State University Press, 1963), 145; hereafter cited in text.

8. David Worcester, *The Art of Satire* (Cambridge, Mass.: Harvard University Press, 1940), 141; hereafter cited in text.

9. See John R. Harrison, *The Reactionaries* (London: Gollancz, 1967).

10. Walter Lippmann, "H. L. Mencken," *Saturday Review of Literature* 3 (December 11, 1926): 414.

11. H. L. Mencken, introduction to *The American Democrat or Hints on the Social and Civic Relations of the United States of America,* by James Fenimore Cooper (New York: Vintage, 1956), viii, ix.

12. Joseph Wood Krutch, "Antichrist and the Five Apostles," *Nation* 113 (December 21, 1921): 733–34.

13. Maxwell Geismar, *The Last of the Provincials: The American Novel, 1915–1925* (Boston: Houghton, 1947), 376–77; hereafter cited in text.

Selected Bibliography

PRIMARY SOURCES

Bibliography

Betty Adler, comp., with the assistance of Jane Wilhelm, *H. L. M. The Mencken Bibliography*. Baltimore: The Johns Hopkins Press, 1961.
Menckeniana: A Quarterly Review. Published by the Enoch Pratt Free Library, Baltimore; updates Adler bibliography.
Betty Adler, comp., "A Descriptive List of H. L. Mencken Collections in the U.S." Baltimore: Enoch Pratt Free Library, 1967.

Library Collections

The Mencken Room, Enoch Pratt Free Library, Baltimore, Maryland.
The Manuscript and Archives Division of the New York Public Library, New York City.
The Library of Princeton University, Princeton, New Jersey.
The Dreiser Collection, Library of the University of Pennsylvania, Philadelphia, Pennsylvania.

Published Correspondence

Letters of Theodore Dreiser: A Selection. 3 vols. Edited by Robert H. Elias. Philadelphia: University of Pennsylvania Press, 1959.
Letters of H. L. Mencken. Selected and annotated by Guy J. Forgue. New York: Knopf, 1961; new edition with foreword by Daniel Aaron. Boston: Northeastern University Press, 1981.
The New Mencken Letters. Edited by Carl Bode. New York: Dial, 1977.
The Dreiser-Mencken Letters: The Correspondence between Theodore Dreiser and H. L. Mencken, 1907–1945. 2 vols. Edited by Thomas P. Riggio. Philadelphia: University of Pennsylvania Press, 1986.
Mencken and Sara: A Life in Letters: The Private Correspondence of H. L. Mencken and Sara Haardt. Edited by Marion Elizabeth Rodgers. New York: McGraw-Hill, 1987.

Major Separate Works

George Bernard Shaw: His Plays. Boston: Luce, 1905.
The Philosophy of Friedrich Nietzsche. Boston: Luce, 1908; rev. ed., 1913.

A Book of Prefaces. New York: Knopf, 1917.

In Defense of Women. New York: Knopf, 1918.

Prejudices: First Series. New York: Knopf, 1919. Subsequent books in this series, all published by Knopf, are *Second Series,* 1920; *Third Series,* 1922; *Fourth Series,* 1924; *Fifth Series,* 1926; *Sixth Series,* 1927.

The American Language: A Preliminary Inquiry into the Development of English in the United States. New York: Knopf, 1919. Revised editions were brought out in 1921, 1923, and 1936. *Supplements I* and *II* were published in 1945 and 1948, respectively.

Notes on Democracy. New York: Knopf, 1926.

James Branch Cabell. New York: McBride, 1927.

Treatise on the Gods. New York: Knopf, 1930.

Treatise on Right and Wrong. New York: Knopf, 1934.

Memoirs and Diaries

Happy Days, 1880–1892. New York: Knopf, 1940.

Newspaper Days, 1899–1906. New York: Knopf, 1941.

Heathen Days, 1890–1936. New York: Knopf, 1943.

The Diary of H. L. Mencken. Edited by Charles A. Fecher. New York: Knopf, 1990.

My Life as Author and Editor. Edited by Jonathan Yardley. New York: Knopf, 1993.

Thirty-five Years of Newspaper Work: A Memoir by H. L. Mencken. Edited by Fred Hobson, Vincent Fitzpatrick, and Bradford Jacobs. Baltimore: The Johns Hopkins University Press, 1994.

Introductions and Contributions to Books

Introductions to *A Doll's House* and *Little Eyolf,* by Henrik Ibsen. Boston: Luce, 1909.

Men versus the Man: A Correspondence between Rives La Monte, Socialist, and H. L. Mencken, Individualist. New York: Holt, 1910.

"Munich." In H. L. Mencken, George Jean Nathan, Willard Huntington Wright, *Europe after 8:15.* New York: Lane, 1914.

Introduction to *We Moderns: Enigmas and Guesses,* by Edwin Muir. New York: Knopf, 1920.

Preface to *The American Credo: A Contribution toward the Interpretation of the National Mind,* by George Jean Nathan and H. L. Mencken. New York: Knopf, 1920.

"Politics." In *Civilization in the United States,* edited by Harold Stearns. New York: Harcourt, 1922.

Introduction to *The American Democrat or Hints on the Social and Civic Relations of the United States of America,* by James Fenimore Cooper. New York: Vintage, 1956.

Mencken as Editor

NEWPAPERS

Mencken held a variety of editorial positions on both the Baltimore *Herald* and the Baltimore *Sunpapers*. See the Adler bibliography for positions and dates.

MAGAZINES

Smart Set. Coeditor with George Jean Nathan from 1914 until 1923. The Mencken Room at the Enoch Pratt Free Library in Baltimore has a bound set of the magazine from 1908 to 1923.

The American Mercury. Coeditor with George Jean Nathan from 1924 until 1925, and editor from 1925 to 1933.

Newspaper and Magazine Articles

GENERAL

Baltimore *Herald,* 1899 to 1906. Clippings in Enoch Pratt Free Library, Baltimore.

Baltimore *Sunpapers,* intermittently from 1906 to 1948. Two important series were

"The Free Lance," May 8, 1911, to October 23, 1915.

"Monday Articles," February 9, 1920, to January 31, 1938.

Smart Set. Monthly book reviews from 1908 to 1923, plus many miscellaneous articles.

The American Mercury. Monthly book reviews and editorials in most issues from January 1924 to December 1933.

SELECTED MAGAZINE ARTICLES

"The American." *Smart Set* 40 (June 1913): 87–94. The other articles in this series, listed by subtitle, are "His Morals," 40 (July 1913):, 83–91; "His Language," 40 (August 1913): 89–96; "His Ideas of Beauty," 41 (September 1913): 91–98; "His Freedom," 41 (October 1913): 81–88; "His New Puritanism," 42 (February 1914): 87–94.

"Ibsen: Journeyman Dramatist." *Dial* 63 (October 11, 1917): 323–26.

"Literary Capital of the United States." *Nation* [London] 27 (April 17, 1920): 90–92.

"Maryland: Apex of Normalcy." *Nation* 114 (May 3, 1922): 517–19.

"Fifteen Years." *Smart Set* 72 (December 1923): 138–44.

"What's Wrong with *The Nation?*" *Nation* 127 (November 21, 1928): 542–43.

"What I Believe: Living Philosophies XII." *Forum* 84 (September 1930): 133–39.

"Ten Years." *American Mercury* 30 (December 1933): 385–87.

"Notes on Negro Strategy." *Crisis* 14 (October 1934): 298, 304.

"A Proposed Constitution for Maryland." [1937] *Menckeniana,* no. 100 (Winter 1986): 1–14.

Recorded Material

H. L. Mencken Speaks. Caedmon Records, TC-1082.

Anthologies

A Mencken Chrestomathy. Edited by H. L. Mencken. New York: Knopf, 1949.
The Vintage Mencken. Edited by Alistair Cooke. New York: Vintage, 1955.
The Bathtub Hoax and Other Blasts and Bravos from the Chicago Tribune. Edited by
  Robert McHugh. New York: Knopf, 1958.
Prejudices: A Selection. Edited by James T. Farrell. New York: Vintage, 1958.
H. L. Mencken on Politics: A Carnival of Buncombe. Edited by Malcolm Moos.
  New York: Vintage, 1960.
H. L. Mencken on Music: A Selection. Edited by Louis Cheslock. New York:
  Knopf, 1961.
D-Day at Dayton: Reflections on the Scopes Trial. Edited by Jerry R. Tompkins.
  Baton Rouge: Louisiana State University, 1965. Contains Mencken's dis-
  patches on the trial.
H. L. Mencken, The American Scene: A Reader. Edited by Huntington Cairns. New
  York: Knopf, 1965.
H. L. Mencken's Smart Set *Criticism.* Edited by William Nolte. Ithaca, N.Y.: Cor-
  nell University Press, 1968.
The Young Mencken: The Best of His Works. Edited by Carl Bode. New York: Dial, 1973.
The Young Mencken: The Uncollected Writings. Edited by Carl Bode. New York:
  Dial, 1973.
*A Gang of Pecksniffs, and Other Comments on Newspaper Publishers, Editors and
  Reporters.* Edited by Theo Lippman Jr. New Rochelle, N.Y.: Arlington
  House, 1975.
Mencken's Last Campaign: H. L. Mencken on the 1948 Election. Edited by Joseph C.
  Goulden. Washington, D.C.: New Republic Books, 1976.
The Impossible H. L. Mencken: A Selection of His Best Newspaper Stories. Edited by
  Marion Elizabeth Rodgers. New York: Doubleday, 1991.
A Second Mencken Chrestomathy. Edited by Terry Teachout. New York: Knopf, 1994.

SECONDARY WORKS

Biographies of Mencken

Bode, Carl. *Mencken.* Carbondale and Edwardsville: Southern Illinois University
  Press, 1969. Presents the conservative, domestic, and personal side of the
  man.
Goldberg, Isaac. *The Man Mencken: A Biographical and Critical Survey.* New York:
  Simon, 1925. Impressionistic and overwritten. Makes use of Mencken's
  autobiographical notes and reprints some material from his youth.

Hobson Jr., Fred C. *Mencken: A Life.* New York: Random House, 1994. Based on access to virtually all previously restricted material, Hobson provides a detailed and penetrating study, making this the best biography on Mencken available.

Kemler, Edgar. *The Irreverent Mr. Mencken.* Boston: Little, Brown, 1950. Critical and provoking portrait of the "demagogic" Mencken.

Manchester, William R. *Disturber of the Peace: The Life of H. L. Mencken.* New York: Harper, 1950. Readable but rather uncritical romp with Mencken's public personality.

Memoirs

Angoff, Charles. *H. L. Mencken: A Portrait from Memory.* New York: Yoseloff, 1956. A highly critical presentation of the vulgar Mencken. Quotations of conversations are interesting but "from memory." Author never knew when Mencken was joking.

Mayfield, Sara. *The Constant Circle: H. L. Mencken and His Friends.* New York: Delacorte, 1968. Warm, informal portrait of Mencken and his wife, by a close friend.

Critical Studies and Monographs

Boyd, Ernest. *H. L. Mencken.* New York: McBride, 1925. The first and still one of the best books on Mencken from an Irish critic who knew him well.

Dolmetsch, Carl R. *The* Smart Set: *A History and Anthology.* New York: Dial, 1966. Most of the historical section devoted to the Mencken-Nathan years. The serious student will still want to consult the author's doctoral thesis: "A History of the *Smart Set* Magazine, 1914–1923." Ph.D. diss., University of Chicago, 1957. Indispensable for Mencken's role as critic and editor, with much information about contributors during this period.

Douglas, George H. *H. L. Mencken: Critic of American Life.* Hamden, Conn.: Archon, Dawson, 1978. A concise summary of Mencken's philosophy and works.

Fecher, Charles A. *Mencken: A Study of His Thought.* New York: Knopf, 1978. A detailed study of Mencken as philosopher, political theorist, critic, philologian and stylist.

Fitzpatrick, Vincent. *H. L. Mencken.* New York: Continuum, 1989. A useful brief survey of Mencken's life and major works.

Forgue, Guy Jean. *H. L. Mencken: L'Homme, l'Oeuvre, l'Influence.* Monaco, 1967. Published doctoral thesis for the University of Paris. An important study of the sources of Mencken's ideas by the editor of the Mencken letters.

Hobson Jr., Fred C. *The Serpent in Eden: H. L. Mencken and the South.* Chapel Hill: University of North Carolina Press, 1974. A good study of Mencken's relations with southern writers, both as individuals and as groups.

Martin, Edward A., ed. *H. L. Mencken and the Debunkers*. Athens: University of Georgia Press, 1984. Seeks to fit Mencken into a modern American literary tradition. Contains new versions of several of Martin's previously published essays on Mencken.

————. *In Defense of Marion: The Love of Marion Bloom and H. L. Mencken*. Athens: University of Georgia Press, 1996. Letters (Marion's and Mencken's) and diaries of the woman Mencken almost married. Presents an important side of Mencken, especially in terms of his relations to women.

Nolte, William. *H. L. Mencken: Literary Critic*. Middletown, Conn.: Wesleyan University, 1964, 1966. The author, whose own prejudices tend to match Mencken's, presents his case enthusiastically, if somewhat uncritically. His anthology of Mencken's *Smart Set* pieces makes a more convincing argument for Mencken's critical abilities (see section on anthologies).

Scruggs, Charles. *The Sage of Harlem: H. L. Mencken and the Black Writers of the 1920s*. Baltimore: The Johns Hopkins University Press, 1984. A well-documented study of Mencken's influence on and relationship with emerging black writers during the 1920s.

Singleton, M. K. *H. L. Mencken and the* American Mercury *Adventure*. Durham, N.C.: Duke University, 1962. Important study of Mencken's editorship of the *Mercury*.

Stenerson, Douglas C. *H. L. Mencken: Iconoclast from Baltimore*. Chicago: University of Chicago Press, 1971. Largely devoted to the pre-1920s Mencken, this book is a sound study of the origin and development of the critic's ideas.

Wagner, Philip. *H. L. Mencken*. University of Minnesota Pamphlets on American Writers, no. 62. Minneapolis: University of Minnesota, 1966. Brief introduction to Mencken by a friend and colleague.

General Studies

THE DEPRESSION AND THE WAR YEARS

Most commentaries on Mencken in these years tended to reflect the political concerns of the writers as much or more than their views on literature.

Allen, Frederick Lewis. *Only Yesterday: An Informal History of the Nineteen-Twenties*. New York: Harper, 1931. Journalistic in the best sense, this readable yet stimulating book set the tone for future attitudes toward Mencken and the "Age of Ballyhoo."

Cargill, Oscar. *Intellectual America: Ideas on the March*. New York: Macmillian, 1941. Tries to fit Mencken into the context of antidemocratic European influences on modern American literature. The author later sought to make amends for his attack in his less satiric and more balanced "Mencken and the South," *Georgia Review* 11 (Winter 1952): 369–76.

Gold, Mike. *The Hollow Men.* New York: International Publishers, 1941. Party-line Marxist attack from the editor of the *New Masses.*

Hicks, Granville. *The Great Tradition: An Interpretation of American Literature since the Civil War.* New York: Macmillan, 1933. A better-balanced Marxist critique.

Kazin, Alfred. *On Native Ground: An Interpretation of Modern American Prose Literature.* New York: Reynal, 1942. This classic work contains one of the best-informed critical evaluations of Mencken written in this period.

Kronenberger, Louis. "H. L. Mencken." In *After the Genteel Tradition,* edited by Malcolm Cowley. New York: Norton, 1937. Mencken as seen by one of the refugees of the lost generation.

Rascoe, Burton, and Groff Conklin, eds. *The* Smart Set *Anthology.* New York: Reynal, 1934. Contains an anti-Mencken account of the magazine by one of his earliest champions.

THE POSTWAR YEARS

Although some of the old attacks on Mencken are reiterated, writers and scholars in this period are generally more objective and astute in their evaluations of the critic and more interested in fitting him into his cultural context.

Bewley, Marius. *The Complex Fate: Hawthorne, Henry James, and Some Other American Writers.* New York: Grove Press, 1954. An valuable critique that suffers from the author's having taken Mencken's supposed antimoralism at face value.

Brooks, Van Wyck. *The Confident Years: 1885–1915.* New York: Dutton, 1952. A final summing up by an important contemporary.

Geismar, Maxwell. *The Last of the Provincials: The American Novel, 1915–25.* Boston: Houghton, 1947. Contains one of the most important and stimulating postwar essays on Mencken.

Goldman, Eric F. *Rendezvous with Destiny: A History of Modern American Reform.* New York: Vintage, 1960. Contains a brief but provocative attempt to fit Mencken into 1920s liberalism.

Hartschorne, Thomas L. *The Distorted Image: Changing Conceptions of the American Character since Turner.* Cleveland, Ohio: Case Western Reserve University, 1968. Discussion of Mencken in terms of the debate over American character during the 1920s.

Hilfer, Anthony Channell. *The Revolt from the Village, 1915–1930.* Chapel Hill: University of North Carolina Press, 1969. Tries to fit Mencken into the tradition of the "Village Rebels."

Hoffman, Frederick J. *The Twenties: American Writing in the Postwar Decade.* New York: Viking, 1955. Critical of Mencken's love-hate relationship with the middle class.

Leary, Lewis. "H. L. Mencken: Changeless Critic in Changing Times." In *The Young Rebel in American Literature,* edited by Carl Bode. New York:

Praeger, 1960. The final summation of the case of the lost generation against its rejected father figure.

May, Henry F. *The End of American Innocence: A Study of the First Years of Our Own Time, 1912–1917*. New York: Knopf, 1959. An excellent piece of cultural history, this book is important for helping to fit Mencken into the cultural debates of this period.

McCormick, John. *American Literature, 1919–1932*. London: Cape, 1960. A narrowly based, highly critical view.

Ruland, Richard. *The Rediscovery of American Literature: Premises of Critical Taste, 1900–1940*. Cambridge, Mass.: Harvard University, 1967. An important book with a judicious discussion of Mencken's role as a critic and an evaluation of the Mencken-Sherman debates.

Weintraub, Stanley. *Shaw's People: Victoria to Churchill*. University Park: Pennsylvania State University Press, 1996. Contains an essay on Mencken's rejection of his early hero.

Williams, Harold. *The Baltimore* Sunpapers, *1837–1987*. Baltimore: The Johns Hopkins University Press, 1987. Important for placing Mencken within the larger context of the *Sunpapers*.

Yates, Norris W. *The American Humorist: Conscience of the Twentieth Century*. New York: Citadel, 1965. Presents an analysis of the personae in Mencken's satire.

Articles

PUBLISHED COLLECTIONS

Dorsey, John, ed. *On Mencken*. New York: Knopf, 1980. A centennial collection of essays by William Manchester, Huntington Cairns, Alistair Cooke, Charles A. Fecher, Malcolm Moos, William H. Nolte, Carl Bode, and Alfred A. Knopf.

Stenerson, Douglas C. ed. *Critical Essays on H. L. Mencken*. Boston: G. K. Hall, 1987. Excellent collection of reviews and essays from 1908 to 1980, including some original pieces written for this book.

POSITIVE EVALUATIONS BY CONTEMPORARIES

With a few exceptions, Mencken's contemporaries fell into two camps: those who concentrated on the negative side of his position as a critic, and those who, in defending him, emphasized his positive attributes. The three writers who could be called the "independents" belonged to no schools of critics and their comments, usually well balanced and original, survive the partisan battles of the 1910s and the 1920s.

Armstrong, Everhardt. "Mencken and America." *Nineteenth Century* 101 (January 1927): 117–25.

Boyd, Ernest. "American Literature or Colonial?" *Freeman* 1 (March 17, 1920): 13–15.

Fitzgerald, F. Scott. "Baltimore Anti-Christ." *Bookman* 52 (March 1921): 79–81.

Rascoe, Burton. "Fanfare." Chicago *Sunday Tribune,* November 11, 1917. Reprinted in *H. L. Mencken: Fanfare* along with an essay by Vincent O'Sullivan. New York: Knopf, 1920.

Van Doren, Carl. "Smartness and Light, H. L. Mencken, Gadfly for Democracy." *Century* 105 (March 1923): 791–96.

NEGATIVE EVALUATIONS BY CONTEMPORARIES

Anonymous. "Mustard Plaster Mencken." *Bookman* 64 (December 1926): 388.

Anonymous. "The Passing of H. L. Mencken." *Bookman* 70 (October 1929): 186–88.

Babbitt, Irving. "The Critic and American Life." *Forum* 79 (February 1928): 161–76. Beginning of the Humanist counterattack.

Bourne, Randolph. "H. L. Mencken." *New Republic* 13 (November 24, 1917): 102–3. Cogent criticism by a literary radical.

Boynton, Percy. "American Literature and the Tart Set." *Freeman* 1 (April 7, 1920): 88–89.

Canby, H.S. "Federalist: 1925 Model." *Saturday Review of Literature* 2 (December 12, 1925): 401, 409. Mencken as neo-Federalist.

Chesterton, G. K. "The Skeptic as Critic." *Forum* 81 (February 1929): 65–69. Conservative Catholic view.

Johnson, Gerald W. "The Congo, Mr. Mencken." *Reviewer* 3 (July 1923): 887–93. Sharp dissent from Mencken's attack on the South in "Sahara of the Bozart." Author eventually became a colleague and admirer of Mencken.

Kummer, Frederick A. "Something Must Have Happened to Henry." *Bookman* 65 (June 1927): 408–10.

Rascoe, Burton. "Notes for an Epitaph." New York *Evening Post* (March 4, 1922): "Literary Review," 1. Critical reevaluation by a former admirer.

Root, Raoul, Jane Heap, and Margaret Anderson. "Three Views of H. L. Mencken." *Little Review* (January 1918): 10–14. Dissenting opinions from the avant-garde.

Sherman, Stuart Pratt. "Beautifying American Literature." *Nation* 105 (November 29, 1917): 593–94.

———. "Mr. Mencken, the Jeune Fille, and the New Spirit in Letters." *New York Times Book Review* (December 7, 1919): 718. Reprinted in the author's *Americans.* New York: Scribner's, 1922.

———. "Mr. Brownell and Mr. Mencken." *Bookman* 60 (January 1925): 632–34.

Springarn, Joel E. "The Growth of the Literary Myth." *Freeman* 7 (May 2, 1923): 181–83. A just complaint about Mencken's interpretation of the author's theory of the new criticism.

EVALUATIONS BY THE INDEPENDENTS

Krutch, Joseph Wood. "Antichrist and the Five Apostles." *Nation* 113 (December 21, 1921): 733–34.

Lippman, Walter. "Near Machiavelli." *New Republic* 30 (May 31, 1922): 12–14.

———. "H. L. Mencken." *Saturday Review of Literature* 3 (December 11, 1926): 413–14.

Wilson, Edmund. "H. L. Mencken." *New Republic* 27 (June 1, 1921): 10–13.

———. "The All-Star Literary Vaudeville." *New Republic* 47 (June 30, 1926): 159–60.

———. "Mencken's Democratic Man." *New Republic* 49 (December 15, 1926): 110–11. The last two essays are reprinted in Wilson's *Shores of Light: A Literary Chronicle of the Twenties and Thirties.* New York: Farrar, 1952.

ARTICLES PUBLISHED AFTER MENCKEN'S DEATH

Since 1966, *Menckeniana* has published useful articles on various aspects of Mencken, only a few of which are listed below.

Bloom, Robert. "Past Indefinite: The Sherman-Mencken Debate on the American Tradition." *Western Humanities Review* 15 (Winter 1961): 73–81.

Cain, William E. "A Lost Voice of Dissent: H. L. Mencken in Our Time." *The Sewanee Review* 104 (Fall 1996): 229–47. Makes a case for taking Mencken seriously as a literary and social critic.

Cowing, Cedric B. "H. L. Mencken: The Case of the 'Curdled' Progressive." *Ethics* 69 (July 1959): 255–67. An interesting if not quite satisfactory interpretation of Mencken's early political ideas.

Dolmetsch, Carl R. "H. L. Mencken as a Critic of Poetry." *Jahrbuch für Amerikastudien* 19 (Heidelberg, 1966): 83–95.

———. " 'HLM' and 'GJN': The Editorial Partnership Reexamined." *Menckeniana*, no. 75 (Fall 1980): 29–39. A reconsideration of Nathan's role in the famous partnership.

Edwards, Owen Dudley. Article on Mencken in *Encyclopedia of Language and Linguistics,* edited by R. E. Ashur. Vol. 5. New York: Pergamon Press, 1994, 2447–48.

Epstein, Joseph. "H. L. Mencken: The Art of the Point of View." *Menckeniana*, no. 71 (Fall 1979): 2–11. The tragic nature of Mencken's point of view.

———. "Mencken on Trial." *Commentary* 89.4 (1990): 31–39. Reviews and dismisses the charge that Mencken was anti-Semitic.

Fullinwider, S. P. "Mencken's American Language." *Menckeniana*, no. 40 (Winter 1971): 2–7.

Kanigel, Robert. "Did Mencken Hate the Jews?" *Menckeniana*, no. 73 (Spring 1980): 1–7. Reprints some of the unpublished notes (1939) Mencken left regarding Jews.

Martin, E. A. "The Ordeal of H. L. Mencken." *South Atlantic Quarterly* 61 (Summer 1962): 326–38. An interesting attempt to relate the domestic side of Mencken's life to his thought.

————. "Mencken and Equal Rights for Women." *Georgia Review* 35.1 (Spring 1981): 65–75. A excellent analysis of Mencken's views on women.

————. "On Reading Mencken." *Sewanee Review* 93 (Spring 1985): 243–50. Argues that Mencken was a progressive journalist before World War I.

Owens, Gwinn. "Mencken and the Jews, Revisited." *Menckeniana,* no. 74 (Summer 1980): 6–10. Points out that Mencken's comments on Anglo-Saxons were just as savage as anything he wrote about Jews.

Richman, Sheldon L. "Mr. Mencken and the Jews." *American Scholar* 59 (Summer 1990): 407–11. A good discussion of Mencken's alleged anti-Semitism.

Riggio, Thomas P. "Dreiser and Mencken in the Literary Trenches." *American Scholar* 54 (Spring 1985): 227–48. Argues that Mencken's militant metaphors used to describe their literary struggles influenced American literary culture for much of this century.

Rubin, Louis D. "H. L. Mencken and the National Letters." *Sewanee Review* 74 (Summer 1966): 723–38. A reappraisal of Mencken's role as a critic.

————. "The Mencken Mystery." *Sewanee Review* 99 (Summer 1991): 445–63. An excellent discussion about Mencken's divided self.

Schaum, Melita. "H. L. Mencken and American Cultural Masculinism." *Journal of American Studies* 29 (1995): 379–98. An insightful feminist critique of Mencken's attitudes toward women as revealed in letters and in his book *In Defense of Women.*

Scruggs, Charles W. "Finding Out about This Mencken: The Impact of *A Book of Prefaces* on Richard Wright." *Menckeniana,* no. 95 (Fall 1985): 1–11.

Stenerson, Douglas C. "The 'Forgotten Man' of H. L. Mencken." *American Quarterly* 18 (Winter 1966): 686–96. An analysis of the ideas behind Mencken's concept of the ideal citizen.

Vidal, Gore. "The Essential Mencken." *Nation* 253 (August 26 / September 9, 1991): 228–32. A defense of Mencken in the age of political correctness.

Watson Jr., Ritchie D. "Sara Haardt Mencken and the Glasgow-Mencken Literary Entente." *Ellen Glasgow Newsletter* 20 (April 1984): 8–17.

Index

The Author

William H. A. Williams graduated *cum laude* with honors in history from Lafayette College in 1959. Receiving an Edward John Noble Fellowship, he commenced graduate studies in American history at the Johns Hopkins University. He completed his master's degree from Hopkins in 1962 and his Ph.D. in 1972; his doctoral thesis was a critical study of H. L. Mencken.

Williams began teaching in the history department of Southern Illinois University at Carbondale in 1965. In 1966, he took the position of the American historian in the Department of Modern History at University College, Dublin, Ireland. Next, he lectured in American studies at the Justus-Liebig University in Giessen, Germany. He returned to the United States in 1975 as visiting assistant professor in American cultural history at Arizona State University at Tempe. While in Arizona he worked with futurist Robert Theobald on various projects.

In 1985, Williams went to Indiana University, where he earned an M.L.S. and was a project director for the Organization of American Historians. He became a faculty member of the Union Institute's Gantz Undergraduate Center in Cincinnati, Ohio, in 1987.

Williams's first book was *H. L. Mencken,* written for the Twayne United States Authors Series and published in 1977. His second book, *'Twas Only an Irishman's Dream: The Image of Ireland and the Irish in Popular Song Lyrics, 1800–1920* (Champaign: Illinois University Press) was published in 1996 and won a "Deems Taylor" Award from ASCAP in 1997. He has also published articles in the areas of American studies, Irish studies, and ethnic studies. In 1996, he was a consultant for a six-part PBS series on the Irish in America, *The Long Journey Home,* which aired in January, 1998.

The Editor

Joseph M. Flora earned his B.A. (1956), M.A. (1957), and Ph.D. (1962) in English at the University of Michigan. In 1962 he joined the faculty of the University of North Carolina, where he is professor of English. His study *Hemingway's Nick Adams* (1984) won the Mayflower Award. He is also author of *Vardis Fisher* (1962), *William Ernest Henley* (1970), *Frederick Manfred* (1974), *and Ernest Heminiway: A Study of the Short Fiction* (1989). He is editor of *The English Short Story* (1985) and coeditor of *Southern Writers: A Biographical Dictionary* (1970), *Fifty Southern Writers before 1900* (1987), and *Fifty Southern Writers after 1900* (1987). He serves on the editorial boards of *Studies in Short Fiction* and *Southern Literary Journal*.